APM Project Management Qualification Study Guide

APM Project Management Qualification Study Guide

The Association for Project Management

Association for Project Management
Ibis House, Regent Park
Summerleys Road, Princes Risborough
Buckinghamshire
HP27 9LE

© Association for Project Management 2014

First edition 2014. Revised with minor corrections 2015 and 2016.

Paperback ISBN: 978-1-903494-05-9
e ISBN: 978-1-903494-07-3

Cover design by Fountainhead Creative Consultants
Typeset by RefineCatch Limited, Bungay, Suffolk
in 10/14pt Foundry Sans

Contents

MANAGEMENT

List of figures

MANAGEMENT

List of tables

Preface

Welcome to this APM study guide. It has been written by us – practising project management professionals with years of experience of training project managers – and will help you pass the APM Project Management Qualification. It has been developed over a number of years and now appears in this new APM format for the first time with its content having been revised with reference to the *APM Body of Knowledge 6th edition* as well as a number of other publications. The *APM Body of Knowledge* is referenced by the qualification syllabus which describes the learning outcomes and assessment criteria that you will need to demonstrate to be awarded the qualification. It is this syllabus that forms the key to this guide.

We have tried to write the guide in a matter of fact way, trying where possible to cut through the jargon, providing examples and real hands-on practical advice on how to better manage projects and pass the exam. The guide is just that – a guide, it is not intended to be a comprehensive one-stop shop for all things project management but it is intended to deal with the qualification syllabus and all that's in it.

We hope you enjoy the guide, find it useful and that it helps you pass the exam and develop your project management career.

John Bolton and Paul Naybour
Parallel Project Management Ltd

Acknowledgements

APM is grateful to the following for permission to reproduce copyright material:

L. M. Hough for the figure 'Conflict and Negotiation Processes in Organizations' by Kenneth W. Thomas, 1992, in *Handbook of Industrial and Organizational Psychology*, 2nd edition, eds M.D. Dunnette and L.M. Hough, Vol 3, p. 660, Palo Alto, CA: Consulting Psychologists Press. Copyright © 1992 by L. M. Hough. Adapted by permission; Pearson Education, Inc. for the figure 'Hierarchy of needs' from *Motivation and Personality*, 3rd edition by Abraham H. Maslow, eds Robert D. Frager and James Fadiman, copyright © 1987. Printed and electronically reproduced by permission of Pearson Education, Inc., Upper Saddle River, New Jersey; The Centre for Leadership Studies, Inc. for details about Situational Leadership®. Situational Leadership® is a trademark of the Centre for Leadership Studies, situational.com. Reproduced with permission; American Psychological Association for material based on Tudeman, 1965, Developmental sequence in small groups, *Psychological Bulletin*, Vol 63 (6), 384–399; and Belbin Associates for the Belbin 'Team Roles model' figure and table, as defined by Dr Meredith Belbin. Reproduced by kind permission of belbin.com.

Introduction

Welcome to this study guide to help you pass the APM Project Management Qualification (PMQ). In preparing for the exam you should aim to undertake approximately 40 hours of study. This study guide will take approximately that amount of time to read and digest, if you attempt all the exercises and quizzes. Some people will already be aware of a lot of the content and so their preparation time may be less, other people may need more time.

The guide has 12 main sections including numerous questions, tests and opportunities for reflection. You could consider going straight on to sit the exam after spending 40 hours going through this guide. However, experience shows that you will be better prepared after a period of reflection and interaction with a tutor to help ensure that your own personal approach is correct.

By spending about 30 minutes on each of the 73 assessment criteria and answering the associated questions, you will be as prepared as you can be; but we do recommend attendance at a tutor-led exam preparation event, where your exam technique can be honed in the company of an experienced tutor and other professionals.

About APM

The Association for Project Management (APM) is a registered charity with over 21,000 individual and 550 corporate members, making it the largest professional body of its kind in Europe.

APM is committed to developing and promoting project and programme management through its FIVE Dimensions of Professionalism, of which qualifications are an essential part.

The benefits of choosing APM qualifications are:

- Achievement – they offer a progressive structure that demonstrates your project management achievements.

- Recognition – they demonstrate to your employer, clients and suppliers that you are a skilled and committed project professional.

- Knowledge – they are developed using the *APM Body of Knowledge 6th edition*, employing well-established project management knowledge.

For the full range of APM qualifications, please visit apm.org.uk/qualifications.

MANAGEMENT

How this guide is organised

About the exam	A brief overview of the exam including key learning outcomes, common terminology and format.
Sections 1–12	Follow the same basic systematic approach as the APM Project Management Qualification syllabus, each section includes a learning outcome with subsections of groups of assessment criteria; they consider the breadth of knowledge encapsulated within the *APM Body of Knowledge 6th edition* and elsewhere. Please note that this guide does not follow the strict order of the syllabus. We have done this so that we can portray a logical journey through a project using the Whirlwind case study. You may find this an unnecessary complication; however it is our experience that this works best. We have amalgamated some assessment criteria together into groups as in most cases it makes sense to consider a number of them together. For example we have chosen to combine the two assessment criteria *Explain the purpose of a business case during the life cycle* and *Describe who has authorship and ownership of the business case*, into a subsection called 'Business case'.
	It will make that subsection more coherent, meaningful and easier to read. It will also bring together the main themes in one place so that you are not continually turning pages to find the next relevant part.
Case study	Contains the Whirlwind Bike case study; designed to give you something to work with when contemplating the various subjects and their practical application. If you have your own project to use then this is even better. Along with the case study there are also sample templates for you to complete. These templates can be used for any project and you are free to copy them as you wish.
Exam questions	Provides an overview of how the exam papers are structured, together with advice on answering them correctly. There are also sample questions, which you can 'have a go at'. The paper should take you 180 minutes (each question taking about 15–18 minutes). Please note that the questions at the end of sections 1–12 are exam style, not precise APM-worded questions.
Multiple choice answers	Contains the answers to the quick quizzes posed throughout the book.
Glossary of terms	This guide contains most of what you need to know to pass the examination. As the syllabus is derived in the main from the *APM Body of Knowledge 6th edition*, you will find it helpful to have access to that as a reference document, and you may also find that many of the texts referenced are of help.

MANAGEMENT

So ... where to start?

This guide contains most of the things you need to know to pass the qualification. The *APM Body of Knowledge 6th edition* can also be obtained and this will provide some detail over and above what is included here.

Please bear in mind though that the *APM Body of Knowledge* contains material pertinent not just to project management but also programme and portfolio management. These latter two are not examined in depth, but only according to the few assessment criteria that relate directly to them within the qualification syllabus.

APM also produce two key supporting documents – *The Association for Project Management Guidance Notes for Candidates* and the *APM Project Management Qualification Syllabus*. Some parts of these guidance notes are reproduced in this guide along with other hints and tips to help you deal with revision and the exam itself. The syllabus is a very useful document as it describes in clear detail all of those learning outcomes and assessment criteria that you need to be familiar with. These assessment criteria appear in this guide at the start of the section that addresses them but sometimes it helps to have them in a single focused list to use as a checklist to help manage your own learning.

You should obtain a copy of both of these documents (apm.org.uk) just to make sure that you have the latest information.

In reading the *APM Body of Knowledge*, you will notice that there are a number of 'core texts' referenced at the very front of the book. There are also a number of 'further reading' texts identified along the way. For example, you will notice that *BS6079-1 2010 A Guide to Project Management* is referenced. However, as already mentioned, there are also a number of other publications from respected authors and organisations that will give a different (sometimes radically so) portrayal of the subject. You are of course free to browse, purchase or borrow any or all of the above publications (and indeed others) and of course they will help to provide a greater level of detail in particular areas than this document can do.

We have though created this study guide to provide a consistent and usable compilation of the relevant material and information from a number of sources to provide a comprehensive structure and content for your learning.

So go on and start reading and good luck with your studies and exam.

About the exam

What is in the syllabus?

The syllabus is split into 12 main learning outcomes and each of these is covered in a discrete section of this guide (sections 1–12). Within each learning outcome there are a varying number of assessment criteria. The assessment criteria are those that you will be tested on in the exam. The learning outcomes are as follows:

1. Structure of organisations and projects

2. Project life cycle

3. Project contexts and environments

4. Governance and structured methodologies

5. Communication

6. Leadership and teamwork

7. Planning for success

8. Scope management

9. Schedule and resource management

10. Procurement

11. Project risk management and issue management

12. Project quality management

Highlighted throughout these various sections are the assessment criteria that will be used to evaluate your answers in the exam, and whether you have demonstrated sufficient knowledge of them. We would remind you that we have grouped the assessment criteria together in some cases in a ' subsection' where it makes sense to consider them as one.

In some of the assessment criteria you will find reference to a number of theories usually introduced by the term 'such as'. We have not tried to describe all of these. The exam is inclusive of much relevant theory according to the demand of the question; you can refer to any material of which you are aware – so long as it is relevant. For example there are quite a number of motivation theories (just look on the internet), we have chosen to describe two here, but if you refer to a third and it is relevant then that will be fine. The material in this guide is enough but in most cases the minimum you will need.

Terminology

There are numerous publications on project management. A quick web search will reveal hundreds of thousands of entries for project management and related topics. If you tried to read them all though you would a) take an enormous amount of time and b) probably have so many competing views that you would become confused. So, which are important and which are not? A key benefit of this guide is to help you sort the good

MANAGEMENT

from the less relevant. We have been able to draw on multiple sources and experience to do that for you.

This guide uses a consistent form of words so that there should be no confusion about terms and it provides sufficient ways of describing the various aspects and suggests terminology that is valid that you can learn and use. Sometimes though, the examiners may choose to use different words so as to be inclusive across industry and reference works. The term 'product' for example may also be termed 'deliverable'. Technically there is a difference but in most cases people will be using them interchangeably. You may of course already experience some or all of these concepts, but recognise them with a different name or term. In most cases you do have the opportunity to 'flex' the language to suit your own experience or industry. Markers will give credit for answers that are relevant to the question posed even if alternative vocabulary to that within the *APM Body of Knowledge 6th edition* or this guide is used. In the exam, provided you are clear about the use of the term and use it in a suitable context you will not be marked down for using a different one. Sometimes though, the context demands adherence to a term phrased in a particular way (the use of the PESTLE acronym where this is specifically mentioned in the learning outcome, for example – see p. 16). The phrases used in this guide are suitable; if you have no other alternatives then learn these.

The format of the exam

The exam is a three-hour, closed book written paper, invigilated under exam conditions by an APM representative or by a self-invigilator organised by an accredited training provider. When you arrive, you will usually be able to choose a desk (unless you arrive last and there are only just enough); you are not permitted to take anything into the exam room with you apart from pens, rulers and calculators and may take nothing away that was given to you for the purposes of the exam. You will also need some form of photo ID. The qualification is highly regarded and as such valuable. You should be proud to obtain it, and respect the need to maintain its credibility and confidentiality.

APM seeks to test only knowledge, not competence, in the PMQ examination. More information can be found in the syllabus, the examination notes and this document, but you are strongly advised to refer also to the text of the *APM Body of Knowledge 6th edition*, and the further reading recommended there. The examination seeks to ascertain your knowledge by setting a series of 16 questions which examine specific learning outcomes in the syllabus.

- You need to answer 10 of these questions.

- You need to score an overall percentage of 55 across all of the 10 questions which you are required to answer.

- Each question carries a total of 50 marks.

- The mark you need to pass therefore is 275 out of a total 500 marks possible.

The qualification assessment specification includes advice on the use of certain 'keywords' in the questions you will encounter. Note these well as they will be significant and have very specific connotations in the context of the exam. For more information see the guidance notes on the APM website apm.org.uk.

MANAGEMENT

You should also be aware that APM offer considerable help for people with disabilities or medical conditions that interfere with their ability to engage fully with the standard exam. You should contact APM if you feel you would like to discuss this or your accredited training provider will be able to help.

Specific details on the exam structure, format and how you should approach it (including hints and tips) can be found in the Exam questions section at the back of this guide.

Contexts and environments

1

Subjects covered in this section

1.1 Projects and business-as-usual

1.2 Projects, programmes and portfolios

1.3 The project environment

1.4 The legislative aspects of project management

1.1 ## Projects and business-as-usual

By completing this subsection you will be able to:

■ distinguish between projects and business-as-usual.

We have put this assessment criteria in its own section because it is a vital core element of project management and it needs to be read in conjunction with some of the basic attributes of projects and their various characteristics.

The main characteristics of projects

Before we can really go on and start to consider the APM Project Management Qualification syllabus in detail, there are a few basics that need to be established.

■ In order to derive benefit a project will be required to produce a planned set of deliverables (or products).

■ Projects are transient; they have a finite time in which they will deliver those deliverables, and as such they need to acquire temporary resources.

■ They are of various sizes, there are overheads associated with any project and they are therefore normally a significant endeavour involving risk that must be managed.

■ They are directed at the achievement of benefits, we do not typically do projects merely because we can. We expect to derive some long-term benefit from them potentially way beyond the end of the project itself.

■ They operate within a predetermined and planned budget (for the project).

■ Projects are the vehicles of change in an organisation. They are not the repetitive business-as-usual types of activity.

Projects are normally referred to by virtue of their various 'success criteria' the key ones of which appear as in Figure 1.1 below.

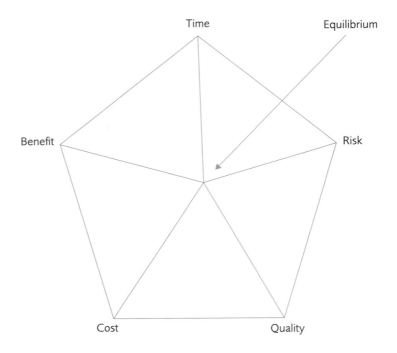

Figure 1.1 The balance of competing project criteria

Each of the vertices of the pentagon has a definite quantified criteria associated with it. These are called 'success criteria'. It is relatively common to hear the term 'quality' used instead of 'deliverables'. You may also often hear the word 'product' used. The broad term 'quality' is interpreted as 'fitness for purpose' or to put it crudely, the products 'do what it says on the tin' (the tin being the specification). Use of the term 'quality' however has advantages as it implies that it is not just any old deliverable or product but one that actually fulfils the stated requirement.

There is a point of equilibrium somewhere within the pentagon. The exact nature of the various success criteria is what the project manager has to balance throughout the project (after they have been agreed and documented in the business case and the project management plan [PMP]). Some of these success criteria may not be compatible with each other. For example there may be situations where a particular end date (a big sporting event opening ceremony, for example) is absolutely paramount. It must be achieved almost at any cost, although what usually happens is that the scope (or quality) is scaled back to fit within the time and the budget constraints. The scope of the project is loosely defined as all of those things that the project will do and all of those things that will be produced.

There are usually trade-offs to be made between the resultant benefit of a project (saving 20 per cent on our inventory costs, for example) and the costs of implementing a computer system to allow us to do so. A cheaper system may allow us to save 19 per cent and it may be that the extra one per cent comes at a too high price. We will consider success or failure of projects later, but suffice to say here that it is often the misunderstanding of the nature of the relationship between these criteria that causes projects to be perceived as failures.

The project sponsor is responsible for making and agreeing the success criterion trade-offs. They are the arbiter of the beneficial outcomes that may be achieved and the cost of achieving them. This is a fundamental aspect of a project sponsor's role and means they can create and own a viable business case. The business case will normally be 'approved' by the sponsoring organisation and the sponsor will own it through the life cycle.

Projects are different from business-as-usual

Projects are formulated and undertaken in order to introduce a change to an existing status quo (e.g. a new computer system, a bridge, a new product launch, etc). This distinguishes them from operational tasks. Consider the following examples:

- Open heart surgery: to the surgeon and the patient this may seem like a project, to the theatre nurse it may seem like a repetitive operation.

- A factory manufacturing 300 washing machines a day: the factory that makes the washing machines would have been the result of a project, each washing machine though is simply business-as-usual.

- Building a new footbridge over a major river: never been done before, this is a project.

- Manufacturing a new aircraft type: the first prototype is probably a project, as is the second and maybe third, eventually though even a large manufactured product becomes 'business-as-usual'.

- Implementing a prototype software system: never been done before, probably a project.

Which is the project? The differences are summarised in Table 1.1 on page 4.

The benefits of project management are that:

- The organisation is able to deploy their projects in a consistent way, with a consistent set of processes and commonality of approach.

- Risk is reduced and opportunities maximised through the use of tried and tested processes and with skilled and talented project managers risk can be managed proactively and a judicious amount of risk taking considered.

- Success happens more readily and frequently, the culture of the organisation improves to encompass the normality of success and failure becomes less frequent and more unacceptable with ill-founded or non-viable projects being terminated.

- Individuals work in a more successful environment, where appropriate controls innovation can flourish, and a variety of approaches and tasks can keep everyone challenged with the continual firefighting kept at bay.

- Stakeholders become more accustomed to success and the opportunity to contribute positively is enhanced as there is less need for conflict when things go wrong.

MANAGEMENT

Table 1.1 The key differentials that separate a project from business-as-usual

Project	Business-as-usual
Seeks to introduce change.	Seeking to maintain a stable platform for efficient production.
Limited by time.	Repetitive and continues indefinitely.
Teams working with unique, bespoke plans and risks.	Highly procedural working practices to enable complex operations to be delivered in a consistent way.
Specified scope so we understand what the project work and products are.	The first few prototypes of a mass-produced item may be a project; once production is ongoing they become business-as-usual.
Produce specific one-off deliverables.	Produce specific deliverables, but repeatedly.
They have a discrete number of steps (delineated by the finite time), called a project life cycle.	Products go through a life cycle from build, through operations to disposal, called a product life cycle.
Projects seek step change and transformation.	Business-as-usual is seeking continuity, consistency and slow incremental improvement.
Requires a specific authorised business case.	Normally funded from operational budgets rather than capital budgets. Business cases are less relevant.

Quick quiz (answers on page 271)

	Question	Options	Your answer
1	The interaction between projects and business-as-usual is. . . .?	a) Incidental b) Irrelevant c) Essential d) Always the same	
2	A project will require a business case.	True or false?	
3	Projects can be undertaken many times in the same form.	True or false?	
4	Projects have a distinct start / finish.	True or false?	

	Question	Options	Your answer
5	Projects introduce slow incremental change.	True or false?	
6	Business-as-usual is repetitive and continues indefinitely.	True or false?	
7	An example of a success criteria might be.....?	a) The time a project takes b) How experienced the project manager is c) Assumptions made d) Who the sponsor is	
8	Which of these is a project?	a) Running a marketing department b) A prototype software system c) Making washing machines d) Running a finance department	
9	A key element of project management is the management of risk.	True or false?	
10	Projects require an authorised business case.	True or false?	

MANAGEMENT

Use this space to make some notes

What kind of question might there be in the exam?

1	List five key attributes of a project and describe how each differs from business-as-usual.
	50 marks (10 marks each)

1.2 | Projects, programmes and portfolios

By completing this subsection you will be able to:

■ differentiate between project management and portfolio and programme management;

■ outline the characteristics of programme management and its relationship with strategic change;

■ explain the challenges a project manager may face working within a programme;

■ describe where the use of portfolio management may be appropriate.

It is not easily possible to describe the difference between quite complicated concepts like these without first describing each, which we have done in this subsection.

The context of portfolio management

Organisations face many challenges when running their projects. There are numerous key questions that they may feel they need to answer in order to make sure they are not only running the right projects but also that they are able to vouch for the fact that they are running them well. The term 'portfolio management' is used to describe this overarching form of governance exerted by the organisation over its projects and programmes. A portfolio in essence is the sum of all those projects and programmes. Portfolios therefore contain programmes and projects.

The portfolio manager may need to consider a number of things when deciding which projects and programmes should be within the portfolio. Some of these considerations might be:

■ Balancing the number and type of projects to suit changing strategic objectives.

■ The nature of the overall risk exposure – organisations could not take on too many risky projects.

■ Efficiency through 'weeding out' those projects and programmes not directly contributing sufficient value.

■ Effective use of scarce resources, making sure that the business is able to fund the entire workload.

■ Better focus on the achievement of benefits.

In Figure 1.2 we see that the 'host organisation' has choices about which projects, portfolios and programmes it will be running. In some organisations the overheads associated with portfolio and programme management may be unnecessary. In this case they may just run projects and any governance follows this path (the hatched arrow). As organisations become more and more mature with regard to their project management disciplines it may be appropriate to consider formal portfolio and programme management. This will assist

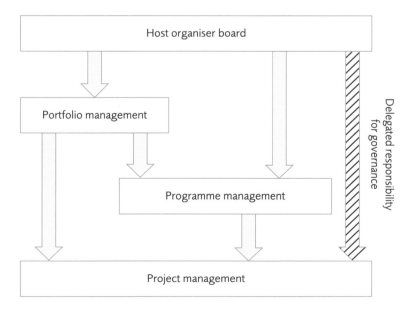

Figure 1.2 Governance structure

with prioritisation, project control, risk management and reporting because they will all be managed as a collective 'whole' within that portfolio or programme.

The role of managing the portfolio falls to the host organisation. They should choose to undertake the programmes and projects that best suit the strategic direction of the business. Each project will be commissioned in response to a specific business case; this is also true of a programme. It is these business case decisions that will be fundamental in deciding whether a project is in (or out) of the organisation's portfolio.

A portfolio manager has the job of ensuring that the whole range of projects and programmes that are underway represent the most appropriate mix of projects applicable to the organisation's needs at any given time. They will need to:

■ Screen projects to ensure they do in fact conform to the organisation's needs at the time.

■ Prioritise projects to make sure that they are optimised in terms of the available resources and return on investment.

■ Continually reassess throughout the accounting period, and add or remove some projects over time, because they may no longer be appropriate in changing business circumstances.

■ Make sure that any considerations external to the portfolio are reflected and taken into account.

The governance of project management (as we will see later) has a significant role to play in the management of a portfolio and therefore there are significant aspects of portfolio management that overlap with those of governance.

A lot of students of the subject have significant problems with the concept of a portfolio. Very simplistically it is the organisation's collection of everything to do with projects or programmes.

The appropriateness of using portfolio management

Where the management of organisational risk is needed. By having a holistic view of the whole workload, organisations can better co-ordinate all the different projects and programmes, enabling a better flow of risk information from senior management to project teams and vice versa. This means that contingencies can be transferred between different projects and programmes, providing a more efficient use of those funds and resources. Furthermore, the overall risk profile can be better understood. We may have one very risky project where our efforts need to be directed, while other less risky ones can manage their own risk exposure.

Where organisational capacity is a limiting factor. With a global view of all the projects and programmes it is possible to avoid capacity bottlenecks, where multiple projects and programmes compete for the same resources. It is imperative that organisations are able to divert scarce resources quickly and seamlessly from one area to another so that delays and issues on one project, which can yield under-utilisation, can be diverted elsewhere.

Where standardisation and consistency of approach is needed. Common methods and tools can be established and maintained at portfolio level, avoiding duplication and confusion. An organisation would not really want its project managers all coming up with their own way of doing things. A corporate project office might be instrumental in reducing these overheads and governance arrangements will have an influence.

Holistic view of the workload. Here, senior management can make far more effective judgements on how to best ensure that investment resources are most appropriately allocated. The portfolio can be balanced to find a compromise between the desire to do everything as soon as possible and actually making sure that the most beneficial projects are done first.

Co-ordination of the impact on business-as-usual. When an organisation embarks upon a range of projects and programmes there is a need to make sure that these do not have a combined effect on the business that is so great as to put the maintenance of business-as-usual at jeopardy.

Programme management

We saw in the earlier section how a project is characterised by its:

- delivery of a specified product;

- uniqueness;

- introduction of change;

- constrained budget;

- specified schedule;

- differentiation from business-as-usual.

What are the implications for organisations that have more than one project on the go at any one time though? Some organisations will have literally hundreds of projects. What do these organisations need to do to control them? What organisational components need to be in place to help manage them?

Where an undertaking is so significant that it is introducing a large component of organisational change into the business, to a wider audience, perhaps even society in general, then the concept of a project does not have sufficient scope to allow these bigger challenges to be dealt with. For this circumstance we need to discuss programme management.

Programme management can be summarised as being the co-ordinated management of a range of projects and change management activities. It is basically a wrapper that surrounds the projects and provides a framework of control that enables a more co-ordinated approach to a number of these associated and (importantly) interdependent projects.

Programmes consist of multiple projects and an interaction with business-as-usual. Each of these is dependent on the others, the exact projects contained within a programme will vary with time, and some will start sooner than others and some later. Which projects exist within a particular programme is a result of their contribution to the overall programme objectives. If they are fundamental to the achievement of the strategic objectives, then they should be in the programme; if they do not, then they should be omitted.

Programmes and projects have an impact on business-as-usual. This is because they clearly deliver products into the business and proper transition arrangements need to be made. A programme will have much clearer visibility of these issues and may also have a lot of them within its own scope.

Large programmes may also have their own specialists drawn from the business dedicated to the programme itself. Projects need this support also but to a much smaller degree and may well share resources rather than have dedicated long-term commitment as in programmes. For example, a programme may well incorporate its own HR team to deal with staff issues. Other significant areas where this may happen is in the areas of procurement, risk management and finance services.

Projects can exist in isolation and not as part of a programme. These will usually be single highly focused activities that have a relatively small or low impact on the organisation and its objectives. This is not to belittle projects not in programmes, but merely to acknowledge that programmes are in place to provide co-ordination and control of large multidisciplinary endeavours of strategic importance.

The layer of programme management control made possible through the use of the structure can add significant extra cost, but the better control of risk and focus on benefits can make it worthwhile.

Programmes and the achievement of strategic change

1. **Interdependence of the component projects to each other**. Only by linking each project with each of the others in the programme can we be sure of having a consistent set of them, managed collectively. For example the relationship between the project to build the data centre needs to be managed tightly aligned to the IT hardware project to equip it.

2. They are normally associated with **a 'vision' and a top-down approach**: "We want to be the world's best employer." The vision set by the senior managers in the organisation will dictate which projects are in and which are out of the programme. By definition this vision is the key cornerstone of intent. If projects contribute to the vision they are in the programme and if they do not they are not.

3. **They can adopt a flexible evolutionary model**. Not all programmes have certainty over the outcomes, sometimes in a multi-year programme complete predictability is impossible and delivery in tranches with the objectives continually evolving may be a preferred approach.

4. **They are strategic in nature**.They are generated as a consequence of some larger organisational imperative. "We want to be the largest seller of XYZ in the world," may be the vision for the programme. This will yield overall strategic deliverables focused squarely on the needs of the organisation in the broadest sense. This vision is the highest level of intent applicable to the programme and needs to accurately reflect the strategic direction of the company.

5. **They focus on the overall benefits to be derived by the organisation** – they are benefits-focused (Figure 1.3) in that they are clearly reliant upon the needs of the end beneficiary to describe what success looks like in benefit terms. "We need to reduce a hospital waiting time because of XYZ . . ."

Benefits of programme management

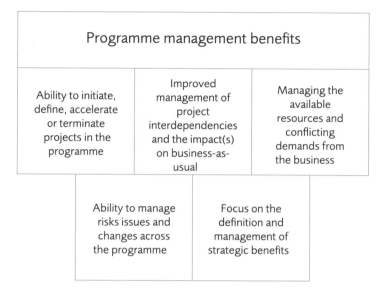

Figure 1.3 The benefits of programme management

Projects versus programmes

Programmes have some key differences from projects – see Table 1.2 on page 12.

Programme management roles

Project and programme managers share a number of attributes. They both need to be strong communicators, be able to manage resources and schedules, influence stakeholders and attend to detail, but programme managers have a number of these attributes (and responsibilities) that are different in proportion to those of project management counterparts. They need to be a strategic thinker, able to operate at the higher echelons of an organisation, able to juggle multiple projects, have a highly developed approach to risk and be comfortable with uncertainty.

The programme manager has to:

- Plan the programme including scheduling the projects and trying to ensure early delivery of benefit.

- Prioritise individual resources across projects and if necessary move them from one project to another.

- Make sure that risks (and lessons learned) are communicated across the projects in the programme through networking and other sessions.

- Make sure that all the programme processes are properly executed: this will usually be through a programme management office.

- Support the project managers through team-building and individual interventions, working with them to mentor and coach them where appropriate.

■ Ensure the business is ready to receive the outcome of the projects by working with the operational managers to make sure they are ready and able to implement the solutions as they come on stream.

■ Ensure proper assurance is carried out by commissioning audits on the projects within the programme and submitting the results to the programme sponsor.

Table 1.2 The key differentials between projects and programmes

Project	Programme
Constrained by specific objectives understood at the start.	Objectives evolve and can (to a degree) be modified as the programme matures.
Tactical single solution to single requirement.	Strategic in nature tackling large change programmes or major changes at an organisational level.
Projects deliver outputs which will subsequently deliver benefits after the end of the project.	Programmes will deliver benefits throughout their life cycle and have a highly developed benefits-management focus.
Focused teams with a systematic and structured approach with clearly defined roles and responsibilities.	Complex inter-project relationships call for highly developed communication and influencing skills.
A project may have a single customer defining the requirements and accepting specified products.	Programmes have multiple customers at different times through their life – because each project is a separate undertaking.
Satisfaction of a single tactical objective.	Top-down 'visionary' approach, projects assembled into a programme where they contribute to the vision.
A known scope means a clear view of the necessary tasks is possible.	Cyclical development means projects can come and go from the programme as necessary (but always to achieve strategic benefit).

In the same way projects have a project sponsor, the programme also has a programme sponsor, who has the job of making sure that the programme and the programme manager have support and guidance. Due to the overtly strategic nature of the programme, the programme sponsor has to be a senior individual, capable of 'paving the way' for the programme, providing an escalation route and also a source of communication in support of the programme. They need to have a high degree of political acumen, and be able to negotiate at board level.

The challenges of programme management

Some of the problems a project manager may experience when working within a programme structure can be quite difficult to overcome. The programme manager will need to work closely with their project managers to ensure that they are supported in their endeavours.

In particular a project manager may experience the following difficulties:

- They may need to recognise that the programme manager is their sponsor. This may not be the case when working in an isolated project but as part of a larger programme structure the programme manager will have control of their activities.

- The programme will usually instil its own governance arrangements upon its constituent projects thus requiring the project manager to conform to these rather than have some autonomy over their own particular activities directly.

- The project manager may not be trained on the specific method being used to govern the programme.

- Working alongside other project managers may mean more reliance on managerial meetings and time spent co-ordinating activities with others.

- The project manager may feel distant from the end customer because the products (as they are produced) will be delivered to the client through the programme. This layer of translation opens up opportunities for misinterpretation and confusion unless managed well.

Work-based exercise

What sort of programmes do you encounter?

Seek out your organisation's project or programme management office and see if they can point out examples of programmes.

Speak to colleagues about this.

See if you can think of areas where organisations (either ones you have worked in or those you are aware of) have used programmes to help deliver strategic change.

Some examples of programmes might be:

- A merger or acquisition in the financial service sector where one organisation merges its own people, processes and systems with those of another. Look for a key reason for this programme happening e.g. "We want to be the leading supplier of XYZ services."

- A car company developing a model through a number of key stages. This form of development programme is cyclical, the end result is never completely clear, but, for example, to satisfy a desire to be a market leader will lead the programme through a number of product launches and upgrades.

- Where there are a large number of diverse but complementary activities, with products that are not always clear or tangible. One example might be lobbying governments to get support for funding a charity aid project.

Use this space to make some notes

....

....

....

....

....

....

Quick quiz (answers on page 271)

	Question	Option	Your answer
1	Programme managers are just senior project managers.	True or false?	
2	Programmes are just big projects.	True or false?	
3	The interaction between portfolios and business-as-usual is. . . .?	a) Incidental b) Crucial c) Where relevant to make sure projects deliver maximum benefit	
4	The scope of a programme is fixed throughout its life cycle.	True or false?	
5	Portfolio management has a linkage with corporate project office management and governance.	True or false?	
6	The words vision, benefits focused and 'strategic' are associated with programmes.	True or false?	
7	Portfolios have a distinct start and finish.	True or false?	

	Question	Option	Your answer
8	Programme management and portfolio management are the same thing.	True or false?	
9	A portfolio manager would be interested in making sure that individual projects were initiated, mobilised and terminated in line with the strategic business plans of the business.	True or false?	
10	Which of these could be classified as a programme?	a) The integration of two large financial institutions b) Installing a small new computer network c) Building an estate of new houses	

What kind of questions might there be in the exam?

1   Explain <u>five</u> key benefits of using a programme management approach.
50 marks (10 marks each).

2   List and describe <u>five</u> features of a programme.
50 marks (10 marks each)

MANAGEMENT

| 1.3 | **The project environment** |

By completing this subsection you will be able to:

■ describe how environmental factors affect projects (including the sector, geography and regulation);

■ explain tools and techniques used to assess a project's context (including PESTLE, SWOT).

The environment within which a project operates can range from the relatively simple to the very complex. We have grouped both of the relevant assessment criteria relating to these here so that they can be studied and digested as one.

The project environment

A project does not operate in a vacuum. It will have a number of influences that either constrain or liberate it. These are many and varied and can be influenced only to a greater or lesser degree depending on their nature. The project manager must be fully aware of these so-called environmental factors so that they can prepare for and manage them as well as they can.

Extraneous environmental factors such as the election of a new mayor or the changes to a technical specification can have a very marked influence on the way in which the project operates. If we know a technical standard is about to change we can either work fast to avoid having to change our products with it or delay until it has been implemented so we have the latest version. By adopting a formalised way of assessing a project we can work towards understanding all of these many and varied influences.

The context of projects

As mentioned it is necessary to understand the context of a project for many reasons. The context of a construction project versus a project to implement an IT system will vary greatly depending on the bias and emphasis of some key factors. These are usually categorised according to the acronym of PESTLE shown in Table 1.3.

Table 1.3 The context of projects: PESTLE explained

	Construction project	**Implementing a software system**
Political	A publicly funded capital programme will have a large number of politically motivated stakeholders and decisions on the strategic direction will be difficult to determine.	External political influences may be quite small, but internally bringing together a number of internal departments and gaining consensus across a company can be significant.

	Construction project	Implementing a software system
Economic	Funding a large capital project is usually almost wholly dependent upon public funds (either directly or indirectly). Quite often things like public finance initiatives or private partnerships will be relevant. Also, long-term projects are much more susceptible to the uncertainty around interest rates, for example.	An IT project to automate internal processes will have an impact over the whole investment case for the project. The benefits of the system are usually less measurable and they may not occur until well into the future. The cost of the software and implementation will be offset against a more intangible business case.
Sociological	Projects need to be aware of, and may be constrained by, their position and impact on society in general. Power stations, bridges, railway lines, etc., require a deep understanding of the sociological trends surrounding the project; this will make the stakeholder identification process critical.	The interaction between the users of the system and the system itself will need to be understood. Understanding the needs of the society will mean more attention to ease of use and accessibility. Making it available to homeworkers or those with disabilities, for example, are areas that other projects may not need to consider.
Technological	If the project is in a safety-critical area (e.g. replacing rail track outside a mainline station), it will require a much greater understanding of the technological specifications relating to the expected implementation timescales, specifications and anticipated through life reliability.	A software system requires some form of hardware infrastructure on which to operate. Typically computer-related technology races ahead at high speed, so there needs to be consideration given to the availability of such systems and also the anticipated time before it becomes beyond 'end of life'.
Legal	Significant attention to health and safety and other critical safety issues will be needed. The nuclear and rail industries have a very high degree of regulatory requirements and frameworks within which they operate.	Software systems need to be covered by processes including the storage and dissemination of personal data.

	Construction project	Implementing a software system
Environmental	The disposal of waste from a construction site is heavily regulated, partly to protect the surrounding environment. For example, a site such as a large brownfield development would need a very high degree of cleansing and preparation prior to actual construction. Clearly necessary, but it will probably delay construction and affect the timing and schedules.	Power consumption for a software system was something not actively considered even a few years ago. Greater attention to these energy consumption issues now means that careful thought needs to be given to the installation of the machinery, the times it is available (and not available).

So we can see that two different types of project have different contextual issues to deal with. Using the **P-E-S-T-L-E** helps to identify what they are. See if you can think of some areas from your own project back at work where these are evident.

There are other aspects of a project's context you may need to consider, summarised in Table 1.4:

Table 1.4 The context of projects: other considerations

Area	Impact
Procurement processes	May need to plan a long time ahead if procurement is heavily directed by the organisation or elsewhere (e.g. European Union procurement regulations).
Regulatory requirements	Banks and insurance companies have to be aware of the regulatory framework they operate in. This can place significant constraints over their projects.
Use of structured methods	Operating within an organisation with highly structured project methods will be instrumental in how quickly or slowly progress can be made.
Appetite for risk	If the organisation does not have a large appetite for risk then this will have a big effect on the type and number of projects undertaken.
Strengths, weaknesses, opportunities and threats (SWOT)	The organisation needs to be aware of what it is good at and not so good at. Analysing these factors will provide a significant insight into how a project ought to be managed. Organisations with a poor record of managing subcontractors may wish to run the project in-house, for example. If the strength of the business is a healthy cash flow, then it may mean early payment schedules can be used as a way of securing discounts.

WHIRLWIND BIKES

Consider the case study on page 259. What specific areas of project context can you observe? Use PESTLE to structure your observations.

Use this space to make some notes

Quick quiz (answers on page 272)

	Question	Options	Your answer
1	A project context is only concerned with external factors.	True or false?	
2	An example of a political context might be the impending election of a new mayor.	True or false?	
3	APM sometimes calls a project's context the project environment.	True or false?	
4	Accommodating a more elderly passenger base on a transport network is an example of which of the PESTLE factors?	a) Political b) Sociological c) Legal d) Environmental	
5	The project will need to understand the context to help understand the need and wants of the stakeholders.	True or false?	

What kind of question might there be in the exam?

1

This question has <u>two</u> parts. Answer both parts.

Explain what is meant by the term 'project context'.

10 marks

Explain <u>four</u> distinct factors that may influence project context.

40 marks (10 marks each)

1.4 The legislative aspects of project management

By completing this subsection you will be able to:

- explain the importance of relevant legislation applicable to projects (such as health and safety, environmental, employment, contract, data protection, freedom of information).

The legislative context

The primary areas for consideration here are:

■ health and safety regulations and law;

■ contract regulations and law;

■ employment regulations and law;

■ environmental regulations and law;

■ freedom of information.

Health and safety law and regulations

The main enabling act of parliament was the Health and Safety at Work, etc. Act 1974. Its objectives were that of:

Securing the health, safety and welfare of persons at work and protecting persons, other than persons at work, against risks to health or safety arising out of or in connection with the activities of persons at work.

The Act introduced a new system based on less-prescriptive and more goal-based regulations, supported by guidance and codes of practice. For the first time, employers and employees were to be consulted and engaged in the process of designing a modern health and safety system.

The Health and Safety at Work, etc. Act 1974 also established the Health and Safety Commission (HSC) for the purpose of proposing new regulations, providing information and advice, and conducting research.

The HSC's operating arm, the Health and Safety Executive (HSE) was formed shortly after in order to enforce health and safety law, a duty shared with local authorities.

The importance of the Act is to enshrine in law the acceptable standards and mechanisms to achieve the objectives. The benefits of the Act are to provide:

■ a healthy and safe environment for employees;

■ protection to the general public who may be affected by work;

■ a clear reporting and management structure to ensure that the processes are in place;

■ guidance on the interpretation of the law;

■ codes of conduct to be followed in specific industries.

Health and safety – what does a project manager need to be aware of?

In order to provide a proper working environment, the project manager (as part of the organisation's management structure) must consider the following:

Making sure that a health, safety and environmental management plan is in place

This document (possibly part of the project management plan [PMP]) will include the scope of the project, the roles and responsibilities associated with it, particular external standards that may need to be adopted, reporting mechanisms, specific project-related procedures, training record keeping and other pertinent information. The plan will be developed in conjunction with stakeholders in the sponsoring organisation and approved by the relevant health, safety and environmental body in that organisation.

Making sure that risk assessments are carried out

The project manager may not be able to carry these out themselves, but must make proper provision and funding available to ensure that they are done, properly recorded and any resultant actions completed. A typical example of a risk assessment is a specific one for the use of display screens in office environments.

That the project team is properly trained

Project staff may think that due to the temporary nature of the project they do not need to follow HSE regulations or are in some way immune. Accidents can happen anywhere and the project manager will need to instil in the employees a robust and serious attention to these issues.

There is open and honest disclosure

One of the main things that the project manager establishes is a safety culture in which staff are comfortable reporting dangerous situations and not be penalised for it. HSE is the responsibility of everyone. One of the areas required by law is the Reporting of Injuries, Disease and Dangerous Occurrences Regulations (RIDDOR) to be adhered to where near misses are required to be reported.

That regular reviews are undertaken

So that minor situations do not develop to become dangerous. Sometimes where a particular environment has been occupied for some time and familiarity becomes complacency there is a grave danger of accidents happening. Continual assessment and restating of the issues and procedures will make sure this doesn't happen.

That everyone is aware of stress as a potential HSE issue

Where a project has strict deadlines, difficult problems and resource shortages there can be a temptation to drive the team too hard, thus inducing stress. The project manager should ensure that working hours are not unreasonable, that proper relaxation facilities are available and the project team are consulted as part of work allocation, all of which will help in this area. But as with all health and safety matters the project manager should seek support from their professional HSE colleagues.

Proper safety equipment is provided

Personal protective equipment (PPE) should be made available to staff where the circumstances dictate. Codes of practice help to guide what is the minimum requirement, although many organisations seek to exceed this minimum. Fluorescent jackets, hard hats and rubber gloves are all examples of PPE. Machine tools guards, scaffolding, electrical equipment and working at height are all specific areas with stringent requirements for health and safety attention.

Environmental issues are addressed

As well as the protection of employees and the public, the project manager will have to be aware of and conform to any relevant legislation relating to the environment. Rehabilitation of contaminated land, recycling of printer toner and disposal of waste are all issues that will need to be considered; once again the circumstances will vary depending on the project.

Please also note that it is advisable to obtain proper health and safety advice when the need arises.

Contract law and regulations

Contracts are simply an agreement between parties where one offers to sell (products or services) and the other offers to buy (those products or services).

For a contract to be enforceable in English law, there are a number of things that need to be considered. These include:

- Who are the parties and a description of the works or services, what are the relevant company names, registration details and are they actually legally entitled to enter into this agreement.

- The provider's responsibilities with regard to design, approvals, subcontracting and assignment: this is particularly pertinent in construction projects. If the designers design something that is unsuitable then it is they that will need to rectify the problems.

- Timings, costs, milestones, when exactly will things be done, are there any damages for late payment or incentives for early payment?

- Quality and other standards to be followed, if there are standards to be followed who will assess those standards and where will project quality assurance and control be exercised?

- Payment and when payment is due etc., this will be very concerning to subcontractors where their cash flow may be sensitive and the need to have swift payment may be vital to their survival.

- What happens if things go wrong; liquidated damages, penalty clauses, consequential loss are all phrases used in and around contracts.

- Who owns what during and after the contract particularly intellectual property rights (IPR) and copyright, the intellectual property vested in a project can be substantial and the ownership of it may be vital to understand. Some knowledge-based suppliers will have a huge vested interest in the acquisition and reselling of IPR.

- Assignment and management of risk, who owns the responsibility for dealing with risk and can they in turn assign that responsibility to others.

- How disputes and arbitration will be carried out, in the UK most contracts are subject to the jurisdiction of the UK court system under UK law. Where multinational agreements are in place then this may not be the case.

There is more detail relating to the nature of contracts and procurement terms in general in Section 12. Please also note that it is advisable to obtain proper legal advice when the need arises.

Employment law and regulations

Project managers are sometimes in a strange position effectively directing the activities of people who are actually line managed elsewhere. This concept will be discussed when considering matrix organisations. They therefore may (or may not be) that person's legal employer. Nevertheless project managers will need to be aware of potential employment issues as they may have a direct influence over individuals covered by any relevant legislation.

Project managers must be aware that absence from work may be a sign of something more sinister. If an employee feels stressed at work they may be more inclined to stay away. Project managers must be aware that in a project environment there is a risk that people are put in stressful situations that are unreasonable and this must be avoided.

The Public Interest Disclosure Act 1998 covers the case of whistle-blowing. If staff feel that they are being directed to undertake activities they feel are in some way illegal or otherwise irregular they have protection should they inform others of the facts without fear of recrimination. The project manager must ensure that open and honest communication is encouraged and team concerns are taken seriously and dealt with.

The Working Time Regulations 1998 prescribe rules regarding the amount of time an employee can work, have breaks and holidays. Employees have rights under this law and project managers must be aware that again there is a risk that in a pressured environment there may be the urge to work longer than is strictly allowed. Project managers must ensure that objectives and targets are fairly set and do not overburden the team.

It is illegal to discriminate on the basis of sex, gender, race, sexual orientation, age or disability. Project managers, like their line management colleagues, need to be aware of the implications of contravening these regulations. Project managers must engender an environment of inclusion and fairness in all the project activities.

The Data Protection Act 1998 lays down the rights of the individual with regard to the storage and retention of information. Project managers may inadvertently be storing personal data either of their team or of other individuals as part of the project they are running and be unaware that this may in fact represent a breach. Project managers must ensure that there is an appropriate information management plan that everyone can abide by.

Please note that this is not an exhaustive list and once again, professional support may need to be sought.

884 of8888888

Environmental law and regulations

These days project management is constrained by environmental considerations in ways that it never was before. There are literally hundreds of pieces of applicable legislation and the following are just a few considerations:

Projects may need to consider undertaking an environmental impact assessment. This will take into account the wider range of environmental aspects that a project may affect or be affected by. It might include the discharge of water, traffic congestion, noise, smoke, etc. It would need to be done at an early stage, usually as part of the planning stages, and may be needed to support a planning application.

In construction projects the use of contaminated land to build on will result in the need to carry out proper surveys, along with the correct disposal of any waste from the site and recycling of any that can be re-used on the site.

ISO 14001:2004 (BSI, 2004) sets out the criteria for an environmental management system that an organisation can be certified to. It does not state requirements for environmental performance, but maps out a framework that a company or organisation can follow to set up an effective environmental management system.

Energy consumption will be closely monitored, for example on an IT project. While there are still large rooms full of expensive and energy, hungry computers there is a growing need and desire to throttle back the energy consumption of these installations, leading to a number of revisions to plans that only a few years ago would have seemed perfectly reasonable.

The 'waste hierarchy' ranks waste management options according to what is best for the environment. It gives top priority to preventing waste in the first place. When waste is created, it gives priority to preparing it for reuse, then recycling, then recovery, and last of all disposal (e.g. landfill). The stages include (consider Figure 1.4):

■ Prevention entails using less material in the first place. Designing in a longer product life cycle will help to keep the re-manufacture impact to a minimum. Computer design techniques have been a huge contributor to this avoiding 'over engineering'.

■ Reuse involves taking the parts (machines, motors, etc.) and using them in similar applications after refurbishment. Car breaker's yards are good examples of this.

■ If materials cannot be reused then they can possibly be recycled into a new product. Copper is extracted from old heating systems and melted down and used in electric motors.

■ Recovery includes the use of the product to extract energy for use instead of fresh supplies. An example of this might be anaerobic digestion to power heating plants.

■ Disposal, landfill and incineration without energy recovery should be the last resort.

MANAGEMENT

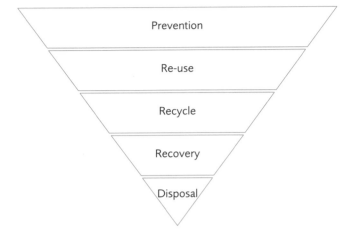

Figure 1.4 Environmental considerations

Freedom of information

The Freedom of Information Act 2000 means that most public authorities are obliged to provide the public with access to information it holds. (This is not information held about individuals as that is covered under the Data Protection Act.) The Act states that public bodies must a) publish certain information about their activities and b) individuals can ask to see copies of the information they hold. Government departments, local authorities, the NHS, state schools and police forces are all covered by the Act.

More information is available from the information commissioner's website ico.org.uk.

Please note: where consideration of employment or other legally orientated subject matter is proposed these notes should not be taken as comprehensive and are for the illustration of potential areas for examination only. Individuals should seek further guidance where appropriate.

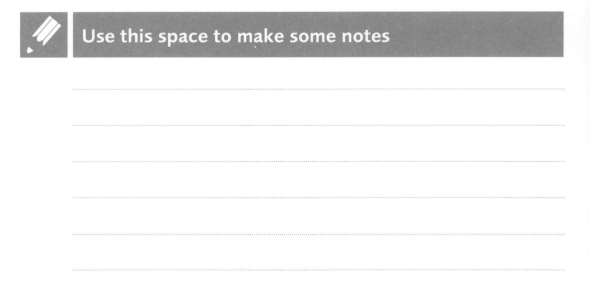

Use this space to make some notes

WHIRLWIND BIKES
Consider the following case study on page 259. Are there any potential legal issues on Whirlwind Bikes? What steps might you take to ensure that the road testing trials are accident free?

Quick quiz (answers on page 273)

	Question	Options	Your answer
1	Providing safety equipment is an employer's responsibility under HSE legislation.	True or false?	
2	The Health and Safety Executive informs and enforces safety law.	True or false?	
3	Which of these can cause stress?	a) Urgent timescales b) Working longer hours c) Working away from home d) All of the above	
4	RIDDOR is unique because it covers which of the following specific issues?	a) Nuclear contamination b) Food allergies c) Near misses d) Car crashes	

MANAGEMENT

	Question	Options	Your answer
5	Which of these is concerned with environmental management?	a) ISO 14001 b) BS6079 c) BS5750 d) ISO 100001	
6	IPR stands for...?	a) Intellectual property rights b) Internal paper rights c) Inspection of personal records d) Implementation of paper receipts	
7	The layers of environmental considerations are Prevention, Reuse, Recycle, Recovery, Disposal.	True or false?	
8	The Public Interest Disclosure Act includes what could be described as...?	a) Stress at work b) Near misses c) Whistle-blowing d) Regular reporting	
9	The project manager must ensure a health and safety plan is in place on all projects.	True or false?	
10	Contracts require agreement.	True or false?	

What kind of question might there be in the exam?

1 This question has two parts. Answer both parts.

Explain the purpose of a project health and safety plan.

10 marks

List and describe four components of a project health and safety plan.

40 marks (10 marks each)

2 Organisations and structures

	Subjects covered in this section
2.1	Organisation structures
2.2	Organisational roles
2.3	Project office

2.1 Organisation structures

By completing this subsection you will be able to:

■ differentiate between types of organisation structures highlighting advantages and disadvantages of each (including functional, matrix, project).

Three different types of organisation structure

There are a number of potential ways in which a business may choose to organise itself and these ways are generally considered to fall into one of three main categories, a functional, project or matrix structure.

The authority and influence of the project manager differs according to the type of structure, as shown in Figure 2.1. Typically, as an organisation becomes more 'project-based', so the project manager's authority increases, while the authority of the line manager decreases.

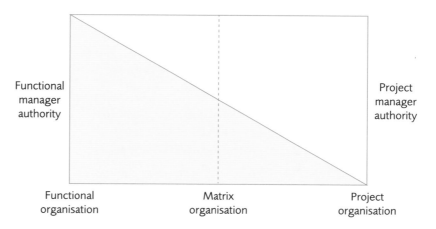

Figure 2.1 The relative authority of the project and functional managers

The functional organisation

A purely functional type of organisation is one which has very clear lines of reporting and accountability up and down through the organisation. Examples of this type of organisation are where key skills need to be developed and maintained, and there is a relatively low level of change going on. An example of this type of organisation structure appears in Figure 2.2, along with the strengths and weaknesses in Table 2.1.

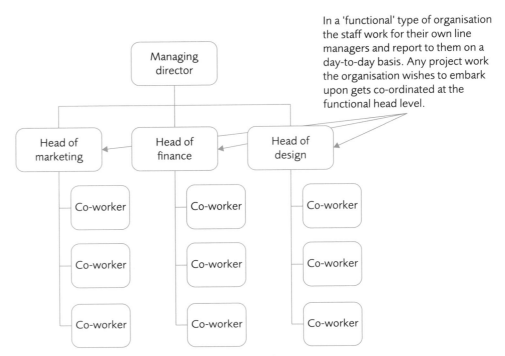

In a 'functional' type of organisation the staff work for their own line managers and report to them on a day-to-day basis. Any project work the organisation wishes to embark upon gets co-ordinated at the functional head level.

Figure 2.2 The functional organisation

Table 2.1 Strengths and weaknesses of a functional organisation

Strengths	Weaknesses
Maintains a cohort of very skilled staff, experts in their own chosen field. This can be very valuable where capability needs to be maintained (e.g. a fire service).	Less flexible and less able to adopt project working. The only way a project will happen is at the functional head level.
Allows for a lot of organisational learning due to its stable nature. The teams will be able to embed and utilise their specialist knowledge.	Does not provide variety for those that want it, thus affecting motivation. Staff will have no visibility of potential opportunities in other parts of the organisation.
Staff know who they report to and can easily determine priorities. This reduces conflict and associated stress.	Can lead to under-utilisation as there is an opportunity for under-utilised staff in one part of the structure to not have access to potential opportunities in other parts.

The project organisation

At the other end of the continuum lies the project organisation. In this type, the project manager is in charge and the organisation only exists for the purpose of running its constituent projects. Once they have all finished then, in theory, the organisation ceases to exist. Some examples of this might be a construction consultancy or film production unit where the holding company is only a skeleton and the project teams are brought together when needed and disbanded when not. Diagrammatically, it looks like this (see Figure 2.3):

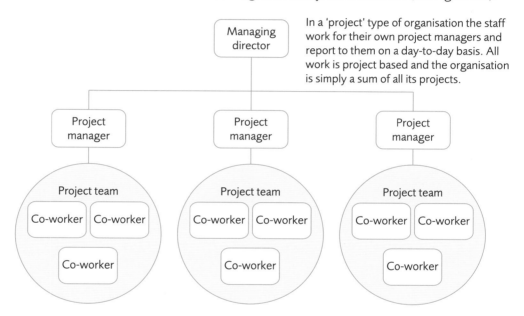

In a 'project' type of organisation the staff work for their own project managers and report to them on a day-to-day basis. All work is project based and the organisation is simply a sum of all its projects.

Figure 2.3 The project organisation

Project organisations, too, have pros and cons associated with them (see Table 2.2).

Table 2.2 Strengths and weaknesses of a project organisation

Strengths	Weaknesses
They have a very clear focus on the project objectives. They are not distracted by any line management responsibilities.	Little or no career progression and job security. Once the project is over the team members are no longer required.
The project manager is quite clearly in charge and the staff are able to identify and relate to this authority.	Can cause duplication and under-utilisation. For example an under-utilised team member on one project will not be utilised on another.
Easy to identify very clear roles and responsibilities without crossing organisation boundaries. The project managers have a strong project ethic and build their teams personally.	Experience tends to leave the organisation when the project finishes. The overall business does not have access to the experience of the team after the project has been disbanded.

MANAGEMENT

The matrix organisation

The third variation on this theme is a mix between the two main types as above. It is called the matrix type of organisation structure (see Figure 2.4) and has the potential (if implemented well) to deliver the strengths of the other two without too many downsides.

In this type of framework, we see that we still have the staff reporting to a line manager, but now the project managers are able to draw on resources from across the business. In this way the project managers and the organisation get the best of both worlds. The main objective of the organisation is to deploy the right people to the right activities. This framework requires a sophisticated understanding of the organisation and the staff and roles within it, but offers the advantages of optimal resource utilisation while retaining organisational capability. In summary, these matrix organisations have the strengths and weaknesses shown in Table 2.3.

Have a think about what type of organisation you work in.

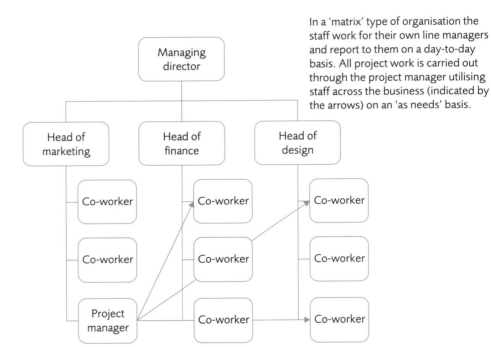

In a 'matrix' type of organisation the staff work for their own line managers and report to them on a day-to-day basis. All project work is carried out through the project manager utilising staff across the business (indicated by the arrows) on an 'as needs' basis.

Figure 2.4 The matrix organisation

Table 2.3 Strengths and weaknesses of a matrix organisation

Strengths	Weaknesses
There is visibility of resource skills and availability. The project managers can 'see' where their potential resources (teams) may reside organisationally.	Needs quite a sophisticated resource management culture otherwise the potential teams are unknown and invisible to the project managers.
The project managers have an organisational authority over staff. The organisation recognises that project managers need to direct others and this concept is familiar to all.	Staff members can find their priorities conflict between project and line manager. If they have more than one person trying to direct their time they may be uncertain about which to satisfy.
Specialist skills are maintained. When one project finishes staff move on to others. This can be balanced against the pastoral needs of the staff (holidays, training, etc.).	Project managers need to be good communicators and good at influencing others to get the job done. They cannot simply rely on an organisational authority in a line management sense.

Work-based exercise

What type of organisation is yours – functional, matrix or project?

What inspires you to say that?

What complications does that cause your project managers?

 Quick quiz (answers on page 273)

	Question	Options	Your answer
1	A matrix organisation helps retain specialist skills when compared to a project organisation.	True or false?	
2	A functional organisation is most likely to retain specialist skills.	True or false?	
3	A project organisation is most likely to retain specialist skills.	True or false?	
4	In a matrix organisation, when the staff member has conflicting priorities between line and project manager, which might they naturally favour?	a) Line manager b) Project manager c) Neither d) Both	
5	Which of these things is <u>not</u> needed in a true matrix organisation for it to work properly?	a) Good influencing skills by the project manager b) Effective resource management systems c) Flexible and motivated staff d) Excessive paperwork	
6	In a functional organisation, who would co-ordinate any project if it took place at all?	a) The functional managers b) The project managers c) Nobody d) The staff themselves	
7	As the organisation becomes more project-focused, the role of the functional manager increases.	True or false?	

	Question	Options	Your answer
8	A matrix organisation has the potential to reduce resource under-utilisation compared to a project or functional organisation.	True or false?	
9	A strength of a project organisation structure is that the teams have a clear focus.	True or false?	
10	Project managers need good influencing skills in a matrix organisation.	True or false?	

Use this space to make some notes

What kind of question might there be in the exam?

1

This question has <u>two</u> parts. Answer both parts.

Explain these types of organisation structures when used in a project context: functional, project and matrix.

30 marks (10 marks each)

Explain <u>two</u> difficulties that a project manager may experience when working in a matrix environment.

20 marks (10 marks each)

MANAGEMENT

| 2.2 | **Organisational roles** |

By completing this subsection you will be able to:

- explain the role and key role and responsibilities of the project manager;

- differentiate between the responsibilities of the project manager and project sponsor throughout the project life cycle;

- describe other roles within project management including uses, project team members and the project steering group/board.

We have chosen to amalgamate these assessment criteria in one place as project roles necessarily interact with each other and these interactions are best dealt with in the context of the others.

Project roles

Project sponsorship is the proactive senior leadership of a project. The sponsor will be the champion and the key inspirational figure for the project. Sponsorship encapsulates the taking of appropriate risk to reap reward and to do so in the context of an organisational framework that can be managed and assured by the nominated sponsor.

The way in which a project sponsor is appointed may well be laid down in the organisation's governance framework. Alternatively, the sponsor may be nominated by the steering group.

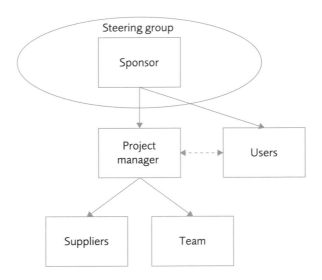

Figure 2.5 The main roles relating to a project

Consider Figure 2.5. There is a fundamental issue at stake when we start to consider organisational roles. The project manager reports to the sponsor for the purposes of the project. This relationship is separate and distinct from any line management or organisational relationship that may exist. As part of a matrix organisation (please refer to section 2.1) the sponsor could be the project manager's line manager but may not be and certainly does not have to be.

Also note that in this model the team is managed by the project manager and so are the suppliers. The suppliers will have a contractual relationship with the project, and the project manager will therefore be managing them as a single entity as opposed to the team members, who the project manager will manage individually. The management methods and techniques for each of these then is clearly very different. Also note that the project manager may be a junior grade to the people they may be 'project managing', as in a matrix structure.

Organisational roles

A summary of the various project roles are shown in Table 2.4 below.

Table 2.4 Organisational roles and responsibilities

Steering group	May nominate the sponsor. The steering group are the agent of the organisation in this respect.
	Helps influence and manage key stakeholders. In some cases simply because of their seniority they will have much more contact with and ability to influence them.
	Supports and advises the sponsor. The sponsor is a nominee of the steering group and as such will need proper and appropriate support at different times throughout the work in hand.
	Authorises the business case. The sponsor alone cannot authorise the business case as they will have been closely involved in its preparation and it will need to be challenged rather than simply accepted as correct and complete.
Team	Deliver the products to time, cost and quality parameters. They will produce the technical products associated with the project under the direction of the project manager.
	Help identify changes, risks and issues. They will be very close to the actual work and as such be the first ones to notice a lot of the detail that may trigger the project processess, such as change control.
	Supports the project manager. The team need to be motivated by the project manager but must reciprocate with adequate levels of support and help and advice to the project manager when it is needed.

MANAGEMENT

Project manager	Manages the project. In so doing they implement the plans and processes incorporated within the project management plan (PMP). They manage the team, report progress and seek support from the sponsor and will be ultimately accountable for the effective delivery of the project deliverables.
	Owns the project management plan. The project manager will keep this document firmly in step with the business case at all times. It must reflect the plans and processes for the future and it is incumbent upon the project manager to ensure that it remains relevant and appropriate for the job in hand.
	Manages stakeholders. The sponsor will manage some of the more major or key stakeholders, but the day-to-day activities of the project manager involve directly liaising with the project stakeholders.
	Liaises with end users. The project manager will need to ensure that the deliverables are meeting expectations and that they will ultimately deliver what they want/need.
	Manages suppliers usually by virtue of some form of contractual arrangement, here they may sometimes be acting as a 'contract manager'.
Sponsor	They own the business case and the realisation of benefits. The project manager delivers the project and delivers the products but the use to which they are put and the effectiveness of that use has to be overseen by the sponsor.
	Helps the project manager manage key stakeholders. They may manage stakeholders directly and may sometimes need to do so personally.
	Usually a peer of the steering group members. They will be selected from a cohort of senior business managers and directors and as such have a collective responsibility for the effective implementation of the project and the embedding of its deliverables.
	The project manager will look to the project sponsor to help resolve those really tricky issues that they cannot deal with. The sponsor in this respect may need to exert their political influence and wider network range to open doors and remove blockers.
	Helps identify key strategic and business risks along with others and in this way pass down information that helps the project manager deliver the project rather than simply dealing with risks and issues on the way up from the project manager.
	Helps the project manager deal with contingencies because the project manager does not own the contingent funds. If they are needed then the sponsor will need to release them when required, thus altering the project budget.

	They approve changes as the project manager cannot necessarily agree alterations to the scope of the project in case it in some way affects the potential for the delivery of the benefits in the business case.
	Arbitrates between different user and stakeholder requirements, perhaps deciding which requirement is addressed at the expense of another.
Users	The users need to define what is required to be achieved from the products once delivered through the requirements management process. They may need to describe in formal terms the requirements of the finished products.
	They advise the sponsor on the suitability of the delivered products as conforming to the specifications and requirements. In practice the sponsor will not be able to accept products alone although they (the sponsor) will actually sign for them upon recommendation of the users.
	They will operate the products, acting as the owner of the finished products they will put them to use and need to make sure that they are operated in a way in which the benefits can be derived.
	They will liaise with the project manager with regard to changes so that the plans and the registers of deliverables are up to date and that any issues relating to the appropriateness of the deliverables can be assured.
	Users need to accept the authority of the sponsor, it is the sponsor that owns the accountability for the suitability of the final solution and as such it is the sponsor that will have final say over which user requirement has priority. In this way any disputes among users will be resolved by the sponsor and not the project manager, releasing the project manager to deliver the project.
Suppliers	Suppliers can help identify key technical aspects and constraints. As the experts they will be able to suggest specific solutions, provide proposals, in turn manage other suppliers (as a prime contractor) and actually deliver the subject of these proposals to the project manager and hence the users.
	Suppliers are distinct from the team as they will be engaged via a contract and as such are required to perform the terms of the contract accordingly.
	They have a responsibility to report progress. This may seem obvious but as they are managed by the project manager it is necessary to instil in any supplier the need to do this and in a consistent and meaningful way.
	It is incumbent upon the supplier to ensure that any issues and risks are properly communicated and if necessary resolved.

The sponsor has involvement throughout the project as indicated in Figure 2.6. This should not be taken too literally, as the sponsor will have varying levels of input at different times, but is an important aspect of their role. The relationship between the sponsor and the project manager is vital to project success and a supportive but separate relationship will need to be carefully defined and nurtured throughout.

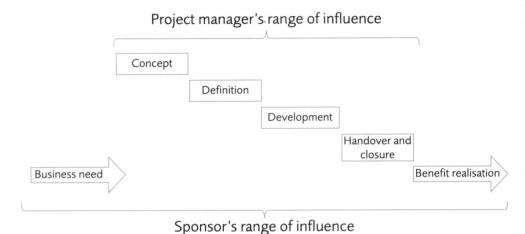

Figure 2.6 The sponsor's range of influence

Work-based exercise
In one of your projects see if you can identify all the roles below

Who is the sponsor?

Who are the users?

Who are the team?

Quick quiz (answers on page 274)

	Question	Options	Your answer
1	The project sponsor is the project manager's line manager.	True, false or maybe?	
2	The suppliers are managed by the project manager, usually through a . . . ?	a) Gentleman's agreement b) Contract c) PMP d) Goodwill	
3	Who owns the business case?	a) Project manager b) Sponsor c) Users d) Internal audit	
4	Who owns the project management plan (PMP)?	a) Project manager b) Sponsor c) Users d) Internal audit	
5	Which of these do the users NOT do?	a) Operate the deliverables b) Specify requirements c) Agree acceptance criteria d) Deliver work packages	
6	The sponsor is a peer of the other members of the steering group.	a) Yes b) No c) Possibly d) Must not be	
7	How many sponsors can a project have?	a) One b) Two c) Three d) Four	

MANAGEMENT

	Question	Options	Your answer
8	Who selects and appoints the sponsor?	a) The steering group b) The organisation's governance framework c) They are self-elected d) The project manager	
9	Changes to the project scope are approved by?	a) The sponsor b) The project manager c) The users d) The suppliers	
10	The organisation's governance structure has a major influence over the appointment of the sponsor.	True or false?	

Use this space to make some notes

What kind of questions might there be in the exam?

1	List and describe <u>five</u> roles associated with a project environment. Include in your answer the responsibilities of each role. 50 marks (10 marks each)

2	Explain <u>five</u> key differences between the role of the project manager and the project sponsor throughout the life cycle of the project. 50 marks (10 marks each)

2.3	**Project office**

By completing this subsection you will be able to describe the functions and benefits of different types of project office, including project support office (PSO), enterprise project management office (EPMO), project services or centres of excellence

The basic project office roles

The basic roles of a project office are described in Figure 2.7:

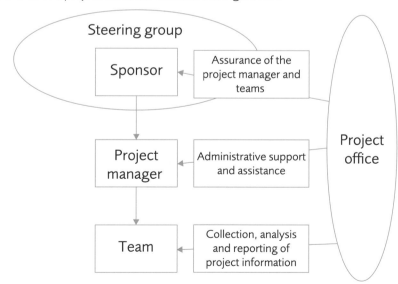

Figure 2.7 The role of the project office

There are as many interpretations of these basic roles as there are project offices. A common manifestation of a project office is that of simple administrative support to the project manager. They are very often tasked with filing, administration, organising meetings and deputising for the project manager. While valuable, these are potentially only part of the role. In a larger organisation, and especially one which has a mature project management approach, the project office can be 'virtual'. That is to say that the different services are provided by distinct different parts of the existing organisation. Some large construction companies have a planning department where the project manager can go for this type of specialist advice. This is therefore an example of this 'virtual' project office team approach. Table 2.5 seeks to illustrate some of the roles undertaken by a project office.

Table 2.5 The project office roles

Key roles	What the project office may do	Describe briefly areas in your organisation where you witness these roles
Administrative support and guidance (project services)	Be responsible for configuration management activities, documentation control and filing. Have experts in given fields such as risk, planning or estimating. Be able to offer some degree of support to the project manager during absences. Be heavily involved in the meetings cycle, issuing agendas and minutes and chasing actions.	
Collection, analysis and reporting of project information	Collate and tabulate the time sheets and other accounting and progress information from the team and elsewhere and provide such reports as the project manager and sponsor may require. Maintain a schedule according to which reports are produced. Sit in on specialist workshops to help gather information on risks and other detailed information.	

Key roles	What the project office may do	Describe briefly areas in your organisation where you witness these roles
Where the project office has expert resources in project management fields	Provide coaching and mentoring to the project managers in the application of tools and various techniques.	
Centre of excellence	Act as the repository for the strategic implementation of not only the individual projects but the portfolio as well. This is sometimes referred to as the enterprise project management office or EPMO.	
Continual improvement	Be instrumental in ensuring the lessons from the project are properly documented and recorded for use elsewhere.	

Project office is a generic term and you may hear it referred to as project support office, project management office, project and programme support office, portfolio support office, enterprise project management office. For the purposes of the exam it is probably best to consider the project office in its most simple form: that is to say as in Table 2.5.

The benefits of a project office are that:

- It relieves some of the administrative burden from the project manager, but it is not just a 'dumping ground' for everything the project manager does not want to do!

- It provides a vehicle for the organisation to standardise approaches through the use of a common method being implemented under control, the project office can be seen as the agent or implementer of aspects of the organisation's project management governance.

- It provides assurance to the project manager that the plans are being followed by checking with the teams and may also provide reports to other stakeholders for their reassurance that things are going as they should.

- It provides consistency of approach, the project office focuses on the project processes and that they are being followed in the right manner.

- It allows continuity in the event that a project manager may need to be replaced.

- It is a vehicle by which common lessons can be learned across the organisation.

Work-based exercise

Does your organisation have a project office? What do they do? Are they centralised or virtual?

 Quick quiz (answers on page 275)

	Question	Options	Your answer
1	A project office has to be a single autonomous unit.	True or false?	
2	A project office manager reports directly to the project manager in all cases.	True or false?	
3	Which of these activities is fulfilled by the project office?	a) Approving changes b) Administering the change control procedure c) Estimating the costs of changes	
4	The project office can deputise for the project manager only if. . . . .?	a) They do not provide an assurance role for the sponsor b) They are competent c) The team agree	
5	EPMO means?	a) Exclusive project management office	

	Question	Options	Your answer
		b) Enterprise project management office	
		c) Everyone's project management office	
6	The team may provide information to the project office for reporting purposes.	True or false?	
7	The team have to follow the direction of the project office.	True or false?	
8	The project office may be responsible for standards and procedures, and provide advice across multiple projects.	True or false?	
9	The project office costs come out of the project budget.	a) True b) False c) Maybe	
10	The minimum number of people in the project office is __ and the maximum is __?	a) 1/4 b) Any number/any number c) 1/any number	

Use this space to make some notes

MANAGEMENT

What kind of questions might there be in the exam?

1

This question has <u>two</u> parts. Answer both parts.

List and describe <u>two</u> key activities that a project office may undertake.

20 marks (10 marks each)

Explain <u>three</u> distinct benefits of a project office.

30 marks (10 marks each)

3

Life cycles

 Subjects covered in this section

3.1 Project life cycles

3.1 Project life cycles

By completing this subsection you will be able to:

- define a project life cycle and project life cycle phases (including concept, definition, development, handover and closure and benefits realisation);

- explain why projects are structured as phases (including the use of end of phase reviews, go/no-go decisions and high-level planning);

- explain the differences between a project life cycle and an extended life cycle;

- outline processes for sharing knowledge and lessons learned throughout projects;

- explain the benefits of conducting reviews throughout the project life cycle (including project evaluation reviews, gate reviews, post-project reviews, peer reviews, benefits reviews and audits).

These assessment criteria have been combined as each one is in itself relatively small and the whole topic represents a more coherent topic to discuss together.

The project life cycle

The project life cycle, Figure 3.1 (Association for Project Management, 2012), allows us to consider a managed and evolutionary progression through the phases of a project. The length of each of these phases can vary considerably between different projects and the naming of the various phases, while important for the exam and consistency, are not necessarily those adopted by organisations in real life. For the purposes of the exam you can use alternate terms if desired. Again though if you are considering this topic for the first time these terms are appropriate.

Within the project management plan (see Section 8.5) will be all the processes that the project will follow to make sure that it is managed in an orderly way. The life cycle describes the broad flow of the project. Think of the life cycle as describing the project journey and the processes work throughout that life cycle. For example risk management is done throughout

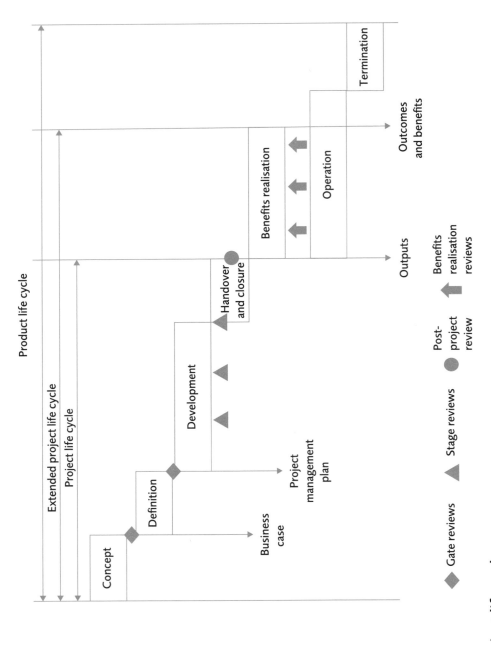

Figure 3.1 Project life cycle

the project, through all the life cycle phases. Section 8.5 will describe some of these processes but they include risk management, stakeholder management, issue management and configuration management among others.

The Concept phase encompasses everything up to and including the production of the business case. It includes the feasibility and 'optioneering' to arrive at the chosen solution for development into the project. It is overseen by the sponsor, and a project manager may well be appointed to develop the business case. The business case may not be final at this stage and may need revision during definition as the project management plan evolves.

The Definition phase includes the production of the project management plan and all of its component plans such as the risk management plan and quality plan etc. It culminates in approval to proceed to development. The primary output is the project management plan (PMP). This documents the entirety of the project and what it will produce. It needs to reflect any changes to the business case and vice versa.

The Development phase covers the construction of the various components that comprise the end product of the project according to the plans constructed in the definition phase. During the development phase there may be many stages (each separated by a stage review) to allow for a proper evaluation of progress. The primary outputs are the products of the project.

Handover is the process of commissioning the products and the migration of them to practical use, and **Closure** is the administrative closure of the project and disbanding the team. Acceptance is the key output as this will signify the users' acceptance of the products into operational service.

During handover the project team will:

- Hand over all the deliverables after checking that as far as they are concerned they fulfil the specifications created at the commencement of the project.

- Create operating procedures and 'as built' drawings, and hand them over along with support arrangements. In addition, insurances will need to be put in place.

- Ensure some form of final acceptance takes place once the product is finally in use. Typically, the project will expect the sponsor and/or the users to sign some form of acceptance certificate to formally demonstrate that they are happy with the products.

- Hand over formal ownership of the products to the users and make sure they have everything in place to cope with any issues arising without continual recourse to the project teams. The project may of course have arrangements in place to provide such a service in the short-term but eventually the users will have to 'stand on their own two feet', so to speak.

During closure, the project team will:

- Ensure the users understand how to operate the products and use them to obtain the benefit they anticipated. In order to do this they may need to embark upon a period of what is called commissioning. Here they will take delivery and begin to move the raw product into becoming an operational asset. With a ship, for example, the commissioning period can be lengthy and will involve many hundreds of people and resources. It may include trial runs, practising emergency procedures, fuelling, etc. For a software system, it may include loading live data, transferring account balances and commencing support arrangements.

- Contribute to appraisals and staff reviews in some instances. This is important so that teams are not simply abandoned once the project is finished.

- Make sure various bookings of time and resources are reconciled and any archiving of materials and documentation can take place.

- Ensure any assets utilised other than people will need to be disposed of, project buildings vacated, hardware returned, waste material recycled, etc.

- Participate in lessons learned activities so that all the lessons learned from throughout the project can be disseminated around the business for the benefits of later projects. The sponsor would commission these and report them back to the sponsoring/steering group.

The extended project life cycle

The extended project life cycle casts the net a little wider and allows the consideration of the wider project life cycle. The extended life cycle along with the consideration of the product life cycle means we have a focus on whole-life costing (i.e. the recognition that the cost of producing the asset must be considered alongside the cost of operating it and decommissioning).

Benefits realisation phase allows us to consider the beneficial outcomes of the project. We don't generally do projects just because we are able to. Most investment is undertaken in order that some longer-term benefit can be derived. We build a railway so people can travel more easily from place to place, for example. This concept is covered in more detail in Section 8.2.

Operations is the component that gives us the framework within which to consider the operational costs. As mentioned, through-life costing necessarily demands that the benefits of having and using the products are valued but this needs to be mitigated by the costs of doing so. Our railway will consume electricity, staff costs, maintenance, ticketing systems, etc. We cannot simply count the income from ticket sales.

The product life cycle

The final component of the life cycle model includes the **Termination** phase. This is intended to draw our attention to how much it will cost to dispose of the product at the end of its useful life. The example often quoted is that of a nuclear power station; would it have been justified had the cost of decommissioning (environmental as well as economic) it at the end of its useful life been considered?

The benefits of having a life cycle

Many organisations and indeed whole industries have their own well understood project life cycle and there are also a number produced and recommended by other professional bodies, such as the Royal Institute of Chartered Surveyors in the UK. This allows a common approach (by industry) and saves organisations developing their own.

A life cycle is an easy way of demonstrating the logical progression through the time frame of a project, with clearly defined activities and outputs for each phase. It also provides an obvious point at which to stop the project (i.e. between phases, at the end of one and the start of the next), where the business case, plans and risks are reviewed and detailed plans for the next phase agreed.

When combined with the principle of project processes it helps us understand in greater detail the evolution of a project, being able to identify areas that need greater attention at different times, such as risk management in the early stages. Other benefits include:

- An understanding of which resources may be required (both in number and nature) and when. This helps the organisation to plan its necessary levels of resource requirements.

- A high-level initial breakdown so that detailed planning can be carried out (within each phase).

- An indication of when key project reviews can take place, ensuring the relevant authorities are in place and things are co-ordinated to proceed.

- An opportunity to ensure that proper attention is given to the early stages by demanding that the project goes through a number of phase gates.

- An opportunity to link progress directly to them and recognise the completion of a phase which will provide increased confidence on the part of stakeholders.

- To ensure that a project continues to be viable through scrutiny at the gate reviews.

The different types of review

When considering life cycles there are some things to note regarding reviews:

At the end of both **Concept** and **Definition** gate reviews will take place. The purpose of this is to review the project against the business case (**Concept**) and project management plan (**Definition**) and decide if the project should proceed to the next phase.

Stage reviews take place throughout the **Development** phase. These reviews evaluate the progress of the project against the agreed plans with the aim of identifying variance and corrective actions.

A post project review is carried out at the end of the **Handover and Closure** phase to ensure complete handover of the project to the customer and learn lessons for future projects.

Benefits realisation will happen during/after **Handover and Closure**.

These reviews are considered in more detail in Table 3.1.

Very often the **Development** phase is split into more than one 'stage' with stage reviews in-between. These stages will offer the opportunity to review the evolution of the project and the resultant products and make sure that things are on track in a formal manner.

Table 3.1 Different types of project reviews

Type of review	Scope of review and outcomes
Gate reviews	This is a formal review, usually commissioned by the sponsoring organisation as part of its governance structure. It will have a formal agenda, usually supported with a checklist of products and criteria. They will happen as a minimum at the end of the Concept and Definition Phases. Very often a gate review will be a formal funding gate, granting permission for the project to proceed. There are usually three outcomes to a gate review – pass, pass with reservation and fail. The benefits of undertaking gate reviews are: ■ a regular and structured control framework to ensure that progress is as it should be; ■ the development of a relationship between the project manager and their sponsor thus developing trust; ■ a documented statement of progress to demonstrate to the organisation that a requisite level of control is being undertaken.
Post-project review	Carried out soon after the project has finished, these reviews will provide a clear forum to capture lessons learned (see below). Similar to a stage review, they will consider not only the project's satisfaction of its success criteria but will also be a thorough analysis of the effectiveness of the project management methods, tools and practices and team performance. The organisation will receive the assurance that the project has been successful (and if not, why not) such that it can make adjustments to its working practices and systems. It will also document that the project has actually finished and all materials and information have been recorded appropriately. The benefits of undertaking a post-project review are: ■ the capture of lessons learned to help inform future projects; ■ a formal record of the out-turn, this will help in estimating and risk management for future projects; ■ a way to identify excellent behaviours and an opportunity to recognise and reward individuals and teams.

Type of review	Scope of review and outcomes
Benefits realisation reviews	Only after the products have been completed and handover has been carried out can a proper evaluation of the benefits be achieved. Managed and chaired by the sponsor, these reviews will involve the thorough analysis by the business of the relevant achievement of the stated benefits as defined in the business case. The project manager will have moved on (the project has finished after all) and therefore the sponsor's role in achieving these is paramount. The purpose will be for the business to understand whether the project was a success and delivered the necessary products that achieve the benefits. The benefits of undertaking a benefits review are: ■ the project can be recognised for having 'made a difference'; ■ the organisation can review the real benefits obtained and reconcile them with the ambitions stated in the business case; ■ draw out areas where benefits may not be as expected and lay plans to modify and rectify the situation.
Stage reviews	These are carried out during the project using key performance indicators (KPIs – see Section 8.2) established for the purpose, to ensure that activities are progressing as planned. Usually convened by the project manager, supported by the team and chaired by the sponsor and users, they are internal (that is to say they are for the project's use to ratify progress against plans). They review not only the project indicators but also provide an analysis of the effectiveness of the project management tools and processes. Minutes will record progress against time, cost and quality parameters. Any decisions and corrective action will be identified to ensure that the project remains on track. Where significant risks are observed as likely, measures will be put in place to mitigate them. The number of stage reviews throughout the project will be dependent upon a number of factors including the length of the project and associated risks. The benefits of undertaking a stage review are: ■ the project's progress will be measured objectively against its KPIs; ■ corrective actions will be identified and actioned; ■ the sponsor has a formal opportunity to intervene in a project in an organised and predictable manner; ■ risks and issues can be formally and properly addressed and the various logs updated.

MANAGEMENT

Type of review	Scope of review and outcomes
Peer reviews	A peer review can be carried out at more or less any time. They are (as the name implies) intended to use colleagues of the project manager (or potentially the sponsor) to provide scrutiny of the way in which the role is being fulfilled and the manner in which the project is being run. These are sometimes referred to as health checks (when carried out by peers of the person being reviewed). They have the advantage of using people who have first-hand knowledge of the task in hand and who can empathise with particular situations and provide first-hand help if needed. The benefits of undertaking a peer review are: ■ it's a great way of learning through experience – both for the reviewer and the person being reviewed; ■ it capitalises upon recent, up to date knowledge; ■ it is not as onerous or potentially threatening as is perhaps a more rigorous audit.

Sharing knowledge and lessons learned generally

A continual review of project documentation, KPIs, metrics and team performance all provide clues as to where things could be improved. It must be clear that the analysis is only a part of the picture. The organisation should be prepared to take the information available and actually circulate it around the business to make sure that other projects can make use of it. A lessons learned report is not just another piece of bureaucracy to be filed away. Breakfast team meetings, published journals, updated estimate tables, metrics and risk checklists are all examples of where lessons learned can be made available and used productively.

The role of an audit

One formal activity many organisations undertake is an audit. These are external to the project (but may be internal to the sponsoring organisation). They will be more procedural in nature and seek to assure the organisation that the project is conforming to its stated principles and procedures and has a good chance of succeeding. They take many forms, usually financial or procedural but may include health and safety, procurement, etc. They will normally be of use to the organisation and, in some instances, to a much wider audience (e.g. The National Audit Office in the UK) providing information relating to good (and poor) practice.

Work-based exercise

Do your projects have a life cycle? What is it? What documents result from each phase?

 Quick quiz (answers on page 275)

	Question	Options	Your answer
1	There is only one possible life cycle for all projects.	True or false?	
2	When thinking about an extended project life cycle it allows us to consider the termination costs of a project.	True or false?	
3	A project manager would need to understand the nature of the project and the industry it is in to make sure the life cycle is appropriate.	True or false?	

MANAGEMENT

	Question	Options	Your answer
4	Which review takes place during the operations phase?	a) Benefits realisation review b) Phase gate c) Project evaluation review d) Design review	
5	Project audits are normally internal to the project.	True or false?	
6	Benefits realisation reviews happen during which project life cycle phase?	a) Operations b) Termination c) Concept d) Definition	
7	Lessons learned should be recorded all the way through a project.	True or false?	
8	Only a sponsor sees the output from a project audit.	True or false?	
9	The project management plan is finalised during the definition phase.	True or false?	
10	The life cycle model mentioned is the only one that you can use.	True or false?	

Use this space to make some notes

What kind of questions might there be in the exam?

1	Explain <u>five</u> distinct benefits of using a structured life cycle approach. 50 marks (10 marks each)
2	List <u>five</u> key phases of a typical life cycle and describe the activities undertaken during each of them. 50 marks (10 marks each)

4 Organisation and governance

Subjects covered in this section

4.1 Governance

4.2 Methods and procedures

4.1 Governance

By completing this subsection you will be able to:

■ describe the principles of governance of project management (such as policies, regulations, functions, processes, procedures and responsibilities).

What is the governance of project management?

Governance of project management fills the potential void between the project environment and that of the board of the organisation. Just about everything in this syllabus contributes towards project governance, but the concept that an organisation will want to govern its projects and programmes in a certain controlled way gives a clue to the fact that this governance overlaps quite heavily with that of portfolio management. Effective governance will ensure that their projects operate in a predetermined and controlled manner. When talking about governance as a principle, it is necessary to elevate the discussion from that of the single project and begin to consider projects – in the plural.

The absence of project governance may have a significant bearing on the success or failure of an organisation and/or the project.

The governance of project management is intended to complement an organisation's overall governance and to link it and the projects governance together to provide a productive framework in which they can operate in a managed and controlled way, providing effective oversight (see Figure 4.1).

Work undertaken in producing the APM publication *Directing Change: a guide to governance of project management* (APM, 2011) structured the question of project governance into a number of key areas. You may be required to recognise these areas and they are simply included here as headings. The descriptions of the terms in most cases are self-explanatory but these notes are included here to help.

Portfolio direction is associated with the way in which the organisation organises its projects and programmes, groups them, sifts and filters them and ultimately includes or terminates them according to their specific needs and appropriateness.

MANAGEMENT

Figure 4.1 **The nature of governance of project management**

Disclosure and reporting is concerned with the need to be open and honest with regard to how the projects and programmes are progressing and to be in full possession of all the relevant facts and details in order to govern the portfolio adequately.

Project sponsorship is concerned with the overall organisational commitment to a project or programme and its relationship to the portfolio.

Project management capability is concerned with the advancement and control of the project management resources and teams and how they are best able to perform their duties commensurate with the needs of the governance structure.

These various principles fit broadly into a number of more generic categories. The suggested categories are annotated at the end of each description (e.g. portfolio direction, etc.). The questions that project governance is intended to resolve (and the benefits of practising governance) are:

■ How do we know our projects are on track? All projects have an approved plan containing authorisation points at which the business case is reviewed and approved. Decisions made at these authorisation points are recorded and communicated. This could be an example of **Portfolio direction**.

■ Where does the responsibility for governance of projects and programmes lie? The board of directors has overall responsibility for the governance of project management. This means they have to set policy and define the governance framework to be used. This could be an example of **Portfolio direction**.

- How do we know the information we are getting to make decisions is correct? The organisation fosters a culture of improvement and of frank disclosure of project information. This implies that project managers and staff should feel able to discuss the true state of projects with senior managers. The roles, responsibilities and performance criteria for the governance of project management are clearly defined. This would be reflected in the organisation's governance documentation. This could be an example of **Disclosure and reporting**.

- What are the governance arrangements – have they been agreed and documented? Disciplined governance arrangements, supported by the appropriate methods and controls and ensuring they are applied through the project life cycle. This implies an agreed and implemented reporting system that has some consistency across projects. This could be an example of **Portfolio direction**.

- How do we know we are doing the right things? A coherent and supportive relationship is demonstrated between the overall business strategy and the project portfolio, i.e. the projects are aligned to support the organisation's goals and objectives. This could be an example of **Portfolio direction**.

- How does the organisation know when things are going well (or not so well)? The board, or its delegated representatives, decide when independent scrutiny of projects and project management systems is required, and implement such scrutiny accordingly. For example, they should make the time to attend gate reviews. This could be an example of **Disclosure and reporting** and possibly **Project sponsorship**.

- Are risks being dealt with appropriately? There are clearly defined criteria for reporting project status and for the escalation of risks and issues to the levels required by the organisation. Again, this implies a standardised reporting process. This could be an example of **Disclosure and reporting** and possibly **Project sponsorship**.

- How do we know the organisation is doing the right things? The business case is supported by relevant and realistic information that provides a reliable basis for making decisions. The word 'realistic' is key; the organisation should not allow itself to follow an unrealistic plan. This could be an example of **Project sponsorship**.

- Are all of our stakeholders in agreement with what we are doing? Project stakeholders are engaged at a level that is commensurate with their importance to the organisation and in a manner that fosters trust. For example, the stakeholders should make time available to understand the challenges the project faces. This could be an example of **Project management capability**.

- Are we actually competent to govern ourselves? People appointed to make decisions must have delegated authority and be able to exercise that authority in a competent way. This could be an example of **Project management capability**.

These are fine and noble principles but to bring them to life, think about your own organisation. For the purposes of the exam, if you can relate some of the principles of governance to your own organisation you will be more likely to be able to remember them. Have a think about the organisation you work in.

MANAGEMENT

Work-based exercise

What components of governance do you witness in your organisation?

How does your organisation govern its portfolio (decide what is in and what is not in it)?

How does your organisation sponsor its projects (does it have nominated sponsors)?

What arrangements are there for governing the projects (are there set methods to use for example)?

What do project managers do by way of periodical reporting and how does the organisation respond to this?

Quick quiz – you will need to mark these yourself

These are questions derived directly from *Directing Change: a guide to governance of project management* (APM, 2011). Again think about your own organisation and use these questions to prompt in your own mind what your organisation does well and what it does not so well. Combine it with your observations from page 64. Give each a score of 1 (poor) to 10 (excellent).

	Question	Provide a score 1–10
1	Do all projects have clear critical success criteria and KPIs and are these used to inform decision-making?	
2	Is the board assured that the organisation's project management processes and project management tools are appropriate for the projects that it sponsors?	
3	Is the board assured that the people responsible for project delivery, especially the project managers, are clearly mandated, sufficiently competent, and have the capacity to achieve satisfactory project outcomes?	
4	Are project managers encouraged to develop opportunities for improving project outcomes?	
5	Are key governance of project management roles and responsibilities clear and in place?	
6	Are service departments and suppliers able and willing to provide key resources tailored to the varying needs of different projects and to provide an efficient and responsive service?	
7	Are appropriate issue, change and risk management practices implemented in line with adopted policies?	
8	Is authority delegated to the right levels, balancing efficiency and control?	
9	Are project contingencies estimated and controlled in accordance with delegated powers?	

Use this space to make some notes

What kind of question might there be in the exam?

1 This question has <u>two</u> parts. Answer both parts.

Explain what is meant by the term project governance.

10 marks

Explain <u>four</u> effects there might be on the organisation's projects if project governance is not implemented adequately.

40 marks (10 marks each)

4.2 Methods and procedures

By completing this subsection you will be able to:

■ explain how project management methodologies can be used to support the governance structure;

■ explain the advantages of using standard project management methodologies across an organisation.

We have combined these two assessment criteria as essentially they are two aspects of the same topic.

What does a project management methodology contain?

A project management methodology contains the procedural framework within which the project can operate.

There are two types of project management methodology: the public ones, such as PRINCE2®, and the proprietary methods within a specific given organisation. Many organisations write their own so that they can integrate it with their own systems and procedures, enabling project management teams to work in a co-ordinated manner across the business.

Generally speaking, a project management methodology has a number of key elements:

People and organisation

A method will have a standard way of describing the individual roles and effectively who does what. Some common terms to be adopted are those of the sponsor, project manager, project office and so on. In this guide we have used these terms consistently, although some methods such as PRINCE2® have other specific roles such as a project board which consists of representatives from the user, supplier and business.

Products

The term product is used to describe all of those things produced by the project. They can fall into one of two different categories:

- products that help run the project, which includes items such as a project management plan, schedule, risk log and so on; and

- products which are those that are directly related to the output from the project and form part of the deliverables to the client, such as a product marketing plan, a bridge, software system, etc.

They are differentiated because a) they have a different target audience; b) the first type are there to assist in the running of the project while the second are delivered to users and accepted by them; and c) by drawing attention to them it makes sure that they are considered when it comes to the scope planning of the project. Methods normally describe which products are produced and when.

Processes

The processes are those steps that need to be followed in the running of the project, the framework in which the project will be managed. An example might be the way in which risks are identified, assessed, planned and managed through the life cycle. One example can be found in APM's *Project Risk Analysis and Management Guide* (2004) but other organisations may well have their own, adapted to their own specific needs. A lot of these processes will be documented or referenced by the project management plan (PMP).

Templates for documentation

Typically, the business case, PMP, risk log and product specifications will all have predetermined formats and they are quite often already populated with text and helpful hints that have been incorporated as a result of experience in earlier projects.

Tools

Some methods include specific tools that can be deployed. In others, references to specific tools mean that the project teams can be directed to practical solutions to assist them in their day-to-day activities. These might include planning software, document management systems and flowcharting techniques and so on.

Advantages of a standard project methodology

A method provides links to organisational governance – it requires us to think hard about how the project interacts with the organisation. Part of the governance framework will impose authorisation gates where funding is approved for example, how sponsors are appointed, what delegated authority applies. These are all areas where a project method provides the clear manifestation of an organisation's governance framework which helps achieve co-ordination across the business of various projects and the adoption of a single method will mean they are all executed in the same manner, thus providing:

Consistency: Everyone does similar things in similar ways producing similar recognisable products at the same time in the life cycle.

Continuity: Processes and templates are properly documented and recorded meaning it is possible to swap key staff in and out of the project as needs arise.

Communication: A method has a very clear layout, is easily described and forms a basis for a common language across different projects. It also provides for integration between multiple projects which again helps enable teams to be interchangeable.

Clarity: Everyone knows what is going on. There is no ambiguity about roles, the purpose of the product or its route through the system from creation, through testing to approval.

Capability: A method encourages the retention of documentation that can be used for future analysis of success and failure, better informing those projects that come after and thus enhancing the organisation's capability.

Project methods are not used instead of a project life cycle, but complement it. Quite often a project life cycle is documented within a method and may be used consistently across the organisation.

Quick quiz (answers on page 276)

	Question	Options	Your answer
1	Project methodologies _____ guarantee the success of a project.	a) Always b) Never c) Help contribute to d) Get in the way of	
2	A method replaces a project life cycle.	True or false?	
3	Properly documented methods overlap with some areas of project governance.	True or false?	
4	The main areas that a project method is NOT intended to help with are what?	a) Consistency b) Clarity c) Communication d) Bureaucracy	
5	The project manager can work to one project method while the team can work to another.	True or false?	

Use this space to make some notes

MANAGEMENT

 What kind of question might there be in the exam?

| 1 | List and describe <u>five</u> key components of a project management method.
50 marks (10 marks each) |

5

Communications

Subjects covered in this section

5.1 The communication plan

5.2 Conflict and negotiation

5.1 ## The communication plan

By completing this subsection you will be able to:

- describe the key contents of a project communication plan;

- explain the benefits of a project communication plan;

- explain the importance of effective communication in managing different stakeholders;

- identify factors which can positively or negatively affect communication.

All these assessment criteria relate to communications or the communication plan so we thought it wise to discuss them all under one subheading.

The role of the communication plan

The communication plan (or communication management plan) is a component of the PMP (owned by the project manager) and includes a number of key areas. Typical contents of the communication plan might include the following:

The target for the communication – the work done on stakeholder analysis in the early parts of a project will be vital in identifying who the project needs to communicate with. The list of stakeholders is very helpful in understanding which individuals and groups need to be influenced for the project to be successful. The stakeholder analysis helps to prioritise the project's communication efforts and should be updated as the project progresses, so that the changes in the attitude of stakeholders to the project can be mapped. This enables a demonstration of the effectiveness of the communications strategy.

What communication will be undertaken – the plan will describe the information that needs to be communicated into and out of the project. This may include reports and other formal documents produced on a regular basis and also describes what informal information needs to be disseminated and when.

71

How will it be communicated? – the plan must have a clear strategy for the various communication channels available. These fall into the following main categories:

- Formal verbal – includes such things as meetings, interviews, presentations, briefings, etc. They may be formal phase gate reviews, team meetings, stakeholder briefings, etc. They are recorded in minutes or other means so they can be referenced if required.

- Informal verbal – which includes 'water cooler' conversations, unrecorded telephone conversations, etc. It is exceptionally difficult to script these types of communication, but some organisations will give their staff a large amount of training to deal with the press interviews, for example, so it is possible. Good practice dictates that any verbal communication be followed up with a written record.

- Formal written – includes reports, presentations, minutes, specifications, designs, etc. They are anything planned to be produced and which is a fundamental component of the project. As their production is planned it is intended to be formal.

- Informal written – includes things like 'Post-it notes', email (although very often considered formal), blogs, forums, etc.

- Non-verbal – this type of communication relates to how individuals convey messages directly one to one or one to many. They are related to our own personal mannerisms and our way of depicting ourselves, which is usually referred to as body language. The main principle is that our body language cannot be denied and will often convey more of the message than the words spoken or written. The tone and pitch of our voice can also communicate 'non-verbal' information. The frequency and volume of digital communication and its impact also needs to be taken into account.

In all cases we anticipate that the recipient will respond based upon the communication, and a measure of its effectiveness will be whether the attitudes, behaviours or actions of the recipient do actually change as a result. Informal communication is more difficult to manage and dependent upon the culture and networks existing in the organisation and, being unplanned, it can happen anytime. Care is needed when considering informal communications as a channel as there is usually a record of proof required.

Use of various channels – the project has a number of channels available to it in order to disseminate and receive any information. The most common channels are the traditional written word (or, more usually, typed on computer and emailed). There are now a huge and growing number of options available to most organisations in the way they disseminate information. Obviously these include all of those approaches above, but also social networking sites, workspace shared files on computers, websites, podcasts and other more innovative ways of getting a message across.

Understanding the audience – the communication plan must consider the nature of the audience and how they may wish to receive information. The plan should take into account the options for delivering messages in a different format to different individuals, while balancing that with the costs, time and effort involved.

Costs – communication costs money. The type and volume of communication is largely dependent upon the resources required to deliver it. Face-to-face meetings are valuable but can be terribly expensive, especially if long-distance travel is involved. Each of the activities associated with communication on the project will need to be included in the scope and therefore costed into the budgets.

Feedback – know how feedback will be collected and what will be done as a result. Communication is a two-way process and if you are continually in 'send mode' you will not be able to adapt the message to accommodate changes or pick up on the impact of barriers.

What happens when project communications go wrong?

The benefits of a communication plan are that if written and followed then the following problems can be avoided:

- Different groups or individuals get differing messages, which causes doubt, concern, confusion and rework. Just think back to a meeting where not everybody got the same invitation!

- The costs are not automatically included in the budget. We need to hold a team meeting to discuss a topic and call people from around the world but nobody has a budget for it.

- We fail to understand the needs of the stakeholders, the risks, benefits and costs are not fully appreciated and different stakeholders believe they are getting one thing when in fact the plan is for them to get something else.

- Stakeholders do not know where to go for data, causing the wrong information to be used and incorrect decisions being taken.

These are just some of the things that might cause problems. Refer to your own experience to see what problems you have had where communication has broken down or been ineffective.

Barriers to communication

The project manager must be aware of the potential barriers to communication, refer to Table 5.1 on page 74, and make allowances for them. We typically think of physical barriers, but there are also cultural and psychological ones.

Table 5.1 Typical barriers to communication

Barrier	What can be done to overcome	If you witnessed it, what did you do?
Perception on the part of the receiver	Make the message clear and unambiguous so that the message is not open to misinterpretation. Use plain language without too much jargon or technical language if it can be avoided.	
The environment, noise, fumes, heat, etc.	Try and make sure that the environment is fit for purpose for the message you are trying to convey. If you are having a personal conversation, do not do it in an open office.	
People's own attitudes and emotional state	Try and understand the person who will receive the information and empathise with their needs. A logical argument in an emotional situation may not have the desired effect.	
Selective listening (pretending not to have heard)	Try active listening, where you become involved in the message, replay it to the sender and recipient and check understanding.	
Time zones and geography	These days it is more common that the project manager will be dealing with people dispersed across the globe. This introduces delays, unreasonable meeting times, etc. Try and get a regime that everyone can be comfortable with.	
Culture and language	Different countries and cultures have different ways of doing things: working time norms in different countries, for example. Language can also be confused by the over use of acronyms.	
Distractions and other priorities	Sometimes you will not appear as high up someone's list as you might like. Make life easy for them; suggest options and offer to go to them, keep meetings short and frequent.	

Quick quiz (answers on page 276)

	Question	Options	Your answer
1	Who owns the communication plan?	a) The project sponsor b) The project manager c) The team d) The users	
2	The stakeholder management activities are included in the plan.	True or false?	
3	The project manager can control indirect communication.	True or false?	
4	When is the communication plan first considered?	a) At the start of the project b) Once the stakeholder analysis has been completed c) At the start of definition d) As the PMP is finalised	
5	How do you know if communication has been successful?	a) Someone tells us b) There is a feedback mechanism c) Whether people like us or not d) If the project wins an award	
6	Which of these is NOT an example of a barrier to communication?	a) Noise b) The office environment c) Body language d) Risk management	

MANAGEMENT

	Question	Options	Your answer
7	Hand gestures in a meeting would be a type of which of these?	a) Body language b) Verbal communication c) Written communication d) Formal communication	
8	The topic of communication overlaps with which other APM syllabus area?	a) Configuration management b) Change control c) Information management d) Business case	
9	Personal preferences on the part of the recipient can be a barrier to communication.	True or false?	
10	The cost of project communications is a project cost.	True or false?	

Use this space to make some notes

What kind of questions might there be in the exam?

1 List and describe <u>five</u> components of a project communication plan.

50 marks (10 marks each)

2 Explain <u>five</u> implications of project communications being dealt with ineffectively.

50 marks (10 marks each)

5.2 | Conflict and negotiation

By completing this subsection you will be able to:

- identify sources of conflict within the project life cycle and ways in which it can be addressed (such as Blake and Mouton, Thomas and Kilmann, and Pruitt);

- explain how to plan and conduct different negotiations (including formal, informal, competitive and collaborative).

Conflict and negotiations seem to fit quite well together and have been combined as one subsection for the purposes of this guide.

Positive and negative conflict

These two types of conflict can be prevalent on any undertaking. Because a project by its nature is seeking to introduce change, there is a large opportunity for conflict to occur. People sometimes baulk at the idea of changing the way they work, where they work etc., and the project manager must be able to deal with it all in a proactive and constructive manner.

We often think of conflict as a bad thing. It is very cogently argued, however, that conflict if handled correctly will provide a huge resource and act as an agent for change. The project manager must be able to recognise this and allow it to take place without it becoming distracting or problematic.

Some significant areas where conflict may arise are:

- Disagreements about timings and dates

- Conflict over money and budgets

- Differing requirements from different users

- Conflict between time devoted to the project and time on other work

- Conflict between individuals

- Not able to obtain acceptance of the project deliverables

- Stakeholders' views needing to be taken into consideration

- Balancing between the various project objectives.

Project managers need to be adept at understanding the nature of the environment they are in and work towards building a network and infrastructure that allows for the resolution of conflict in a procedural and systematic way. This will not be possible in all cases however, and the use of their interpersonal communication and influencing techniques will be crucial to a successful outcome.

Different aspects of conflict can arise at different times in the life cycle. For example, during concept there can be disagreements about the relative values of different requirements and during handover there may be problems obtaining acceptance from the users. During development conflict may arise from challenging deadlines and controlling costs.

Dealing with conflict: the Thomas–Kilmann model

Kenneth Thomas and Ralph Kilmann introduced their Conflict Mode Instrument (Kilmann and Thomas, 1977) (Figure 5.1). The model popularised conflict styles according to an individual's ranking on the co-operativeness and assertiveness scales. Through the use of a self-assessment questionnaire, the candidates are able to determine which style of conflict resolution they would prefer with relation to the two axes in given circumstances.

According to the analysis of a given situation, it is possible to conceive a series of situations where 'opposing' parties, who appear to be in some form of conflict, will adopt a greater or lesser degree of co-operativeness and similarly be more or less assertive.

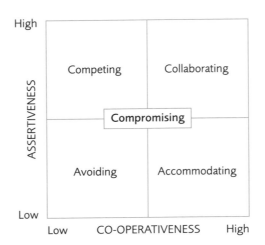

Figure 5.1 The Thomas–Kilmann model
Source: Thomas, 1992. Copyright © 1992 by L. M. Hough.

The various 'modes' were categorised as failures:

Avoiding

If an individual is demonstrating low co-operativeness and low assertiveness they are said to be 'avoiding' the situation. They will not wish to become engaged in the discussions at all and simply avoid the issue. This is not a very good state of affairs as usually the problem will simply re-emerge at a later date.

Accommodating

A highly co-operative person exerting little or no assertiveness is said to be 'accommodating'. In this situation, they will merely 'go with the flow' and not seek to rock the boat. They will tend to just go along with the proposals. Without a reasonable level of challenge there is always the chance that the wrong ideas get developed.

Competing

A highly assertive but unco-operative person will compete and try and get their way. Clearly this is not ideal, as they may end up winning the battle and losing the war. When faced with this type of individual it might be best to adopt a manner that seeks to increase their level of co-operativeness.

Collaborating

In this space a highly assertive and highly co-operative person will work with you to solve the problem. This is an ideal solution, although in itself may not yield a result, with a further move down both scales to arrive at a compromise remaining necessary.

Compromising

This is where the individual is prepared to sacrifice some of what they have been striving for in order to make the deal. In essence, however, it does mean that if both parties agree to compromise then neither gets all of what they want. In a real world situation, however, this might just have to be the price that is paid to move things forward.

The negotiation process

Negotiation is a process for reaching agreement and where conflict may occur. In principle, each party in the negotiation requires the other to conform. In quite a few instances, negotiations are helped and facilitated by a third party. This objective can be instrumental in removing the emotional context from the issues at stake.

Much of the time negotiations just happen; we negotiate when we need a team member to book a meeting room, when we want to organise a business trip or need to get a lot of diaries in line. However, more difficult and contentious negotiations will demand a much higher degree of attention to the process than might otherwise be the case.

A project manager will need to be absolutely clear on which role he or she is playing in a particular situation. They may be the broker of a potential deal or someone who wants something out of it. Inevitably, a negotiation goes through a number of stages and if we take the example of a face-to-face meeting in an organised and formal situation, it may take place over a number of days or even weeks.

The types of negotiation

Formal – here, one party wishes to negotiate on a formal basis with another. Examples of this might be where a redundancy package is being discussed or it may be during a corporate takeover. In a formal negotiation, however, one party will need to follow a pre-agreed and measured process, and document its outcome.

Informal – these sorts of negotiations may be more relaxed in style and may not use all of the process and procedure that may surround a formal negotiation. One party may approach the other to undertake a task for them, perhaps cover a day's absence or help review a document.

Competitive – is where a very structured approach may be necessary. For example where goods or services are being procured and the relationship between the buyer and potential sellers may become very competitive in nature (between the suppliers). Referring to the Thomas–Kilmann model, on page 78, this may be where both parties are very assertive and not very co-operative.

Collaborative – is the optimum state (again with reference to Thomas–Kilmann), this is where both parties are very assertive and also very co-operative. In this state there is an opportunity for both parties to get more than either of them could achieve alone.

Steps in a typical negotiation process

Step one: Recognise that a negotiation is impending or necessary (Figure 5.2). The need to negotiate develops over time and in certain circumstances. It might be overt as in the case of arms reduction treaties, or creep up quietly like a contract that needs to be signed in order to proceed. It is important that the parties recognise this and develop a strategy to deal with it in an appropriate fashion. Both parties have to agree that this negotiation will be the one and only forum for discussions.

Step two: Thorough preparation and planning will help understanding of the other side's position. You may also need to:

■ Brief your team to make sure you are all 'on the same page' and there will be no different views expressed from your team that may undermine a position.

■ Look out for their WIFT or 'what's in it for them'. If you can put yourself in the shoes of the people on the other side of the table and begin to understand what it is they want from the arrangements, you will be well-placed to arrive at a mutually agreeable arrangement.

- You will need to explore your own BATNA or 'best alternative to a negotiated agreement'. What happens if you cannot agree? Where do you go, if you walk out and then walk back in, it will not be on the same terms as you had previously?

- Think about the territory of where the negotiation will take place (ours, theirs or neutral offices for example).

- Who has the power to make decisions, are you dealing with an influential person?

- What is the absolute bottom line that we are prepared to accept?

- Do your research, e.g. find out when their year end is, what markets do they operate in, what are the company circumstances, do they need the business, etc.

Seek agreement to all of the above before commencing any discussion or debate.

Step three: During a meeting, observe protocol and pleasantries, build and exchange ideas and offer and accept offers in order to try and build a bridge between the two positions. Watch out for devious tricks to unsettle you like substituting new negotiators, referring for authority, and so on. Be aware of cultural issues, in some environments a nod of the head indicates 'yes I understand', not 'yes I agree'. Understanding this will all have been part of your preparation. As the negotiation progresses, do not get dragged into saying things

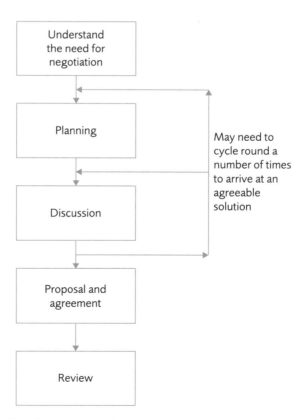

Figure 5.2 A simple negotiation process

MANAGEMENT

because you want to be liked. Separate the issue from the emotion. If necessary, you may call on the services of a third party arbitrator to chair and help mediate.

Step four: Arrive at an agreement and document the settlement arrived at, make sure it is clear and unambiguous. A contract is simply an agreement, if it has been signed then there can be no argument (as long as it is clear).

Step five: Follow up and make sure that the agreement is being enacted as agreed. Review the outcome and learn lessons for the future.

At any stage be prepared to revert back to an earlier stage; there are inevitably a number of rounds to go through, each time the two sides growing closer together and sometimes perhaps for a short period further apart.

 Quick quiz (answers on page 277)

	Question	Options	Your answer
1	Which of these is not a step in negotiation?	a) Preparation b) Discussion c) Bargaining d) Documenting	
2	Referring for authority might be a tactic used in negotiation.	True or false?	
3	Negotiation can happen at any time during the project life cycle.	True or false?	
4	WIFT stands for What's In it For Them.	True or false?	
5	The Thomas–Kilmann conflict model contains the phases Avoiding, Competing, Collaborating, Compromising and _____.	a) Accepting b) Altering c) Accommodating d) Actuarial	

Use this space to make some notes

What kind of question might there be in the exam?

| 1 | List and describe <u>five</u> things a project manager might do to prepare for a negotiation.

50 marks (10 marks each) |

6 Leadership and teamwork

Subjects covered in this section

6.1 Leadership

6.2 Teams and teamwork

6.1 # Leadership

By completing this subsection you will be able to:

- describe typical leadership qualities;

- explain the principles and importance of motivation;

- explain the impact of leadership on team performance and motivation (using models such as Maslow, Herzberg and McGregor);

- explain the benefits of adapting styles of leadership within a project (such as situational leadership, action-centred leadership).

These leadership assessment criteria seemed to go well together and so we have combined them into a subsection of their own. Individually they do not constitute a large enough topic to consider each one alone. You should note that we have not gone into a lot of detail here, and haven't included all the theories named simply because there is so much work available, in books and journals and online. We would encourage you to review these to widen understanding.

What makes a good leader?

"Leadership is the ability to establish vision and direction, to influence and align others towards a common purpose, and to empower and inspire people to achieve success."

APM Body of Knowledge 6th edition (APM, 2012, p. 68)

So much has been written and discussed on the nature and role of leadership, both in the commercial world but also in the worlds of politics and religion, that there are a huge number of varying views and opinions, and it would be impossible to try and encapsulate them all here. We have included a sample and if you wish to pursue the subject further then please do so: anything you learn may be useful in the exam.

APM has specific requirements of candidates of the APM Project Management Qualification and these are summarised in the learning outcomes above. Leadership should take place at all levels in the organisation, with the entire project team taking some form of leadership role, not necessarily a hierarchical one, but often peer-to-peer. This means the project manager needs to build networks and relationships across the organisation to galvanise support for the project from a multitude of disparate colleagues and suppliers.

The syllabus requires you to be able to describe typical leadership qualities. Some examples are shown below:

- Help maintain and promote the project's vision among both the project team and elsewhere.

- Have energy, drive and commitment, leading by doing and motivating the team throughout the project life cycle.

- Reinforce positive relationships, for example, providing clear feedback on performance.

- Build a productive project and working environment in which a focus is maintained on getting work done and moving the project forward.

- Work to raise morale by setting clear achievable goals.

- Act as coach and/or mentor to team members to promote personal growth.

- Help ensure that exceptional events are resolved, and spot opportunities as well as threats which have an impact on motivation.

- Ensure that productive and constructive feedback is provided to enable individual and organisational improvement.

- Protect the project from unwarranted external criticism.

- Lead with a different focus at different times, according to the situational demands at the time (see later).

Principles and importance of motivation/leadership

Motivation is a vital element in leadership, and because of their temporary nature projects require a quick and effective start-up. The project manager will need to demonstrate highly tuned leadership skills to get the team pointing in the right direction as soon as they can, but in a way that lasts. It is necessary for a project manager to ensure that the staff who report to them are fully motivated so that the problems associated with poor motivation can be avoided. These potential problems are many, but as an indication, poor motivation will lead to:

Interpersonal conflict – Individuals may misunderstand their roles and those of others. They may stay insular and apart from people that they do not know or understand, if their respective roles are not made clear and open.

High staff attrition rates – Working in a negative environment with little or no motivation can lead to people leaving after only a short period.

Difficulty in recruiting – If a project has a reputation for poor morale it will be more difficult to recruit staff into the project roles. This may mean the need to offer higher rates of pay or maybe other incentives.

Absence and sickness – This is sometimes prevalent where team motivation is not attended to adequately. People will be more inclined to stay home rather than go into an environment that does not offer opportunity and advancement.

Poor quality of work – Nearly always accompanies poor motivation. If people are not motivated in the right way then they can become a bit slapdash in their approach, not really care about the quality of what they are doing and just end up with 'it's good enough'.

Maslow's Hierarchy of Needs

Often depicted as a triangle, the Hierarchy of Needs theory described that in order to be motivated in any walk or sphere of life, there are a series of tiers of motivational components. Maslow suggested that an individual will look to aspects of the tier above to provide the strongest motivation for them (Maslow, 1943). Thus, individuals always aspire to the next tier up as one level of 'need' has been satisfied. The other overriding principle of the theory is that if any of the lower levels are removed or are lacking, then a person's motivation will revert to the level below and the lost level will be the motivator, despite what has gone before.

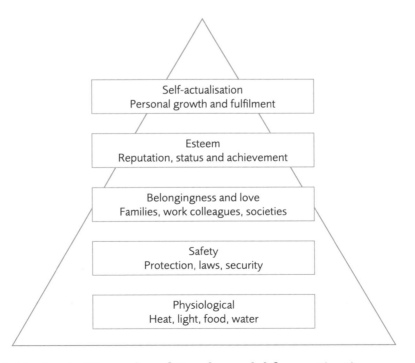

Figure 6.1 Maslow's Hierarchy of Needs model for motivation

Source: Maslow, 1987. Copyright © 1987, Pearson Education, Inc.

The lower levels of motivation include survival (food, light, water for example), family, groups (tribes, clubs, societies, for example), leaders of groups (to become the chairman of a club or society perhaps) or the more ethereal motivator of those things that are more important than all of the others – self-actualisation. Aspiration to the levels above will motivate an individual.

Herzberg's Two Factor theory

Frederick Herzberg developed this concept (Herzberg et al., 1959) which has become a well-cited source of motivation theory. In it he hypothesised that job satisfaction and job dissatisfaction were two independent factors and that there are certain factors which in the workplace cause job satisfaction, while a different set cause dissatisfaction. One of the factors, 'hygiene', was used to represent the fact that if you wash your hands once they will become clean, wash them again and they will become a bit cleaner, and so on. Ultimately though, there can be no point in washing your hands any more as there will be very little benefit. Hence the categorisation of the topics that reside in the hygiene factors column of Table 6.1 below. Ever-increasing attention to the provision of more or greater levels of hygiene factors will not motivate beyond a certain point. It is the motivators that we need to be present in order to be truly motivated. The following table presents arguably the top factors causing dissatisfaction and satisfaction for individuals, when considering their workplace, conditions and so on. They are listed in the order of higher to lower importance, and relative significance in motivating those individuals to do a good job.

Table 6.1 Herzberg's motivation and hygiene factors

True motivators (leading to satisfaction). These are psychological needs to achieve and to grow	Hygiene factors (leading ultimately to dissatisfaction, particularly if they are withdrawn). These are physiological needs; we need money to buy food and shelter
Achievement – being given the opportunity to achieve at one's job, having short definite achievable targets and being clear what is expected. A project manager would be able to support and motivate earlier where shorter timescales for targets are used.	**Company policy** – a typical example would be whether you qualify for a company car. If you have had one for years and then it is withdrawn, this will definitely lead to dissatisfaction as will not getting the exact model you want.
Recognition – being recognised as the expert in one's field, having people seek your opinion. A project manager may be able to direct people to consult with an individual for advice where they are an expert.	**Supervision** – being closely supervised, giving the company the control it desires, will have a detrimental effect on motivation over the long term.
Work itself – actually enjoying what you do, being able to look forward to the day's activity rather than dreading it. The project manager may be able to allocate work according to an individual's preferences.	**Work conditions** – we expect a certain level of health and hygiene to be prevalent in our workplaces. Again though, continually enhancing the facilities and amenities will not motivate, and the removal of them will have the opposite effect.

Responsibility – giving people more responsibility for their work, and making them accountable for it, has a huge motivating influence. Making someone a work stream leader may be motivational.	**Salary** – it is not possible to continually pay individuals more and more salary. There comes a point where this no longer motivates and just becomes 'the norm'.
Advancement – as individuals grow, so they need new challenges to take them to the next step on their career for non-monetary reward. Perhaps supporting a team member to speak at a conference and become recognised outside of the team.	**Relationship with peers** – we expect a certain civility and professionalism. Once this has been achieved though there is little else to be gained from further enhancing the environment.
Growth – we all seek to grow in one way or another, whether to learn new skills, make new contacts or simply realise our career ambitions. Allowing a team member to research new ideas or provide a very challenging task might be motivational to some.	

Work-based exercise

Take some time to think about times when you have been demotivated. What particularly about those circumstances was it that inspired that reaction and which side of the Herzberg model did it stem from?

See if you can draw any conclusions from your reflection and the basis of the theory.

True motivators (e.g. being given the chance to advance)	Hygiene factors (i.e. was your reaction based around the company policy, pay, etc.)

MANAGEMENT

Hersey and Blanchard's leadership model

The Situational Leadership® model is a behavioural theory published by Paul Hersey and Ken Blanchard (Hersey and Blanchard, 1977) who theorised that leadership can be categorised as being of one of four styles. Each of these can be categorised by virtue of the relative levels of Support or Direction that is provided by the leader to the follower. The leader should adapt their attempts to influence to meet the needs of their followers based on their readiness to perform each specific job, task or activity. A follower's readiness is determined by their ability and willingness to complete the task at a sustained and acceptable level.

When managing a team of individuals it is important to recognise the fact that they may have different needs when it comes to leadership style. They may be more ready to take on one task as opposed to another based on their relevant knowledge, experience and skill. In order to be effective, a leader needs to take these variables into account:

Low Readiness – Someone new to the organisation is likely to be committed and willing to do the job but may be ignorant of the specific steps to be undertaken to accomplish that and may need a high level of instruction about the job and their role in it as well as praise for steps taken in the right direction. Consider the new graduate, intelligent and willing but does not know yet how to undertake the task being asked of them. In this case the leader will need to explain not only what is required but also a lot about how to do it and why they are doing it the way they are.

Moderate Readiness – As this person develops their capabilities they may need to rely less on the leader to provide this oversight. Slowly becoming more able they begin to need less 'how to' instruction and more reassurance that they are doing it just fine on their own without the leader directing their steps.

High Readiness – Once they are proficient in the activity and exhibit confidence in their ability to complete it they may start to question the manner in which the job is undertaken and begin also to adapt their working practices and manner to make improvements. The leader will provide input into their proposals and help them act out these modifications and improvements to the process and procedures followed.

The project manager needs to recognise these attributes and abilities, seek out the strengths (and weaknesses) of the individual and produce a 'personalised' approach that will seek to accentuate the positives and minimise the negative aspects of the individual's ability. A leader may wish to consider adopting one of four 'styles': delegating, coaching, supporting or sometimes just telling the follower what to do. As a further piece to consider, it may be helpful to think of a time when you have seen a very capable person 'over managed'. Some of the things you will hear said will include the accusation of 'micro management'. Similarly where team members require a higher degree of engagement they may be heard to complain of being left to get on with it. Clearly the role of the leader is to spot these occurrences and seek to alter their approach accordingly.

The advantages of altering the leadership approach depending on the situation are:

■ The leader can provide the most appropriate amounts of support and direction according to the maturity of the people being led, thus making sure that they are not left alone to fail or become unnecessarily micro managed.

- The people being led feel that the leader is in tune with their needs and will respond positively as a result.

- Delegation will not be confused with abdication (of the responsibility).

- Staff that need direction will be approached and led in an appropriate manner.

 ## Quick quiz (answers on page 277)

	Question	Options	Your answer
1	Which of these is NOT a hygiene factor?	a) Salary b) Advancement c) Work conditions d) Company policy	
2	Maslow's theory of motivation includes low, moderate and high readiness	True or false?	
3	Which of these is NOT a motivator?	a) The work itself b) Growth c) Salary d) Responsibility	
4	A project manager does not have a role to play in the motivation of project staff.	True or false?	
5	Which of these may occur if the motivation of a team is not good enough?	a) Sickness b) Poor quality c) Absenteeism d) All of the above	

MANAGEMENT

What kind of questions might there be in the exam?

1	This question has three parts. Answer all parts.

State a definition of leadership.

5 marks

State what is meant by the term situational leadership.

5 marks

List and describe four ways in which a project manager may adapt their style to suit the circumstances.

40 marks (10 marks each)

2	List and describe five ways in which a project manager may seek to motivate their team.

50 marks (10 marks each)

6.2	**Teams and teamwork**

By completing this subsection you will be able to:

■ describe the characteristics and benefits of effective teams and teamwork;

■ explain factors involved in the creation, development and management of teams (models such as Belbin, Margerison-McCann, Myers-Briggs, Tuckman, Katzenbach and Smith).

Teams and team development have been combined because they both approach the same topic from different standpoints but using the same main principles. You should note that we have not gone into a lot of detail here, and haven't included all the theories named simply because there is so much work available written in books, journals and online. We would encourage you to review these to develop the principles.

Team development

"Teamwork is a group of people working in collaboration or by cooperation towards a common goal."

APM Body of Knowledge 6th edition (APM, 2012, p. 76)

Good teamworking is vital in any project. At a very early stage in their career, a project manager has to come to terms with the fact that they cannot do everything themselves. They therefore need to be able to motivate others to want to do the work required. Individuals will rarely have the ability to do all of the diverse tasks on a project and therefore we need more than one. This in turn, leads us down the road of having teams of multidisciplinary individuals, all working towards a common goal – the essence of a team. These teams demonstrate mutual accountability, a supportive environment for each other and are able to relate to and deliver a common set of objectives.

The key benefits of having a team of people are that the team is able to:

- Deliver more than the individuals could do independently through a coherent approach and more effective hand offs between tasks and individuals improving the use of team members' time and reducing rework.

- Be more efficient in communication between individuals within the team as everyone knows each other and understands each other's behaviours thus speeding things up.

- Provide reassurance to stakeholders through a unified and confident approach that the job is in hand and under control.

- Provide a rewarding place to work for individuals, and facilitate an aura of mutual support and respect that is motivational and improves morale.

- Help develop healthy, constructive conflict, thus enabling creativity and the more thorough development of solutions to problems.

In order to understand teamwork better, we will consider here two distinct theories to help understand what is important both:

- **Before** the team has formed and how we might select that team. The syllabus contains a team roles model, the most common of which was developed by Meredith Belbin and is often used to explain the nature of team members and their preferred 'style'.

- **After** the team has formed helping to understand the team's evolution. One that gets mentioned in the syllabus is the Tuckman model of group development.

The Belbin Team Roles model

Meredith Belbin studied at Cambridge in the UK and with associates he developed the concept of Team Roles (Belbin, 2010). It has become one of the most recognisable and well-used tools to help analyse the nature of individuals and their preferred style within a team environment. One of his main conclusions was that an effective team needs to have members that between them cover nine major roles within the team. These roles are shown in Table 6.2:

MANAGEMENT

Table 6.2 Belbin's Team Roles descriptions

Team Role		Contribution	Allowable weaknesses
Plant		Creative, imaginative, free-thinking. Generates ideas and solves difficult problems.	Ignores incidentals. Too preoccupied to communicate effectively.
Resource Investigator		Outgoing, enthusiastic, communicative. Explores opportunities and develops contacts.	Over-optimistic. Loses interest once initial enthusiasm has passed.
Co-ordinator		Mature, confident, identifies talent. Clarifies goals. Delegates effectively.	Can be seen as manipulative. Offloads own share of the work.
Shaper		Challenging, dynamic, thrives on pressure. Has the drive and courage to overcome obstacles.	Prone to provocation. Offends people's feelings.
Monitor Evaluator		Sober, strategic and discerning. Sees all options and judges accurately.	Lacks drive and ability to inspire others. Can be overly critical.
Teamworker		Co-operative, perceptive and diplomatic. Listens and averts friction.	Indecisive in crunch situations. Avoids confrontation.
Implementer		Practical, reliable, efficient. Turns ideas into actions and organises work that needs to be done.	Somewhat inflexible. Slow to respond to new possibilities.
Completer Finisher		Painstaking, conscientious, anxious. Searches out errors. Polishes and perfects.	Inclined to worry unduly. Reluctant to delegate.
Specialist		Single-minded, self-starting, dedicated. Provides knowledge and skills in rare supply.	Contributes only on a narrow front. Dwells on technicalities.

Within the Belbin model (Figure 6.2) there is no suggestion that an individual needs to aspire to one or another of the roles, but rather that behaviours need to be exhibited somewhere within the team, thus there is no 'perfect' profile for an individual.

Action

Figure 6.2 The Belbin Team Roles model

Source: Belbin Team Roles. Reproduced by kind permission of Belbin Associates belbin.com.

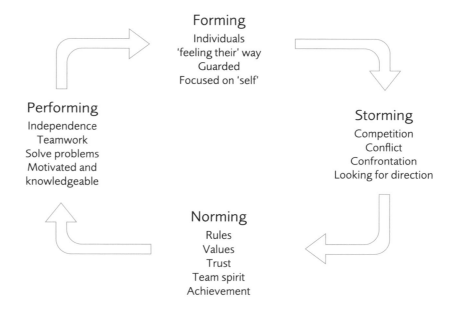

Figure 6.3 The Tuckman model of Team Development

Source: Tuckman, 1965. Reproduced by kind permission of the American Psychological Association.

Bruce Tuckman identified four key stages in Team Development (Tuckman, 1965), see Figure 6.3.

Forming

Tuckman observed that on first coming together the team can be said to be in a forming stage. They are brought together in the first instance of a project. They may not know each other and may be distrustful of their managers and their co-workers. They begin to

understand the task in front of them and will behave independently of each other so they can each understand their role in the endeavour. They are largely uninformed about the team goals and may make incorrect assumptions about what is coming up.

Storming

In this stage the team begins to gel, but struggles to understand how they will inter-operate with the others in the team. There will be competition and confrontation between team members, who each have a view of how things should work, and conflict resolution is a key project management skill during this stage. To help them through this stage, they will begin to be a little more open with their co-workers and between them agree what control structures and leadership influences they are prepared to accept. Some members of the team may be able (through their experience and individual maturity) to coax, coach and coerce others to grow out of the storming stage and into the vastly more productive norming stage.

Norming

Team members are now more accepting of their fellow workers and begin to deliver. They will begin to operate as a unit and support each other in the task. They understand their objectives and will continue to deliver the products in an appropriate manner. The danger is that they fall into a complacent and protective arrangement, whereby they begin to believe that the team is more important than the job in hand. This must be avoided. The team appears coherent and fluid, adapting to changes well but there is always the danger that they are merely in their 'comfort zone' and not being creative or maximising their potential.

Performing

This is the optimum state for the team to achieve. They function as a cohesive unit and demonstrate the ability to get the job done with little or no supervision. They are creative and open to new ideas and actively develop their working practices and methods to achieve optimisation. They are fully motivated and knowledgeable about the job in hand and will be able to solve their own problems. Creative conflict abounds, but the team are more than able to deal with it.

It is possible to witness a team reverting back to one of the earlier stages in the model. This is usually caused by some form of change in the environment, such as people leaving or joining, new supervision, new buildings, etc. Also a team may simply achieve its current objectives and then search for a new challenge. If one is not forthcoming, the team may simply disband. Tuckman termed this as adjourning and this term was added to the model some years later.

As mentioned there is a seemingly limitless number of theories regarding the development of teams but it is pertinent to mention the Margerison-McCann theory who developed the Team Management Systems approach. In a similar manner to Belbin this nominates a number of discrete team roles and uses these to allow analysis of an individual's approach and contribution to a team. The analysis is comprehensive but suffice to say that the categories are Reporter Adviser, Creator Innovator, Explorer Promoter, Assessor Developer, Thruster Organiser, Concluder Producer, Controller Inspector and Upholder Maintainer. Clearly simply allocating a title to an individual is insufficient and the model requires interaction and analysis to conclude a useful and productive assessment so team members can be more effective in their team.

Use this space to make some notes

....

....

....

....

....

....

Work-based exercise

Are you part of a team at the moment? Can you observe where in the development cycle it is? Do you observe any of the individual Belbin styles?

Quick quiz (answers on page 278)

	Question	Options	Your answer
1	Forming is a Tuckman phase of team development.	True or false?	
2	Which of these is not a Belbin Team Role?	a) Implementer b) Completer finisher c) Plant d) Operator	
3	Changes to a team's environment can cause a regression back to earlier team development stages.	True or false?	
4	Fill in the gap forming, storming, _____, performing.	a) Working b) Adjourning c) Failing d) Norming	

	Question	Options	Your answer
5	What does a team NOT demonstrate during the storming phase?	a) Competition b) Conflict c) Hopefulness d) Confrontation	
6	How many Belbin roles are there?	a) 8 b) 2 c) 5 d) 9	
7	Which Belbin role is suited to detailed meticulous work?	a) Shaper b) Completer finisher c) Plant d) Implementer	
8	If teamwork is not treated seriously and developed there may be a lack of motivation among the team members.	True or false?	
9	A 'norming' team are considered as high performing.	True or false?	
10	Plants are the 'ideas' people.	True or false?	

What kind of question might there be in the exam?

1   This question has two parts. Answer both parts.

In a project context explain what is meant by the term 'teamwork'.

10 marks

List and describe four distinct stages through which a team might develop.

40 marks (10 marks each)

7

Scope management

7.1 Defining and managing project scope

By completing this subsection you will be able to:

- define scope in terms of outputs, outcomes and benefits (including use of product breakdown and work breakdown structures);

- explain the way in which an organisational breakdown structure is used to create a responsibility assignment matrix.

What is the 'scope' of a project?

Planning how the project will be managed during the definition stage culminates in the preparation of the project management plan (PMP). One key component of the PMP is a definition of the scope of the project. Scope is a term much used but usually poorly understood.

In essence the scope of a project is all the products to be produced and all of the work undertaken to produce them but importantly includes the benefits to be derived from the use of those products and services. In essence (and we will see more later) they are the combination of the work breakdown structure (WBS) and the product breakdown structure (PBS). Scope management is (put simply) the management activities to ensure the scope is managed.

Scope identification is the first key process of constructing a project schedule. The production of the work breakdown structure will culminate in the generation of work packages and these will have associated products. Scope develops over time as the project becomes known and the content of the scope changes through the requirements capture and analysis and business case definition activities. Throughout the process, various 'freezes' of design are made so that some form of stability can be exerted on the latest version of the design so that uncontrolled change does not cause too much uncertainty and rework. When this does occur it is referred to as 'scope creep'.

During the development phase the scope is further redefined but on an ever-increasing level of detail as more and more becomes known about the products and work until eventually the appropriate level of detail is understood such that the products can be created.

Projects – These are the undertakings that produce outputs.

Outputs – These are the products associated with the project. A nuclear submarine is a product as is the switch that turns on the light in the captain's cabin of that submarine. Sometimes we wish to manage at one level of detail and sometimes at others.

Outcomes – An outcome is the changed circumstance or behaviours resulting from the putting to use of the products. A reduced hospital waiting list time is not a product. The new computer system, more doctors and more wards that make it happen are the products. Collectively they enable an outcome of a shorter time on a waiting list.

Benefits – Stakeholders observe the outcome and choose to put a value on their perspective of it. A reduced waiting time for an operation clearly has a benefit if you are waiting for that operation, if you are not waiting then it will have relatively little value.

Consider Figure 7.1:

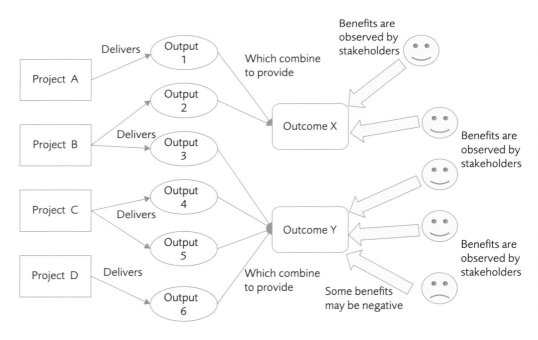

Figure 7.1 Projects – outputs – outcomes – benefits

When the scope of the project is considered early on in the project very generic terms might be used, for example:

■ The project will build a new building.

■ The project will only test the products in Thailand and Indonesia.

■ The scope includes the design build and test stages but not roll-out.

These high-level conceptual statements are fine but they leave quite a bit to the imagination. They are very often found within the business case when the intention is to set the scene and to literally conceptualise the project. As discussed, as the project definition progresses, the PMP requires ever-more detailed refinement of the scope so that the exact nature of the precise deliverables is evidenced.

It is important to keep the business case in mind so that the PMP does not diverge from it and to make sure that the resultant project does in fact adhere to the principles and materiality of the requirements in the business case.

The two key components (products and work) that help us to develop the eventual plans and schedules ensure that we are able to manage properly. It can be helpful to think of the project work breakdown structure and product breakdown structure as two sides of the same coin. One describes the work required (to produce the products) and the other describes what will be produced (as a result of the work). Very simplistically, the WBS is a hierarchical structure that is normally conveyed as a diagram, as in Figure 7.2.

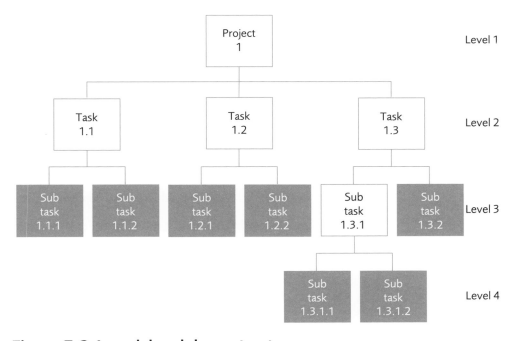

Figure 7.2 A work breakdown structure

Work breakdown structures

The WBS is a tool for defining the hierarchical breakdown of work required to deliver the products of a project. Large pieces of work are broken down into smaller components. These may again be subdivided until the lowest required level of detail is established. The lowest units of the WBS become the work packages in a project. The WBS defines the total work to be undertaken on the project and provides a structure for project control systems such as Earned Value.

There are a few key components to recognise in a WBS:

■ In Figure 7.2 all of the shaded boxes represent work packages.

■ Each level is clearly identified (through the numbering structure) as being a breakdown of the level above (1.1.n. etc.).

■ The levels start at one and develop as the granularity and precision of definition increases.

■ At the lowest level of each of the nested levels of the structure there are work packages.

■ Each work package can comprise of a number of activities. It is these activities that would find their way into the precedence diagram alongside any existing work packages.

■ There are no predetermined numbers of levels, it is a judgement that must be made for each project or workstream.

■ The activities typically include project management as this is a component of the project work and must therefore appear in the WBS.

■ The WBS includes all the work that is in the project scope.

Work packages

Work packages are the level of definition or unit of work for which a budget is estimated and reported. There can be different levels (as above). A typical work package should:

■ Have a discrete estimate associated with them so that proper recording can be maintained for lessons-learned purposes.

■ Have a discrete budget allocated to them, so an accurate cost can be compared to them.

■ Be allocated to a single accountable person, to avoid confusion.

■ Not overlap, each containing a discrete self-contained package of work.

■ Have some form of consistent numbering to identify them.

■ Have a relatively short duration, or be divided into a series of activities whose status can be measured objectively.

Product breakdown structures

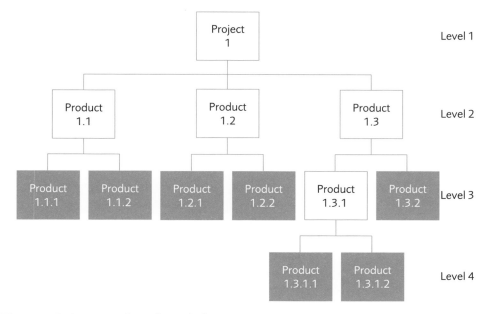

Figure 7.3 A product breakdown structure

Those eagle-eyed among you will notice very little difference in practice between a PBS and WBS as far as the two diagrams (7.2 and 7.3) are concerned. The main point to note is that the WBS talks about work and will use verbs while the PBS talks about products and will therefore use nouns. You can use either as the primary breakdown and may want to do both. Quite often your organisation will have a stated preference and will dictate how these breakdowns are constructed and indeed which type to use. The key advantage of the PBS is that it gives you a definitive list of interrelated products that will prove invaluable when you come to do configuration management as it will form the backbone of the configuration library.

Organisational breakdown structure

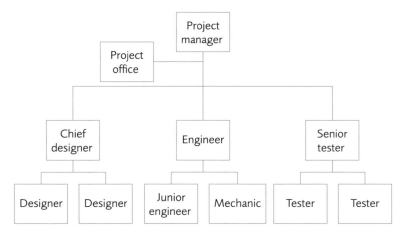

Figure 7.4 An organisational breakdown structure

There are a few key components to recognise in an organisational breakdown structure (OBS) (Figure 7.4):

■ Each person who has a role in the project should be identified in the OBS.

■ It is not merely a cut and paste from the company's organisation chart, careful thought will be needed.

■ Anyone who has a role must appear, even if it is just a small involvement.

■ The OBS demonstrates a reporting hierarchy for the project; it does not necessarily represent line management roles.

■ Each role ought to have either a role description, terms of reference, statement of work, or some other mechanism to clearly identify what is required of that individual.

The primary use of the organisational breakdown structure is to be able to communicate to stakeholders the relevant parties associated with the project. However, the real power of the OBS comes when it is combined with the WBS to provide a matrix of roles called a responsibility assignment matrix.

The responsibility assignment matrix or RACI chart

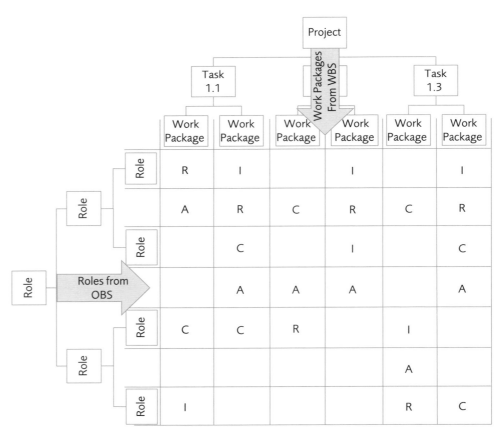

Figure 7.5 A responsibility assignment matrix (RAM) or RACI chart

The responsibility assignment matrix (RAM), also known as RACI matrix or sometimes RASIC matrix, describes the participation by various roles in completing tasks or deliverables for a project (Figure 7.5). It is especially useful in clarifying roles and responsibilities in cross-functional/departmental projects and processes.

RACI is derived from the four key responsibilities most typically used: *Responsible, Accountable, Consulted*, and *Informed*.

R – Responsible. Those responsible for carrying out the task; the person who will do it. (Only one person should be responsible for the task.)

A – Accountable. Those accountable for getting the job done. They may choose to make another RACI role responsible (to them).

C – Consulted. Those consulted in the execution of the task.

I – Informed. Those informed about the activity and provided with the output.

RASIC includes an additional role, *Support*.

S – Support. Resources allocated to Responsible. Unlike Consulted, who may provide input to the task, support help complete the task.

RAM, RACI or RASIC charts would all be acceptable in the exam.

The real benefit of them is that, at a glance, it is possible to identify who is doing what. There should be no missing responsibilities and likewise there should not be more than one. It is a very powerful tool for the project manager and is a key component of the PMP.

In most cases it will be preferable to nominate a single person associated with each role although on some occasions it may be better to simply nominate a group or perhaps another organisation (a contractor perhaps).

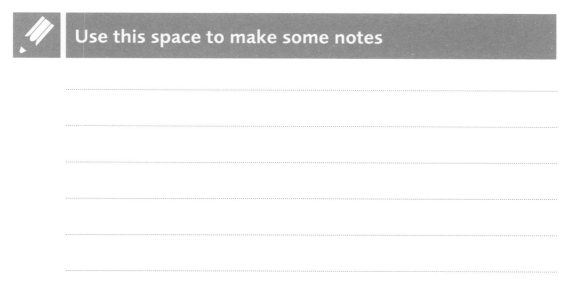

Use this space to make some notes

MANAGEMENT

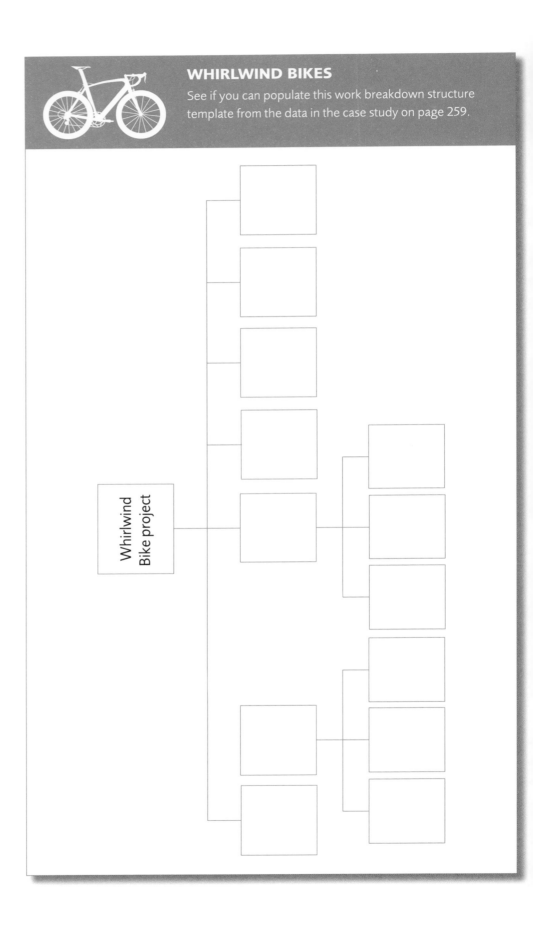

WHIRLWIND BIKES

See if you can populate this work breakdown structure template from the data in the case study on page 259.

Whirlwind Bike project

Quick quiz (answers on page 278)

	Question	Options	Your answer
1	OBS means?	a) Organisational breakdown structure b) Outline breakdown structure c) Organisation benefits structure d) Organisational benefits system	
2	WBS means?	a) Work benefit system b) Work baseline system c) Work bottom system d) Work breakdown structure	
3	Each level of the WBS will be easily identifiable as a sublevel of the level above.	True or false?	
4	An example of a component of a scope statement might be what?	a) Which sites are included b) When the project will take place c) Who will manage the project d) Why the project is taking place	
5	The project manager is responsible for producing the scope breakdown.	True or false?	
6	A RAM chart shows what?	a) The task and when it will take place b) The task and the person involved in it c) The person involved and when it will take place d) The risks associated with the task	
7	The scope statement is a key component of the project management plan.	True or false?	

MANAGEMENT

	Question	Options	Your answer
8	A WBS shows the decomposition of tasks.	True or false?	
9	The lowest level of a WBS is called a . . .?	a) Work package b) Task c) Activity d) Change module	
10	Stakeholders will place a value on the benefits of a project.	True or false?	

What kind of questions might there be in the exam?

1   This question has <u>two</u> parts. Answer both parts.

Explain what is meant by the term 'project scope'.

10 marks

With the aid of suitably labelled diagrams where appropriate explain <u>four</u> aspects of defining a project's scope.

40 marks (10 marks each)

2   Explain <u>five</u> uses of work breakdown structures, including how their use is of benefit.

50 marks (10 marks each)

7.2   Requirements and configuration management

By completing this subsection you will be able to:

■ explain how to manage scope through requirements management processes (such as capture, analysis, justifying requirements, baseline needs);

■ configuration management processes (such as planning, identification, control, status accounting, audit and verification).

These two components are combined in the syllabus and so they are similarly combined here.

Requirements management process

Given we are in the area of understanding the stakeholders' requirements and trying to make sense of them, we will need some form of process and the following one is suggested. Each of the steps has a particular purpose and collectively they will ensure that the stakeholders have their requirements documented and properly managed through to completion.

The manner in which requirements are captured should be specified in the organisation's governance or portfolio management procedures. It is inappropriate for a project to generate its own requirements; they are totally reliant upon stakeholders to provide the necessary 'need'.

Requirements capture

There are a number of generic techniques that can be used here and also some specific techniques. The project may consider:

- Brainstorming sessions.

- Questionnaires and data collection.

- Analysis of pre-project documentation.

- Review of any relevant legislation.

- Contract requirements.

- Prototyping.

- Written requirements specification based on the outgoing system/product.

- A 'user case', where we try and identify the use to which a product will be put.

- User forums and focus groups around new products.

In some circumstances the project itself may be the source of requirements, especially where research or innovation products or work is required. For example, the search for a new drug cure may be driven itself by the project team as there are no 'users' as such.

Requirements analysis

Once we have been able to identify what the stakeholders require of the system, we can begin to build an idea of how this may be achieved. We might need to build a preliminary database (computerised or otherwise) of what these requirements look like and then commence evaluating them in an orderly and systematic way. It will also be necessary to look for overlaps and gaps between different requirements.

There are a large number of tools to help evaluate requirements but they all concentrate on a few key issues:

Value – does the requirement have any value in the marketplace into which it will be introduced? This area has a large degree of overlap with that of benefits management.

Priority – is the requirement of sufficient priority to be considered as needing to be within scope of the project and is this particular requirement more or less significant than others?

Time – at what point does this requirement need to be met? Sometimes where there is a non-discretionary project to be undertaken, having the product ready by a certain time is the fundamental requirement.

Process – how can these requirements be met, are they routine or innovative? What can we do to understand how they can be satisfied?

The analysis process weighs up all of these topics together with the organisation's strategic objectives, people and resources available.

Justify the requirement

Quite often when considering requirements the team will consider a mechanism for prioritising and justifying these requirements using a technique such as a MoSCoW list, a term used to establish a common framework for the evaluation of requirements (International Institute of Business Analysis, 2009).

M – Must have – these are things that are vital to the acceptability of the product at this release.

S – Should have – these are things that are high priority that should be included if time and resources allow. If not possible then a work around may be needed to compensate for its absence.

C – Could have – these are desirable but strictly speaking can be done without. They can wait for later releases.

W – Won't have – these are things that definitely will not be in this release and most likely no other releases.

This mechanism will allow a structured approach to the evaluation of the requirements with a common understanding of the criteria applied.

Document the requirements baseline

We encounter many terms like functional requirement, system requirement, technical requirement, user requirement etc. The project manager will have to identify these specific terms and steps that will work on their project. It will then be a case of recording them in the project management plan so that everyone is clear. The analysis will be preceded and succeeded with a period of documentation, so that everyone concerned is clear about the nature of the requirements and subscribes to them. Once documented the requirements form a fundamental starting point for the development of more refined and detailed levels of requirement. Once the high-level business requirement has been identified, it will need to be distilled (a part of the scope definition activity) into lower levels and different types of requirement.

Once the requirements have been documented then the configuration management process applies, as they are effectively part of the project's baseline. Any changes to the requirements can have a huge knock-on effect to other aspects of the project and the integration of all of these discrete components therefore is of paramount importance. If we decide to build the bridge 20 metres longer, having already built the foundations, we will experience a high degree of cost and time delays and potential project failure.

Requirements test

The requirements are tested both after being first constructed and thereafter throughout the project. There needs to be a structured flow down between the various levels of requirements and each lower level may need to be validated by a different audience. This process is often demonstrated through the V-shaped diagram model in Figure 7.6:

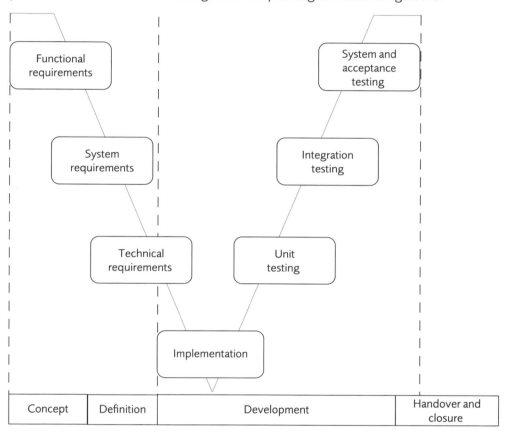

Figure 7.6 The V-shaped model for understanding and testing requirements

This one might apply to a software system, but others that are available will relate to engineering, petrochemical, retail and so on. The principle is that the relevant level of specification is tested and validated by the relevant level of user through the use of an appropriate test. As the life cycle develops so we analyse and test the various requirements at ever-increasing levels of detail as the technology becomes more specific, then towards the end of the project we revert back to the original 'need' and compare our products with it. The test we use for the functional requirements (e.g. processing 10,000 records per hour) will not be the same as the tests applied to the hardware itself.

Requirements linkage with quality

For the project to be perceived as a success it will need to be able to demonstrate that it has delivered according to the requirements. Therefore, quality and requirements must go hand in hand. The quality management section will focus on the achievement of quality, but suffice to say that if you do not understand what is required there is very little chance of being able to deliver it.

Work-based exercise

How does your organisation collect requirements and how does it record them?

Is there an automated system?

How do you know if all relevant stakeholders have been consulted?

Configuration management process

The purpose of configuration management is to ensure that at any time throughout the life cycle the project manager can be confident that all of the products that have been produced conform to their own relevant specifications, but also that they have been demonstrated to have worked with all of the products with which they interact.

Consider a building; if the design calls for a distance between two walls to be 10m, all the drawings and specifications will be based on this fact. The foundations will have been dug and the concrete poured, the roof beams ordered and sufficient roof tiles purchased for the necessary span. We will have checked the drawings, the surveyors will have calculated the quantities and everything will be going to plan.

Let us assume that the person fabricating the roof beams was given an older version of the drawings that was made earlier in the project before the design was finalised but showed the walls to be 9m apart. When the beams arrive they will not be long enough. Whose fault would this be? The beam supplier has done what they have been told, the people building the walls similarly. Who ends up with the problem? The project manager will, and to avoid being in this position they need a configuration management system that will make sure that everyone is working to the same drawings.

Configuration management can often be overlooked as the benefits are not immediately obvious and it is also not very easy to implement configuration management later on in the project once problems have started to occur.

If the configuration management system is not in place and being operated correctly, we run the risk of:

- Individual products not working together (as per the building example above).

- Poor quality of deliverables (we will not be able to test the product against the requisite specification).

- A lot of rework (the beam supplier will need to build new beams).

- Confusion, to the detriment of morale (the tradesmen have all done their job, but the end result is incorrect).

- Unsafe products in operation (especially problematic in safety-critical software systems).

- A high degree of warranty work and bug fixes (especially software).

- Other suppliers having difficulty interfacing with the project (we cannot describe what our finished product will look like).

In the above example the simplest of configuration management systems might do. If someone on the project was charged with looking after the various drawings/documents, who made sure that they had a reasonable version control, that a list of people who needed them was maintained and that those people got a revised version as and when it was changed, then the problem could well have been avoided. Please note that the area of document control overlaps quite a lot with that of configuration management and quite a lot of organisations will have a document management system that may well satisfy a lot of the requirements of a configuration management system. Because of the implications on the ability to produce a quality product, configuration management is often seen as a quality technique and should arguably appear as part of the project quality plan.

The activities contained in a configuration management process

If a more comprehensive configuration management process is required there are a number of accepted steps that can be adopted which together represent a configuration management procedure.

MANAGEMENT

Configuration planning

The project manager will make sure that an appropriate configuration management procedure is in place and is being followed. In practice they will work very closely with the configuration librarian in this regard. They will make sure that the procedure is briefed out and that all the stakeholders are aware of the implications of the system in operation. They will need a configuration management plan which defines all of the project-specific configuration management activities, roles and responsibilities. Some of these roles are listed later in this section.

Configuration identification

This activity is concerned with the correct and consistent identification of all the various components that go to make up the whole 'configuration'. Each component and subcomponent should have an easily identifiable and recognisable label so that it can be quickly and easily discernible where the component fits and how it may or may not interact with other components. A product breakdown structure can help here with its hierarchical numbering system; it is a key component of the cataloguing effort. The components and subcomponents classified in this way are also termed configuration items.

Configuration control

Configuration control is concerned with the process to be adopted in the management of the library. There should be clearly documented procedures to be followed by all involved in the project. The project manager will be instrumental in prescribing this as part of the configuration management plan and thereafter will need to make sure that suitable assurance is being undertaken.

Typical steps in the configuration control processes might include:

■ Interaction with the change control process as this is the source of potential configuration item amendments.

■ The checking in and out of items to the project team for amendment/usage.

■ Checking to make sure other configuration items are not affected (and if they are, potentially raising another change request).

■ Approvals from the configuration controller to implement the change.

■ Notifying all relevant parties of the change.

■ Making sure all records are up to date.

Configuration status accounting

This is the recording and reporting of all information relating to each configuration item in order that the various versions can be tracked. This enables the tracking of modifications to configuration items. A status account would include for each configuration item:

- Its identifier (from the PBS).

- Its owner (the person who created it and manages it).

- The date of last update.

- Its current status (e.g. is it being updated at present?).

- Its latest version number.

- Any other products that might be affected if this item is updated.

Configuration audit

Configuration audit is a key component of configuration management. It is carried out at regular predetermined stages to ensure that all the planned configuration items are where they should be in terms of their life cycle (i.e. the correct version is being used) and that there is sufficient evidence to demonstrate that all the change configuration and testing processes have been completed.

The roles associated with configuration management

The configuration librarian – this person is the custodian of the configuration library. They will be responsible for the proper management of the library and will liaise with other team members and the project manager to ensure that the procedures are followed.

The project manager – will be ultimately accountable for the proper execution of the configuration management process as indeed they are for all of the processes in the PMP. The project manager may need to prepare the team for an audit of the process (undertaken by impartial auditors). They will also be instrumental in championing the process as very often it is seen as onerous and unnecessary.

The configuration item controller – will have responsibility for individual configuration items. They own the technical specifications and are responsible for producing a product that conforms to the specification. If changes are to be made to a configuration item, then it is the configuration controller who will have responsibility for making sure that all the other items have been checked and updated as necessary. The configuration item owner is often a team member of a contractor or supplier.

The change control board – in a large project with complex interdependencies it might be appropriate to convene a change control board (comprised of at least the configuration item controllers) to make sure that the entire scope of the change is understood, acknowledged and approved (if appropriate), rejected or deferred.

The project team – the project team will need to follow the process. They may see this as a hindrance to their work, but if communicated properly they can see that it is in the best interests of the project.

MANAGEMENT

Use this space to make some notes

Quick quiz (answers on page 279)

	Question	Options	Your answer
1	The requirements are the same as benefits.	True or false?	
2	The configuration management plan forms part of the project PMP.	True or false?	
3	The ways in which requirements are gathered are usually driven by . . . .?	a) The project manager making it up b) The organisation's governance framework c) The procurement process d) The sponsor	
4	When should the requirements be tested?	a) At the beginning b) At the end c) All the way through d) Once	

	Question	Options	Your answer
5	Which of these is not a component of configuration management?	a) Work breakdown structures b) Control c) Assurance d) Planning	
6	Changes to the requirements are instigated by . . . .?	a) The project sponsor b) The project manager c) The procurement department d) The users	
7	Which of these roles is not associated with configuration management?	a) Project manager b) Configuration item controller c) Configuration librarian d) Procurement specialists	
8	Which of these is not a step in the requirements management process?	a) Identify b) Analyse c) Reiterate d) Test	
9	The configuration librarian checks products out and into the configuration library.	True or false?	
10	A status account would not include.	a) WBS number b) Owner c) Latest version d) ID number	

?	**What kind of questions might there be in the exam?**
1	This question has <u>two</u> parts. Answer both parts List and describe <u>four</u> steps in a typical requirements management process. 40 marks (10 marks each)
2	Explain why requirements management is important 10 marks

7.3	**Change control**

By completing this subsection you will be able to:

- explain the different stages of change control (such as request, review, assessment, decision, implementation);

- explain the relationship between change control and configuration management, and the concept of change freeze;

- explain the advantages and disadvantages of a change control process.

What are changes and why do they need controlling?

A change is something that will affect any of the key baselines associated with a project – the time, cost, quality, risk exposure or benefits case. Some changes may be welcome, some not. Either way, they need to be managed.

Change comes about for a number of reasons:

- External influences, for example, a change of government or organisational strategies.

- A new and innovative technique or process apparent after the business case has been agreed.

- Efficiencies of process and changes associated with getting things done quicker/cheaper that have emerged.

- Changes to the benefits model: perhaps doing a little more may have a huge return.

- Evolving designs and emergence of new information.

- Contractual changes generated by the client or other stakeholders.

A large proportion of the *APM Body of Knowledge 6th edition* is devoted to the construction of plans of one form or another. Having gone to so much trouble to make sure that the plans are coherent, viable and communicated, it would be very counterproductive to allow uncontrolled change to undermine all of the good work. One of the major causes of problems with projects is uncontrolled change, because ultimately it ends up with no one knowing what is going on. The purpose of a change control process is to make sure that the baselines of the project are secured and only changed with appropriate controls, checks, agreement and communication.

One of the reasons that so much time is spent planning is to counteract the effects identified in Figure 7.7. As time progresses, the ability to have an impact on the shape and direction of a project diminishes. Similarly, as time goes by, the cost of any changes will rise.

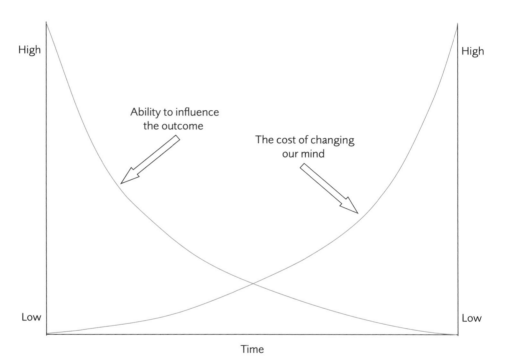

Figure 7.7 The cost of change curve

Other key aspects of projects, examined in a number of earlier sections, are that of the role of the sponsor and the business case. Once commissioned, a project is coherent in terms of understanding what will be done when and why. The cost is also considered and understood. Any changes to these parameters may call into question the viability of the project as a whole.

The emphasis is on control and the ability of the project manager to keep track of and make sure that proper authorisation has been received for changes to the project's baseline.

Figure 7.8 describes the minimum steps that should be included within a change control process to be sure to control a project's scope.

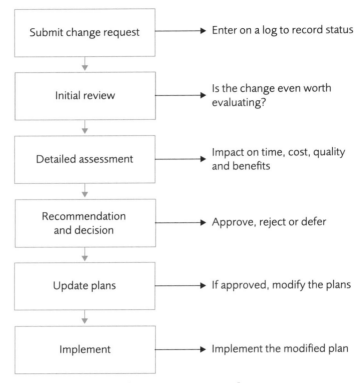

Figure 7.8 Steps in a change control process

Change request

A change can be requested from a number of sources. They can emanate for any of the reasons described previously. Stakeholders generally will instigate changes and the project manager must make sure that they are recorded. Potentially changes can be submitted many times if that is justified. A simple change control log should include a minimum of fields to properly record it. Generally the fields to include are:

■ Number – some form of identifier to uniquely identify the request.

■ Originator – who requested the change?

■ Description – a brief overview.

■ Date – date it was raised.

■ Status – has it been approved, rejected or deferred?

■ Impact – what will the effect be on the time, cost, quality, benefits and risk parameters for the project?

Each change control form is catalogued on a change control log and these details are recorded in summary for each change request.

Initial review

An initial review is carried out to determine whether or not the change is viable, potentially acceptable and has the support of a quorum of stakeholders. This initial review should be relatively short and focused. There is a potential for a lot of change requests and the analysis of them can end up derailing a project simply because while the team are analysing them, they are not doing the work on the plan. The initial review therefore is a form of filter to ensure that only sensible and viable changes should be taken forward to the next stage with the cost and effort implications of a full-scale review.

The configuration librarian, change control board (if there is one) and the configuration item controller may all need to be consulted to ensure that any changes to other parts of the system or product reflect the business case and strategy. This will help in the initial stages to understand the scope of the change and how much work may be involved.

Detailed assessment

The main use of the change control log (or register) is to keep track of the various changes, the detail of which will be recorded on the change control forms. These will generally be more detailed and will usually have a significant amount of reference documents associated with them. A change control form would carry detailed analysis of the material in the change control log. They will in essence be a 'mini business case' for the change. All of the aspects of a business case need to be considered when reviewing a change request (including time, cost and impact on scope) because of their potential to change the business case. The sponsor will need to have enough information on the impact of the change to make rational decisions about whether to approve them or not.

During the detailed assessment, all the product specifications from the configuration libraries are analysed and the impacts of changes to the products are properly evaluated to make sure that they are properly understood and any subsidiary change requests are raised. Once again there is a strong interaction with the configuration management process.

Recommendation and decision

The person with the authority to approve a change is typically the project sponsor (possibly taking advice from a duly appointed change control board). They have the responsibility to make sure that the stakeholders are consulted and any differences are resolved. They will liaise with the project manager and any other advisors to make sure that they are in essence 'doing the right thing'. The options for the sponsor are:

- Approve the change and authorise its inclusion into the plans.

- Reject the change and not approve its implementation.

- Defer the change until later.

At all stages the stakeholders need to be communicated with and kept up to date with progress and decisions. Ultimately, the project manager will need to co-ordinate the implementation of the change to make sure that it is done seamlessly and incorporated into the plans.

MANAGEMENT

Update plans and implement

This stage involves the project manager introducing the new tasks into the plan. Most of the normal planning process would already have been carried out during the detailed feasibility, but now the live schedules, budgets, specifications and risk registers will need to be formally updated and managed through the configuration management procedures. Changes must be considered alongside the existing frameworks of product descriptions and specifications. Once again the configuration librarian will be involved to make sure that the appropriate version number, modification levels and releases are co-ordinated.

Everyone who needs to know must be told about the change or errors due to incorrect information may creep into the system. It should not be forgotten that a prospective change is substantially easier to implement than a retrospective change to products already completed.

The implementation of a change is concerned with actually carrying out the approved work. At this point, the change control process merges with the normal managerial activities of the routine management of the PMP. The project manager should maintain any changes within the main project. Once approved, the changes will be absorbed into every level of planning and the new activities will be undertaken in exactly the same way as the original task load.

The relationship between change control and configuration management

Whenever a change is considered there may be an impact on the products the project is seeking to produce. The totality of these products is described as the project configuration. These principles were discussed in section 7.2. However, for the purposes of change control it is worth noting here that the two processes are inextricably linked and the failure to consider one without the other may result in the following problems:

■ Changing a product may have an effect on other products. This may lead to a mismatch between the two, potentially causing problems later, when two components are to be connected for example.

■ Uncontrolled changes undertaken by configuration item owners without reference to the controlling influence of the configuration librarian and their library will cause major problems later on when others are using the wrong versions.

The checking-out and checking-in procedures can add time to the changes being enacted. In a live environment it is not uncommon to find conflict between those trying to get changes enacted and the configuration librarian and their staff.

Change freeze

As the project progresses from one stage to another and as the requirements begin to be collected and converted into products, so the necessity for change also rears its head. It is virtually inevitable that the stakeholders will have forgotten something or changed their minds. The change control process is designed to protect the project from uncontrolled changes.

However, there will come a time when more changes cannot be considered and this is called a 'change freeze'. It is implemented so that the products as they are currently specified can be finished and delivered. It is not uncommon for products (especially software) to be delivered at various stages of modification. These interim stages are usually referred to as a 'release' – most people will be familiar with the process where their mobile phone software gets updated for example.

It is quite easy to see how this method could relate to software but with a construction job (building a bridge for example) it is far less feasible to accommodate emerging requirements and so the change freezes are usually quite significant events requiring top-level approval.

Advantages and disadvantages of change control

The advantages of change control include:

- The project scope is managed and control is maintained because there is a clear baseline that describes the current state of the project time, cost and quality parameters.

- The formal process ensures proper record-keeping and that everyone is clear on the nature of the current baseline.

- Proper adjustments can be made to expectations about schedule, cost and quality, ensuring the various stakeholders have been properly informed about what the project is producing.

The disadvantages of change control are:

- It can cause delay while the process wheels turn and this can cause frustration.

- It can cause friction between the project manager and the user community because the project manager will be seen as blocking changes and hiding behind the process.

- The process itself can cost money to implement as there needs to be an appropriate level of bureacracy and effort to investigate requests.

- It can seem like burdensome bureaucracy and sometimes individuals will not want to follow it, preferring to circumvent the process to 'get things done'.

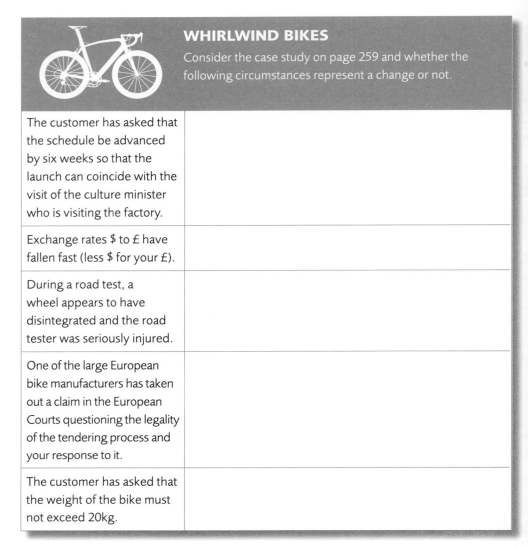

WHIRLWIND BIKES

Consider the case study on page 259 and whether the following circumstances represent a change or not.

The customer has asked that the schedule be advanced by six weeks so that the launch can coincide with the visit of the culture minister who is visiting the factory.	
Exchange rates $ to £ have fallen fast (less $ for your £).	
During a road test, a wheel appears to have disintegrated and the road tester was seriously injured.	
One of the large European bike manufacturers has taken out a claim in the European Courts questioning the legality of the tendering process and your response to it.	
The customer has asked that the weight of the bike must not exceed 20kg.	

Use this space to make some notes

Quick quiz (answers on page 280)

	Question	Options	Your answer
1	The steps in a change control process include request, _____, detailed evaluation, recommendation, _____, implement.	a) Initial investigation; control b) Changes; configuration c) Initial investigation; update plans d) Update; appraisal	
2	A project sponsor has ultimate authority to approve changes.	True or false?	
3	The project manager has ultimate authority to approve changes.	True or false?	
4	Which of these does a change control process not seek to deal with?	a) Morale b) Quality c) Cost d) Benefits	
5	How many times can a change be submitted?	a) Once b) Twice c) Three times d) As many as is justified	
6	Which of these is not an outcome from the recommendation stage?	a) Deferral b) Rejection c) Absorption d) Approval	
7	Which of these is not an entry on a change control log?	a) Date b) Number c) Impact d) WBS number	

	Question	Options	Your answer
8	On a change control form, the project manager would want to record everything except . . .?	a) Who raised it b) Costs to implement c) Was it approved d) The probability of it happening	
9	Configuration management is tightly linked to change control.	True or false?	
10	A configuration librarian would be consulted during the initial investigation of a change control.	True or false?	

What kind of questions might there be in the exam?

1 List and describe <u>five</u> steps in a change-management process.

50 marks (10 marks each)

2 Explain <u>five</u> potential consequences of changes not being properly managed on the project.

50 marks (10 marks each)

8

Planning for success

8.1 Business case

By completing this subsection you will be able to:

- explain the purpose of a business case and its importance during the life cycle;

- describe who has authorship and approval of the business case.

The purpose of the business case is considered as a single topic here alongside the roles of those who input or interact with it.

The importance of the business case

The development of the business case can be viewed as a funnelling arrangement, whereby the problems or opportunities an organisation may face are analysed and reviewed in order to determine the correct project response.

Figure 8.1 describes this 'funnel'. These 'potential projects' enter into the concept phase as a result of some initiative on the part of the sponsoring organisation. These may be problems the organisation faces (such as rising maintenance costs on existing equipment) or capitalising on an opportunity (such as a new product launch).

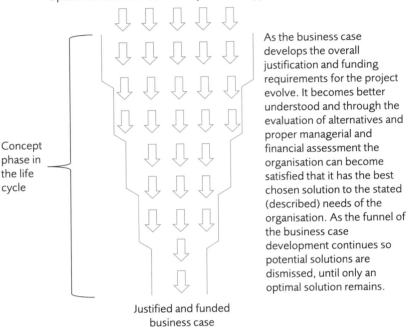

Options to deal with described problems/opportunities

Concept phase in the life cycle

As the business case develops the overall justification and funding requirements for the project evolve. It becomes better understood and through the evaluation of alternatives and proper managerial and financial assessment the organisation can become satisfied that it has the best chosen solution to the stated (described) needs of the organisation. As the funnel of the business case development continues so potential solutions are dismissed, until only an optimal solution remains.

Justified and funded business case

Figure 8.1 Business case development

Contents of a typical business case

The business case balances the following three major topics:

Benefits – How much might be recovered from the investment, who might witness it and when will it be evidenced?

Costs – How much will it cost to produce the products that will collectively deliver the benefits?

Risks – What might go wrong with either of the above? The risks a business case is mostly concerned with are strategic ones (what might cause problems for the business?). Clearly, opportunities that have not been previously considered may emerge and also need managing.

Other key headings might include:

■ The strategic case for the project (what problem or opportunity has it been commissioned to deal with?).

■ Benefits to be derived from the project, which can be financial or non-financial, or both.

■ Options appraisal and justification of the chosen option (see financial investment appraisal below). As the funnel forces a gradual filtration and selection process so the various options will be discarded in favour of ultimately just one. This one option is then developed in the definition phase.

■ Investment appraisal – generally an assessment of the relative costs and benefits of the project using financial and statistical modelling to understand how these balance.

■ Constraints (the things that are perceived as barriers) – an example might be being unable to gain access during certain hours. They are generally things over which the project has little or no control.

And for the chosen project option:

■ High-level description of the project scope (what's included and what isn't).

■ Estimated costs – these will evolve over time and it is not unusual to witness high-level budgetary estimates in the business case with an ever-increasing level of accuracy and detail emerging over time.

■ Target schedule (key dates and milestones) – this again will be a high-level schedule, possibly just a list of key deadlines to be met and further decomposed in the PMP later.

■ Assumptions (the things we have taken to be true in order to proceed) – all through the business case development there is a need to act upon assumptions, but care is required later as these will inevitably lead to risks being created.

■ Dependencies (what else needs to happen) – these need to be captured, recorded and managed to make sure that any external factors (mayoral elections, perhaps) do not impede progress.

■ Success criteria are in the business case to make clear those things that the project is seeking to achieve. They are the end points, not the measure of progress. These are the project KPIs.

■ Impact on business-as-usual. This is the disruption that may interfere with the normal operations of the business; for example, replacing a school hall floor may mean problems for the staff who need to hold large examinations there.

Roles in the preparation of the business case

The question is always asked – who writes the business case? The answer is typically the sponsor and project manager with input from others.

So who does contribute?

The sponsoring group (steering group or project board) are the representatives of the organisation for whom the undertaking is being carried out. They oversee the construction of the business case in collaboration with the nominated sponsor. They will be able to approve it and thereafter the sponsor will use the business case as the reference point for the project.

The sponsor oversees the construction of the business case in collaboration with the sponsoring group. They may well have specialised knowledge but must remember to use the experts that work for them and not presume too much based on their own expertise (or lack of it). For smaller projects the sponsor may have delegated authority to approve the business case.

The project manager may physically write the business case, or more likely (on a large project) will manage a 'mini project' to write it and in doing so may employ other staff.

The suppliers may well have significant detailed knowledge to make the writing of the business case possible; for example, they may be experts in a particular process that the client is unaware of, thus placing them in a good position to add value.

The users know what they require by way of products and benefits; they need to separate musts from wants, prioritise the relevant aspects of the specification and provide advice to the sponsor as to the exact details of some of them.

Subject matter experts, such as procurement specialists, management accountants, marketing professionals, drawn from within the organisation. These staff can be co-opted onto the team to enable proper analysis and decisions to be made.

External consultants will often be engaged to prepare the business case for a project. This has the distinct advantage of making the decision-making process dispassionate and impartial.

How does the business case evolve through the life cycle?

During the concept phase the business case is developed by the project manager and their advisers to produce an outline business case. It will contain the necessary evaluation and detail to enable the project to proceed to definition. It will represent a 'one-stop shop' where the primary justification for the project can be found and referenced. The original estimates generated during concept will be fairly high level and will be in need of further refinement: this happens through definition alongside the PMP. The business case is quite flexible at the start and will reflect the need to consider a number of options before narrowing down thinking to arrive at the recommended solution.

During definition the business case needs to be reviewed alongside the evolving PMP and will eventually be produced as a final document. In truth the PMP is probably started during concept as the business case development will be subject to some of the procedures in the PMP and so they ought to go hand in hand. As the PMP develops it will take a guide from the business case and will evolve from some of the risk, success criteria and assumptions therein.

During development the business case will form the cornerstone of the project evaluation. The PMP will govern the project but the business case sets out the benefits. If anything in the project has a potential to render the business case unachievable, then the project manager and the sponsor will need to take appropriate action (potentially even terminating the project if this mismatch is serious and significant enough). The business case benefits need to be reviewed during the gate reviews, this is in addition to the project performance and progress data.

During handover and closure the business case needs to be checked to ensure that the products as delivered are suitable for acceptance as capable of yielding the anticipated benefits. The users will be in a position to advise the project teams and sponsor about this.

During benefits realisation, the business case will form the main point of reference for the business to be assured that the benefits are being realised and to the value and timing anticipated.

WHIRLWIND BIKES

Consider the case study on page 259.
See if you can write a draft business case using the template produced here.

What are the key timescales?

What are the business risks?

What are the main costs?

MANAGEMENT

 Quick quiz (answers on page 280)

	Question	Options	Your answer
1	Who owns the business case?	a) The client b) The sponsoring group c) The project manager d) The project sponsor	
2	A project will only be justified if the benefits outweigh the costs.	True or false?	
3	A project will always require a business case.	True or false?	
4	When are benefits realised?	a) During operations b) During termination c) During definition d) During development	
5	Suppliers may be able to provide specialist knowledge to help construct the business case.	True or false?	

Use this space to make some notes

What kind of questions might there be in the exam?

1   List <u>five</u> roles that may have an interaction with the development of a project business case and describe the contribution of each of those roles.

50 marks (10 marks each)

2   This question has <u>two</u> parts. Answer both parts.

Explain the primary purpose of a business case.

10 marks

List and describe <u>four</u> components of a business case.

40 marks (10 marks each)

8.2 | Benefits management

By completing this subsection you will be able to:

■ explain benefits management (including success criteria and key performance indicators and their uses in measuring project success).

Project success

Benefits management is the mechanism for understanding what organisational benefits will accrue from the project and the systematic management of them until they are realised.

There are two complementary views of success here.

Take the sponsor's perspective; they are tasked with the realisation of benefits because they own the project business case. The project manager is focused on delivering to time, cost and quality. These do not compete, but it is important to understand the nature of the differences.

Take an example of a new road bridge over a river. The project manager can build the most cost-effective structure possible on time and to budget (as per their project management plan) but if nobody uses the bridge then there will be no practical benefit and any benefits inserted into the business case will obviously not be realised.

Question – is it possible to have a successful project which delivers to time, cost and quality that does not deliver benefit? Or conversely, is it possible to have an unsuccessful project (one that overspends, perhaps) that does realise benefit?

The answer, of course, is yes to both. The difficulty arises if we do not have a sufficiently well-developed understanding of each: we find ourselves unable to really classify the project as a success or failure.

MANAGEMENT

Fear not, there are solutions, but it does involve some terminology. Consider the introduction of a new high-speed rail service:

Table 8.1 Defining project terms

Term	Definition	Example
Success criteria	The measures by which the success of the project is judged.	Was the project finished on time? Can we operate at the advertised speed? Is the system safe?
Benefits*	The quantifiable and measurable improvement resulting from completion of project deliverables that is perceived as positive by a stakeholder. It will normally have a tangible value, expressed in monetary terms that will justify the investment.	People travelling get to their destination quicker. The train operator makes a profit. Stations on the route encourage regeneration. N.B. It will be necessary to put a value on these if we want to fully conform to the definition.
Key performance indicators	Measures of success that can be used throughout the project to ensure that it is progressing towards a successful conclusion.	During the project we might want to measure the rate at which we are laying the track. We might want to make sure that we have a happy team environment (survey, perhaps).
Success factors	Success factors are management practices that, when implemented, will increase the likelihood of success of a project.	Defining clear goals and objectives; focus on business value; a proper governance structure, management commitment and clear communication.

* Quantitative benefits are those that can be attributed and measured accurately and objectively such as 'growth in revenue by £x' or 'x years improvement in life expectancy'. Quantitative measures are those that are more subjective such as 'improved ambience' or 'user friendliness'.

The example in Table 8.1 introduces a few things to remember about the terminology and definitions. If you grasp the principles of these here the production of other project management material such as the PMP will be easier.

Once you have defined the success criteria for your project, it ought to be possible to produce a set of deliverables and plans that enable you to meet them.

Benefits management process

Benefits management can be described as a step-by-step process. This is summarised in Figure 8.2.

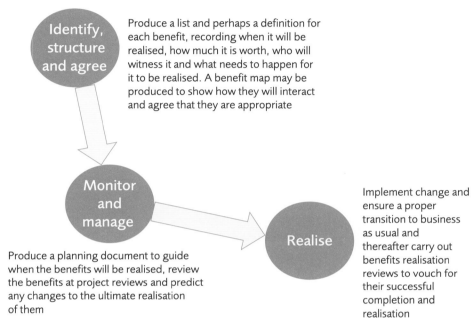

Figure 8.2 A simple benefits-management process

There is a danger in presenting benefits management as a systematic and procedural technique, because some of its importance and implications will be lost. The only reason a project is undertaken is to achieve a change. It is highly unlikely that an organisation would embark upon any project in the ready anticipation of things being worse afterwards. The role of benefits management is crucial to being able to quantify the benefits so that they can be tracked throughout the project and actually realised thereafter.

MANAGEMENT

WHIRLWIND BIKES

Consider the case study on page 259. What are the success criteria, the success factors and the benefits? What might you measure during the project to make sure things are going to turn out as planned (KPIs)? Identify two of each.

Success criteria

Success factors

Benefits

Quick quiz (answers on page 281)

	Question	Options	Your answer
1	The benefits management process includes _____, monitor and manage, realise.	a) Identify and agree b) Shape and agree c) Populate and agree d) Decide and agree	
2	Benefits should be measurable.	True or false?	
3	The business case will include the project benefits.	True or false?	
4	The analysis of the potential benefits is used to ensure they outweigh the costs of a project to make sure it is viable.	True or false?	
5	The business case is always one great big document.	True or false?	

Use this space to make some notes

MANAGEMENT

What kind of question might there be in the exam?

1 This question has <u>three</u> parts. Answer all parts.

State a definition of the term 'success criteria'.

5 marks

State a definition of the term 'benefit'.

5 marks

Explain the term benefits management in each of the following project phases: Concept, Definition, Development and Operations.

40 marks

8.3 | Investment appraisal

By completing this subsection you will be able to:

- explain the use of payback, internal rate of return and net present value as investment appraisal techniques.

Financial investment appraisal

During the development of the business case, the organisation can deploy some key appraisal techniques to help understand the financial aspects of the project's viability. The three you are asked to consider are described below.

Payback method

Using this method a project's projected income can be compared with its initial cost to help understand when the initial investment will be recovered. The payback is expressed as a number of years (Figure 8.3).

Year	Investment £	Income £
0 (now)	24,000	0
1	0	4,500
2	0	4,500
3	0	6,000
4	0	6,000
5	0	6,000
6	0	7,500
7	0	15,000
Total	24,000	49,500

This project will pay back its investment during year 5 (i.e. when the net income equals the investment – between 4 and 5 years in this case)

Figure 8.3 The payback method

Advantages with the payback method	Disadvantages with the payback method
Quick to calculate.	It assumes that money is worth the same now as in the future.
Simple to calculate.	Does not take into account any income after the payback period.
Easily understood.	Does not take into account the future value of money (see NPV later in this section).

Net present value

Using the net present value (NPV) method it is possible to make allowances for how the value of money changes over time. Would you for example prefer to have £100 now or £100 in five years' time? The answer to this is dependent upon a whole range of data, some of which we are unaware of at the time we make the choice. To a business, cash now is much more valuable than cash in the future, partly because businesses often have to borrow money to invest in projects. To adjust for this cost of capital we reduce the value of further returns by a discount factor. These are set for each organisation based on its own policies. An accountant in each organisation will define multipliers (discount factors) to apply to the future income and investments. These adjustments seek to normalise the future values to today's prices so we can compare each to the investment.

Taking the example in Figure 8.3 if we assume a discount rate of 10 per cent the multipliers appear in the table below as the 'discount factor'. The resultant perception of the present value of each of these appears in the right-hand column.

Year	Investment (£)	Income (£)	Discount factor	Present value (£)	
0 (now)	24,000	0	1	(24,000)	The discount factors used here are derived from the assumption of a 10 per cent discount rate
1	0	4,500	0.909	4,091	
2	0	4,500	0.826	3,717	
3	0	6,000	0.751	4,506	
4	0	6,000	0.683	4,098	
5	0	6,000	0.621	3,726	
6	0	7,500	0.564	4,230	
7	0	15,000	0.513	7,695	
Total	24,000	49,500		32,063	
			Net Present Value	32,063 – 24,000 = 8,063	

Figure 8.4 NPV demonstrated with a discount factor of 10%

As mentioned earlier, the calculation of a net present value is very heavily reliant upon the choice of discount factor. If the wrong one is chosen a very different conclusion can be drawn about the viability of the project. Suppose we used a 20 per cent discount rate to drive the same calculations as in Figure 8.4. We would arrive at the figures as in Figure 8.5.

In the case of the previous NPV calculation the profitability of the project is £8,063. Watch what happens if we choose a 20 per cent discount factor:

Year	Investment (£)	Income (£)	Discount factor	Present value (£)	
0 (now)	24,000	0	1	(24,000)	The discount factors used here are derived from the assumption of a 20% discount rate
1	0	4,500	0.833	3,749	
2	0	4,500	0.694	3,123	
3	0	6,000	0.597	3,582	
4	0	6,000	0.482	2,892	
5	0	6,000	0.402	2,412	
6	0	7,500	0.335	2,513	
7	0	15,000	0.279	4,185	
Total	24,000	49,500		22,456	
			Net Present Value	22,456 – 24,000 = (1,544)	

Figure 8.5 NPV demonstrated with a discount factor of 20%

If we compare these two tables side by side the conclusion must be that if we use a 10 per cent rate the project is worth doing, if we use a 20 per cent rate it is not. A reasonably profitable project has turned into one that will make a loss. This is purely and simply down to the choice of the discount rate. This choice of rate can have a huge impact on the decisions an organisation may make about which project to pursue and indeed whether to pursue any at all. There is one final mechanism of analysis that can help remove this problem and it is referred to as the internal rate of return or IRR, which we will cover later.

Advantages of the NPV method	Disadvantages of the NPV method
Takes into account the future value of money.	Quite complex to calculate.
Looks at the whole project life cycle.	Reliant on which percentage is used as the discount rate.
Yields a single predicted figure for profitability.	The more detailed calculation implies greater certainty that is not justified.

Internal rate of return

If we consider the present values of the two scenarios before (i.e. assuming 10 per cent and 20 per cent), then we have some data to analyse using the internal rate of return (IRR) method of investment appraisal (Figure 8.6).

Year	Present value (£) @ 10%	Present value (£) @ 20%	
0 (now)	(24,000)	(24,000)	
1	4,091	3,749	We can plot the two figures from the NPV row on the previous two tables onto a graph
2	3,717	3,123	
3	4,506	3,582	
4	4,098	2,892	
5	3,726	2,412	
6	4,230	2,513	
7	7,695	4,185	
NPV	8,063	(1,544)	

Figure 8.6 NPV variability depending on rate

When we look at this on a graph we can demonstrate the IRR for this project (Figure 8.7). There is a mechanism to calculate the exact figure, but for the purposes of this guide it is merely necessary to describe the principle rather than seek 100 per cent numerical accuracy.

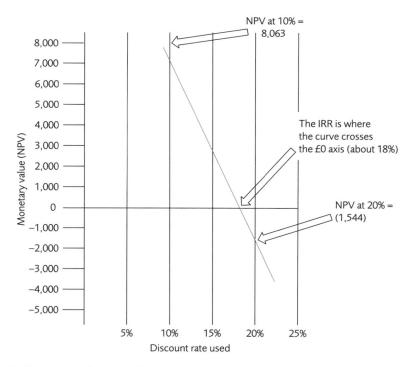

Figure 8.7 Internal rate of return

Advantages of the IRR method	Disadvantages of the IRR method
Takes into account the future value of money.	Quite complex to calculate.
The choice of discount factor is not relevant.	Difficult to calculate with accuracy.
Can compare with an organisation's flat rate expectation of return, i.e. the minimum amount that can be achieved by any option.	Can have multiple results in some particular circumstances.

Managerial judgement

There are a number of ways in which an organisation judges its investments that is not necessarily based on sheer weight of financial evidence. In some circumstances an organisation may choose to do a project even though the investment does not appear to be financially worthwhile, or indeed vice versa. The managers of an organisation have the final say over how their investment capital is spent. If projects have a business case that is not positive (i.e. the benefits outweigh the costs), great care is needed throughout to ensure that incorrect decisions are not made through the life of the project predicated on incorrect financial assumptions.

 Quick quiz (answers on page 281)

	Question	Options	Your answer
1	A weakness of the payback method is what?	a) It is simple to calculate b) It requires a complicated graph to understand it c) It is hard to calculate d) It does not take into account the future value of money	
2	A weakness of IRR is that it is quite complex to calculate.	True or false?	
3	A strength of the payback method is that it is simple to calculate.	True or false?	
4	The discount rates used to calculate NPVs will normally be provided by whom?	a) The project manager b) The project sponsor c) The users d) The company's accountants	
5	Financial investment appraisal takes precedence over managerial judgement.	True or false?	

Use this space to make some notes

....

....

....

....

....

What kind of question might there be in the exam?

1 This question has <u>two</u> parts. Answer both parts.

List and describe <u>three</u> investment appraisal techniques.

30 marks

Explain <u>two</u> benefits of undertaking investment appraisals.

20 marks (10 marks each)

8.4 | Information management

By completing this subsection you will be able to:

- explain an information management system (including collection, analysis, storage, dissemination, archiving and destruction of information);

- explain a typical project reporting cycle including the gathering of data and dissemination of reports and the principles of reporting by exception.

Information is collected to inform the reporting cycle, as such this is considered alongside project reporting.

Information management systems

Accurate information is the life blood of any organisation; in its absence, it is impossible to operate. Project information begins to be accumulated right from the start. The project manager needs to make sure that all the information that is collected (whether planned

or not) is stored securely. In the modern world we often think of information as being electronic; our servers replace filing cabinets, our PCs, our ring binders. There is still a huge amount of information that is stored physically, but most organisations now have computerised workflow and document management processes and systems at their disposal.

Consideration must be given to some of the legislative arrangements around information and how it is used, such as the Data Protection Act, Freedom of Information Act, and perhaps the Official Secrets Act. These are also components of the project context or environment discussed earlier in this guide.

A typical information management system ought to be able to accommodate the following key stages or steps:

Information management plan

As a subsidiary plan in the project management plan, the information management plan would contain the following:

- Scope – what information will be covered in the plan?

- Roles and responsibilities – who on the project does what, regarding information?

- Tools and techniques – what systems are available to be used?

- Process – what processes are going to be followed?

- Audit – how will assurance and verification of the plan be carried out?

Information collection

The project manager needs to think very carefully about how much information is collected, processed and retained. The less that is collected, the less that needs to be analysed and processed. The principle generally is that only the information actually needed should be gathered. Reports should be kept to a minimum, in a standard format, portraying only the information that is needed on which to act properly. It is relatively easy to gather information, the trick is to gather only the right information. Information now falls into many different categories:

- Written – words, reports, specifications, memos, correspondence.

- Video – marketing material, training material, etc.

- Audio – podcasts, voicemail, recorded conversations.

- Web-based or streamed – YouTube, Twitter, e-learning, etc.

- Physical – such as models and prototypes.

- Biological – such as samples or DNA.

All of these might need to be captured and stored. Care may be needed if evidence is required in the future.

Stakeholders may introduce unsolicited information and this is perhaps the most difficult to deal with. The project (as a result of its information management plan) will be able to classify and assimilate the information it knows about, it will be far more difficult to do so with information that it is not or has not been aware of previously.

Information storage

In its simplest form electronic storage is very easy with modern tools and techniques. Care should be exercised though, as there are a number of issues that can, if not dealt with appropriately, cause difficulties. As a minimum, the project should have standards associated with access security, back-ups, version control and accessibility. Document management systems have the potential to resolve a lot of these issues if used sensibly, but are not a replacement for a sound set of management controls.

Information dissemination

The project will need to keep careful records of who needs what information and when. When something changes, who needs to know? How will the information be sent out – is it via email, paper, etc.? What security arrangements need to be wrapped around these processes?

Information archiving

A lot of information needs to be kept for a minimum period of time, for example, tax information, security clearances and training records. The project may need to negotiate with the organisation within which it is operating to understand these constraints and make appropriate arrangements to conform to them. It is not really very useful to archive information without a good cataloguing system so that information can be retrieved when necessary. Where physical information is concerned, then clearly larger and more substantial environments may be required.

Information destruction

Most information may be retained for periods of time without too much difficulty, but care should be exercised so that it is not retained excessively or in breach of any legislative arrangements. The cost of retaining information indefinitely is enormous and regular audits and housekeeping is vital.

Information reporting

Information management is not an end in itself, but a mechanism to ensure the probity of data for the purpose of dissemination. The process of transmitting formal data is via an information reporting process. There are some basic principles around information reporting (Figure 8.8).

MANAGEMENT

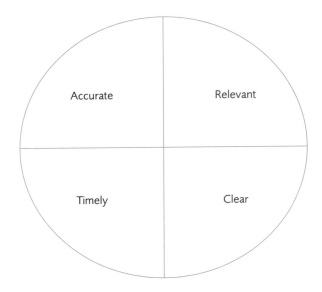

Figure 8.8 Information principles

Keep it relevant – try and keep your information volume to the minimum to achieve the objectives. Examples are template reports, such as highlight reports or exception reports. Make sure you understand the audience.

Keep it clear – use graphs and charts to get the message across without 'clutter'. Examples are the milestone slip charts and Gantt charts.

Keep it timely – monthly reports can report on data up to eight weeks old; on a three-month project, this is not useful. Make sure you know the important cycles and conform.

Keep it accurate – be prepared to be challenged and substantiate any data submitted. The principle of making decisions based on accurate data is well established. If there is any doubt about the accuracy of any of the key data then concerns will need to be escalated.

(Project) Reporting cycle

Typically organisations as part of their governance framework will impose a reporting cycle (Figure 8.9). If they do not, it is good practice for project managers to follow a standard approach each week/month/quarter/year.

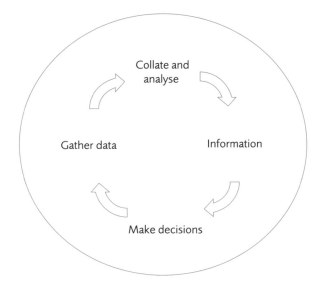

Figure 8.9 A reporting cycle

For example:

- Friday afternoon – time sheets for the project team collected and analysed by the project office who analyse them and make sure the time booked goes against the correct WBS codes.

- Monday morning – the project office produces a summary sheet for the project manager to review and approve.

- The project office then update the relevant schedules to make sure that an accurate reflection of progress is portrayed and all of the project percentage complete figures are up to date.

- The project manager holds a team meeting to review progress to consider the schedules in conjunction with the team's verbal updates at the meeting.

- Any corrections are made and the project progress report is produced, incorporating all other data necessary such as earned value, quality reviews, changes, forecasts etc.

- The report is used at the Wednesday customer meeting where the progress is discussed and any action considered and instigated.

- Each month the latest aggregated weekly reports are considered at the project board meeting where strategic decisions are taken based upon the progress to date and any new matters that need to be undertaken.

- The cycle then repeats itself and so it goes on. This process is not exhaustive and certainly not necessarily fit for all purposes but it is indicative of the kind of process that underpins many projects. Reporting by exception is the process where only those events that deviated from the plan are reported.

WHIRLWIND BIKES

Consider the case study on page 259. What would the reporting arrangement be?

Quick quiz (answers on page 281)

	Question	Options	Your answer
1	Which of these components is not a component of information management?	a) Collection b) Retrieval c) Archiving d) Change control	
2	Personal information can be kept forever regardless if it is needed or not.	True or false?	
3	Every project needs an IT server.	True or false?	
4	Who is responsible for writing the Information Management Plan?	a) The project manager b) The project sponsor c) The users d) The company's accountants	
5	Information management is only important on the largest projects.	True or false?	

Use this space to make some notes

 What kind of question might there be in the exam?

1

List and describe <u>five</u> components of an information management process.

50 marks (10 marks each)

8.5 | **Project management plan**

By completing this subsection you will be able to:

■ explain the purpose of the project management plan and its importance throughout the project life cycle;

■ describe typical contents of a project management plan;

■ outline the authorship, approval and audience of a project management plan.

The project management plan (PMP) is a key document on the project and needs to be developed and owned throughout the project, as such it is necessary to consider all aspects of it in one go.

Why do we need a project management plan?

A project management plan (PMP) is a document that can be used by everyone to help:

■ Explain the nature of the project. Be able to describe its scope, the material deliverables, timescales and roles and responsibilities.

■ Communicate the various strategies and plans to a wider audience. The document needs to be a working document, such that its contents are known, it is up to date and visible to everyone.

■ Provide a baseline from which further measurement and analysis of variation can take place. It is the key document when it comes to recording and reporting variations from the plan.

■ Form a 'contract' between the project manager and the project sponsor. In a client/supplier relationship the PMP may well be part of the contract, but even in an in-house environment, the PMP represents an agreement between the project manager and the sponsor.

■ Provide a basis for continuity throughout the project life cycle. There is no guarantee of continuity of staff and the PMP provides the single document that provides the ability to make sure that all the relevant information necessary to run the project is available and up to date.

The PMP is finalised at the end the definition phase. However, it may well exist in draft form during the concept phase to keep a record of processes and tools as the thinking develops. The PMP is finally issued after the business case is agreed. Much of what is in the business case feeds the PMP and provides the overall strategy and background details (Figure 8.10).

For example, a business case will determine whether to make or buy a particular component. The organisation's decision will need to be reflected in the PMP. The PMP will then take this principle further and develop the specific activities needed to implement this approach. It will turn the business's strategic decisions into practical steps and define the delivery strategy for the project.

Figure 8.10 The concept of the project management plan

Once complete, a PMP is approved by the project sponsor.

Contents of a PMP

The PMP has potentially a large number of contents that fall into different categories (Table 8.2).

Table 8.2 The contents of the PMP

Why	The project management plan is built on the work done in the project business case. The reason for the project will be reproduced or referenced from the business case. Basically, it provides an explanation to the project team as to why the project is important enough for the organisation to invest time, money and effort. The business case 'sets the scene' for the PMP. It is very often a separate document (or series of documents). As a minimum, it contains: ■ a description of benefits; ■ the statement of requirements; ■ the project objectives; ■ strategic fit.

MANAGEMENT

What	This section describes the nature of the project deliverables created to satisfy the project requirements and organisation needs. Particularly, it helps to describe the: ■ scope of the project, including being specific about what is included and excluded; ■ product specifications for each of the main products to be delivered by the project; ■ acceptance criteria, which define how the 'customer' will approve the deliverables; ■ constraints, such as critical time slots; ■ assumptions, of which the plan has been formulated, such as the availability of resources.
Who	This is defined by an organisation chart showing who is involved in the project. Also called an organisational breakdown structure (OBS), it can be used to map the various roles to the individuals using a responsibility assignment matrix (RAM). This yields a valuable document for the project manager to control the project. Contents relating to this typically include: ■ a responsibility assignment matrix, which defines who is responsible for the completion of each product; ■ an organisational breakdown structure, which shows the organisational hierarchy of the project; ■ authority and delegation schedules, which define the delegation of authority within the project for the approval of documents, expenditures and acceptance; ■ role descriptions, which clearly define the overall responsibilities within the project.
How much	This section summarises the project budget, the mechanisms for cost management and how variances are to be dealt with. Being able to predict with some certainty the rate at which the project will be spending its funds is crucial to knowing whether we are on track or not. These include the: ■ budget, including a time phasing, which shows when the funding will be required; ■ earned value arrangements for tracking actual cost and progress against the plan; ■ cash flow forecasts showing the balance of income vs costs for the project. This is of particular importance to contracting organisations; ■ ways that variations are dealt with, describing the procedures for agreeing changes in cost; ■ cost management procedures, including procedures for reviewing the estimated costs and maintaining up to date forecasts.

When	The project schedule is a key document within a PMP. This may be limited to a high-level summary Gantt chart of the key milestones and stages. This is supported by a range of other scheduling information. Specific contents include the: ■ precedence diagrams; ■ resource histograms; ■ gantt charts; ■ project life cycle.
How	This section describes the strategy for running the project. It contains the various subsidiary plans and strategies that will be deployed to arrive at the desired outcome. These ancillary plans are very often separate documents. Indeed a lot of project-based organisations may already have well-developed template plans that can be adopted by the project, rather than inventing new ones from scratch. Specific contents might include the: ■ project methods, which include standards for design work and review of products; ■ health and safety plan, which includes the roles and responsibilities, and a description of how those specific risks will be managed; ■ quality plan, which includes responsibilities for quality and how it will be controlled; ■ procurement strategy, which includes a summary of how goods and services will be acquired, for example, through competitive tendering; ■ communication management plan, which describes the different communication methods that will be used for each group of stakeholders, such as public meetings for local residents; ■ risk management plan, which describes the overall approach to risk, and how risk will be identified and managed; ■ change control procedures, which describe the detailed process for identifying, assessing and approving changes.

Table 8.3 Two distinct types of PMP content

Policies (how the project will be run). These can be thought of as the framework within which the project will operate	Schedules and plans (what exactly will we produce, when, for how much and who will do it)
Stakeholder management policy	Stakeholder analysis
Risk management policy	Risk log
Change control process	Change control log
Configuration management process	Configuration library
Issue management policy	Issue log

(Continued overleaf)

Policies (how the project will be run). These can be thought of as the framework within which the project will operate	Schedules and plans (what exactly will we produce, when, for how much and who will do it)
Quality policy	Quality (defects log)
Resource management policy	Resource plan
Monitoring and control procedures	Earned value reports
Health and safety policy	Health and safety log
Planning and estimating processes	Gantt chart

Please note – Table 8.3 has been produced to indicate the difference between the processes that are followed to run the project on a day-to-day basis and the various schedules or plans that are consequential upon running those processes. There is no one-to-one mapping between the processes identified and the schedules on the right. They are for example only. You will notice though that these 'processes/policies/procedures/frameworks' on the left are all dealt with within the syllabus. They are the things a project manager must do to ensure their project is properly managed.

Use of the PMP throughout the life cycle

It is quite easy to contemplate the use of the project management plan at the start of the project. Maintaining it throughout the project, however, is perhaps a bit more challenging. The PMP is a controlled document. The project manager will own the PMP and ensure that it is continually reviewed and used. The purpose is not to simply just create one and then leave it languishing on a shelf.

- The PMP should be used as a communications tool and be circulated to those who have a need to see it.
- It should be regularly reviewed to ensure it is still accurate and continues to reflect the needs described in the business case.
- Each of the contents can refer to other ancillary documents (such as a risk log). It is important that these linkages are correct and maintained.
- Changes must be conveyed to the audience of the document.
- It can be used as the basis for audits and reviews.

Work-based exercise

See if you can find an example of a project management plan and have a look at the contents. Does it have the following in it?

Definition and information	Policies and procedures

Use this space to make some notes

 Quick quiz (answers on page 282)

	Question	Options	Your answer
1	Who owns the project management plan?	a) The project sponsor b) The project manager c) The procurement department d) The users	
2	Which of these is not contained in the project management plan?	a) The business case b) The risk management plan c) The project objectives d) The success criteria	
3	Changes to the project management plan are approved by who?	a) The project sponsor b) The project manager, users and sponsor c) The procurement department d) The users	
4	If a subsidiary plan (e.g. a risk management plan) already exists, you can use that instead of writing your own.	True or false?	
5	The circulation of the PMP is limited to . . .?	a) The project manager and the sponsor b) The project manager, users and sponsor c) All relevant stakeholders d) The project manager and users	

What kind of question might there be in the exam?

1

List and describe <u>five</u> components of a project management plan.

50 marks (10 marks each)

8.6 | **Estimating**

By completing this subsection you will be able to:

- explain estimating techniques (including analytical, comparative, parametric, three-point and PERT formulae);

- explain the reasons for and benefits of re-estimating through the project life cycle and the concept of the estimating funnel.

We have combined these as they are both heavily concerned with a fairly involved topic that is best explained in one go.

Estimating accuracy

There are numerous published works on the problems associated with estimating. The one truth when considering estimating is that you only know exactly how much something is going to cost just after you have finished it. Project managers, though, are likely to get two questions asked of them fairly frequently – how much is it going to cost and when will it be finished?

The graph in Figure 8.11 shows how estimating accuracy improves as we get further into the project. Here at the end of the concept we have a wider variance from the eventual cost. The detailed estimates that we get are expected to improve as time goes by.

The key factor in accuracy of the estimate is our knowledge about the project as represented by the bottom axis. By the time we commit to the project implementation we ought to be in possession of much more of the available information and this will mean our estimates are far closer to the final end cost (or time). This will be only true if we have made the investment to collect the information needed for an accurate estimate.

It is vital therefore to continue to refine estimates as the project proceeds. The benefits of this are:

- maintain expectations with the stakeholders;

- inform re-planning of the schedule;

- prepare resources (especially human);

- ensure that cash flows and budgets are in step with latest thinking;

- make sure that risks reflect the current state of play.

MANAGEMENT

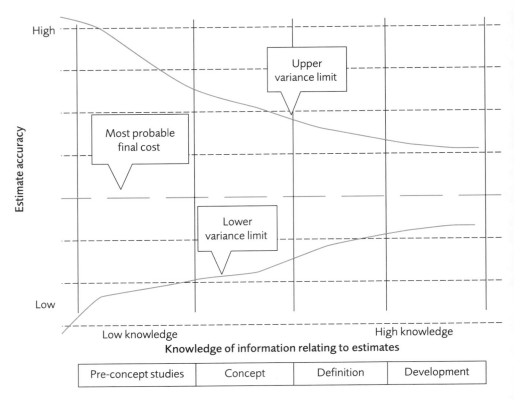

Figure 8.11 The way estimating accuracy improves over time

Difficulties obtaining estimates

There are a number of reasons for poor estimates. Predominantly we are trying to predict the future and it is inherently unpredictable. We can improve our chances of getting a more refined and accurate estimate but there are counter forces at work that mitigate against this.

Subjectivity – almost all estimates contain an element of subjectivity because they rely on an individual's experience and knowledge. Those individuals will have their own bias and prejudices. This will inevitably sway their judgement. The project manager needs to take this into account and try to get to the root of each estimate and reduce any bias.

Assumptions – we make these during a project with the objective of moving things forward. There is a huge opportunity for these to be erroneous and as a result any deductions are incorrect. If these are documented then they can be analysed to give a full picture. The project manager can challenge these assumptions to establish the facts rather than proceeding on unvalidated assumptions.

Not knowing who will do the work – if we make an estimate for a piece of work, we often use our own knowledge and skill and do not make adjustments to compensate for the uncertainty introduced because another person may actually do the work. Wherever possible the project manager will get the estimate from the person who is going to do the work. Where this is not possible the project manager can eliminate the bias through challenge and by seeking different views on the estimate.

Risks – in project work, the element of risk is critical to a good estimate. Inherent risk means that we cannot fully understand the potential for problems, delay or over-run. This in itself is not an estimating issue but our attempts to allow for risk occurrences can merely introduce a further layer of uncertainty. We need to be clear how risks are included within the estimate. Often people will add 'contingency' into a task estimate without declaring it. This is quite dangerous and can inflate some estimates unnecessarily and is usually not systematic, understood or based on any real information.

Lack of previous data – if we have never undertaken this type of project before we will have little or no knowledge of how to do it. We will be unable to arrive at a considered estimate without significant up-front work and even then the element of risk will be increased. Where this data is available then it will clearly be of paramount importance. It should be collected from the actual out-turns of earlier projects and must be used intelligently to ensure mistakes are not replicated.

Despite all of this there are a number of recognised estimating techniques that allow us to systematically understand the problem and provide some tools to help us get better at estimating.

Estimating techniques

Comparative estimating

A comparative estimate is where we take a single known project and simply scale it up and make any allowances that we can to help arrive at a better value. For example, if we built a warehouse last week and it was 300,000m³ and we are building another next year which is 400,000m³, we can scale up the cost proportionately by 4/3. We would then have to take into account any variables that were not proportional; for example, although bigger, the new building may be higher and so the same (or even possibly less) land area may be used thus affecting the cost.

Bottom-up (or analytical) estimating

If we know the component parts through a process of scope definition we can build up a more thorough and detailed idea of the top-level cost.

This type of estimate relies on a very well-developed understanding of the various components and is therefore not really possible during the early stages of a project. The diagram in Figure 8.12 seeks to demonstrate how a top-level project cost can be derived by adding up all the constituent parts from the developed work packages at the lower levels.

Parametric estimating

This form of estimate relies on multiplying out a known number of units by the price of those units. For example, if we wanted to lay 100 miles of railway track and we knew how much it was per mile (say £1m) then 100 miles of track would cost £100m. It is simple and quick. However, of course, the problems are that if there is a small error in the base data then it

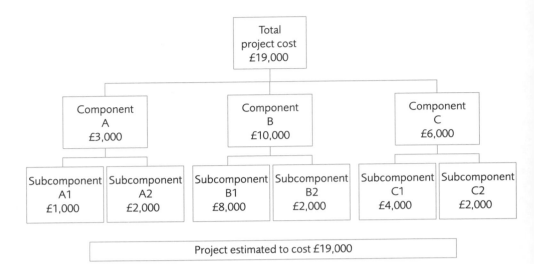

Figure 8.12 An example of bottom-up estimating

will cause significant errors later on. It also relies on a very well-developed body of data on which to draw, which would have been built up over a long period of time and must be representative of the job we are doing now. We could not rely on the price for a mile of road and use that for our railway estimate. Parametric is relatively quick though, as all we need are the raw numbers to put into our model. We might also run into the problem whereby that particular mile of track costs a lot more while another particular mile costs a lot less.

Three-point estimating

A three-point estimate seeks to remove some of the vagaries of calculating a single point estimate. It can be easier to estimate a minimum and maximum cost within which the true cost lies. The estimate can be improved further using a three-point estimate for the best case, most likely and worst case estimate for a cost or duration, consider Figure 8.13.

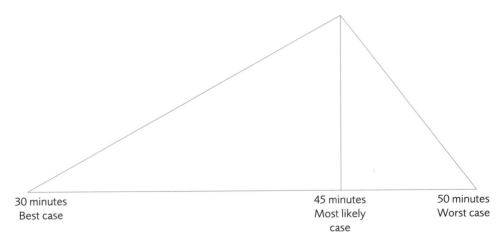

Figure 8.13 An example of three-point estimating

In the 1950s (Fazar, 1959, p. 10) developed the concept of the Program Evalution and Review Technique (PERT) which requires that you carry out the following calculation on three estimates obtained for the same task:

Best estimate = (1 × best case) + (4 × most likely case) + (1 × worst case) / 6

For example, consider your journey to work:

Best case (if no traffic) = 30 minutes

Most likely case (normal traffic) = 45 minutes

Worst case = 50 minutes

The best estimate would be 43 minutes, slightly better than the most likely. This is equivalent to the time it would take you to get to work, assuming your travel pattern followed a PERT distribution. However, your boss would not be very happy because you would be late most of the time if you predicted 43 minutes and always more often than not achieved 45 (the most likely case).

The second use of three-point estimating is to use multiple estimates to run a statistical modelling technique using a computer. This provides the ability to arrive at a statistical estimate by combining a lot of individual three point estimates together. This is called Monte Carlo analysis. In a number of industries you may come across the term quantitative modelling and three-point estimating is the root of that technique. It is not in the APM Project Management Qualification syllabus, but is mentioned only as an extension to the three point technique as above.

Use this space to make some notes

MANAGEMENT

WHIRLWIND BIKES

Consider the case study on page 259. If you had to estimate how long the road testing might take, how might you do it? There are a specific number of miles to be covered and a period of time. What do you need to know? How might you calculate it?

Quick quiz (answers on page 282)

	Question	Options	Your answer
1	A comparative estimate will compare one project with another.	True or false?	
2	A comparative estimate may be most useful at which point in the project?	a) Middle b) Beginning c) End d) Never	
3	What other technique is fundamental to the creation of a bottom-up estimate?	a) PBS b) OBS c) WBS d) Gantt chart	

4	Who should the project manager consult in the creation of estimates?	a) The suppliers b) The users c) The sponsor d) All of the above	
5	Where would the high-level estimates first be recorded?	a) Business case b) PMP c) Risk management plan d) Lessons learned report	
6	Input to parametric estimates might not include what?	a) Price per tone b) Man day cost c) Mile of road d) PERT	
7	A PERT calculation has a divisor of 6.	True or false?	
8	It is easier to calculate the estimate as the life cycle progresses.	True or false?	

 What kind of questions might there be in the exam?

1	This question has <u>two</u> parts. Answer both parts. Explain why accurate estimates are important. 10 marks List and describe <u>four</u> reasons why estimates may be inaccurate. 40 marks (10 marks each)

MANAGEMENT

By completing this subsection you will be able to:

■ describe stakeholder management processes;

■ explain the importance of managing stakeholder expectations.

Stakeholder management process

The definition of a stakeholder is someone who has a vested interest in the outcome of a project. Analysis of stakeholders is necessary because each may have a differing view about the project. They may also have an opportunity to exert influence over the project in a positive or negative manner. There are key stakeholders who may not want a project to go ahead. History is littered with projects that have failed to understand the magnitude of hostility towards their project or indeed the wave of enthusiasm and support that could have been tapped.

There is a danger that the identification of stakeholders is the end of the story. In fact it is only the start. A stakeholder management process is shown in Table 8.4. This would normally be embedded within the overall project management plan.

Table 8.4 A stakeholder management process

Identify	We need to come up with a way of identifying stakeholders. If you work in a well-understood organisation and have been there for some time, you may well have come into contact with all the existing stakeholders. Move to a new project, with a new customer, and you might need to start from scratch.
	Company organisation charts, websites, interviewing people, brainstorming sessions, talking to peers and colleagues, and generally working the system will reveal a whole host of people who may or may not have power and/or influence over what happens on your project.

Assess	Having got a list of the stakeholders, your next challenge is to understand which ones are important. A two by two matrix, below, is a useful tool. 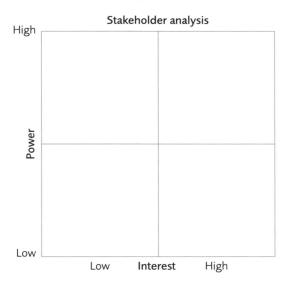 The principle is that you should be able to identify who are the influential people and plot them in their relative positions. It is always difficult when doing these to know whether you are plotting them as at the start of the project or during it. The answer is to produce a stakeholder management plan. The plan implies that you will want to actively manage some of the stakeholders. The action will cause a change of position for some of them. Therefore it is important to place them where they are now and the plan will describe how you will get them to where you want them to be (or possibly stay where they are).
Develop communication plans	To influence people, there are issues that might get in the way: ■ they might not want to be influenced; ■ they might not want to exert any power to help or hinder anyway; ■ they might have a completely different attitude to the one you have anticipated; ■ being able to influence them may come at a price; ■ you may need some help. One of the key documents for any project is a communication management plan to help guide your thinking and to document and substantiate your actions.
Engage and influence stakeholders	Here we need to a) enact the plans, and b) make sure they have worked. So, ensure that the actions that have been planned have happened, and furthermore, if they did not work, do something different. You can use the stakeholder grid to reassess their attitudes and position on a regular basis to determine trends and how effective you have been.

Managing stakeholder expectations

The importance of managing stakeholders cannot be underestimated. The project manager will need to ensure that not only are the stakeholder community properly analysed and categorised but that the appropriate amount of attention is applied to each, depending on their relative power and interest. Failure to do this may result in:

■ Inability to fully understand the requirements. The users represent a significant element of the stakeholder community. Without their input it will prove difficult to obtain sufficient information relating to the nature of the requirements and what acceptability might look like.

■ The risks may be difficult if not impossible to determine, because we would not have had the opportunity to engage with sufficient stakeholders to properly understand them.

■ There may be significant pressure groups or parties against the project such that the progress would be delayed and potentially prevented.

■ The benefits cannot be fully understood. The beneficial aspects of the project are understood by the stakeholders and they are the ones who will be the recipient of those benefits.

■ We cannot truly acknowledge the influence of our own organisation on our success. Internal stakeholders can be just as fundamental to progress as external ones

WHIRLWIND BIKES

Consider the case study on page 259. Carry out a stakeholder analysis for the case study, recreate a stakeholder grid and populate the various boxes with names or job titles. You might need to use your own experience to help in some of the areas.

Use this space to make some notes

Quick quiz (answers on page 283)

	Question	Options	Your answer
1	The axes of a stakeholder grid are what?	a) Power and influence b) Interest and knowledge c) Commitment and power d) Brains and help	
2	Which of these is not a stage in the proposed stakeholder management process?	a) Identify b) Assess c) Develop communication plan d) Negotiate	
3	Which of these is classified as a stakeholder?	a) The sponsor b) The client c) The team d) All of the above	

MANAGEMENT

	Question	Options	Your answer
4	Some of the problems associated with stakeholder management are that in assessing relative power and influence, personal judgement can play a big part.	True or false?	
5	Understanding the stakeholders on a project will be key to understanding which project manager to appoint.	a) True b) False c) Will certainly help d) Never	

What kind of questions might there be in the exam?

1

This question has <u>two</u> parts. Answer both parts.

Explain a key reason why stakeholders should be engaged and influenced.

10 marks

Explain each of the following steps in stakeholder management: stakeholder identification, stakeholder analysis, stakeholder engagement and communication planning

40 marks

9 Schedules and resources

	Subjects covered in this section

9.1	Scheduling
9.2	Resource management
9.3	Budgeting and cost control
9.4	Earned value

9.1	Scheduling

By completing this subsection you will be able to:

- explain the process for creating and maintaining a schedule;
- describe different techniques used for depicting a schedule (including network diagrams, critical path analysis, Gantt chart, milestone chart);
- state advantages and disadvantages of using software scheduling tools.

We have kept all of the material relating to the production of a project schedule together here.

Introduction

This section contains the description of project scheduling. It needs a bit of introduction to try and help put all of the subsequent sections into context. Each of the sections builds on the previous one and the following diagrams help us to understand where these fit into the whole.

We saw in earlier sections how a work breakdown structure is created and the concept that it includes all the work required to deliver the project (Figure 9.1).

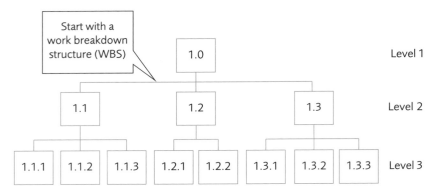

Figure 9.1 Example work breakdown structure

We have taken the WBS and considered the scheduling and logical dependency relationships in order to produce a precedence diagram (Figure 9.2).

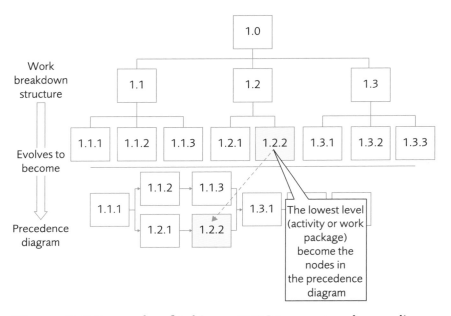

Figure 9.2 Example of taking a WBS to a precedence diagram

We then go on to consider the construction of the Gantt chart, probably the most recognisable tool of modern project management (Figure 9.3).

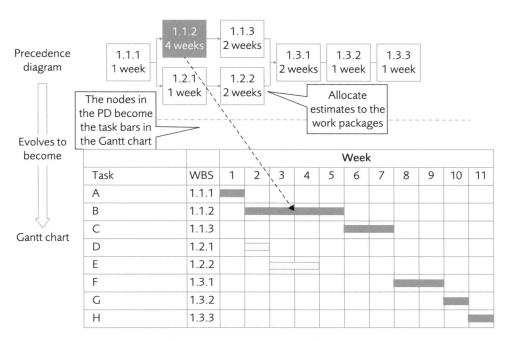

Figure 9.3 Example of how a precedence diagram becomes a Gantt chart

The precedence diagram and Gantt chart are developed to begin to consider where resources will be consumed and what kind of resources they may be (Figure 9.4).

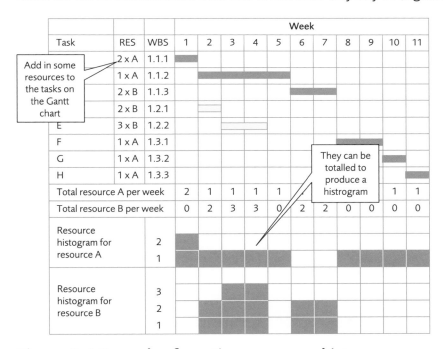

Figure 9.4 Example of creating a resource histogram

Lastly, the overall profiled resource curve is transformed into a project budget by adding actual costs to the volume of resources (Figure 9.5).

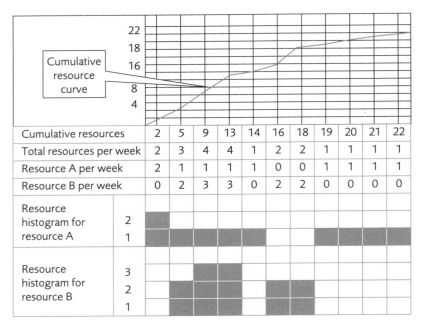

Figure 9.5 Example of adding resources to create a resource histogram

If we assume that these resources cost money, then the total number of them per week multiplied by their respective cost rate (per week) will result in a curve that effectively demonstrates the anticipated cost as it rises over the life of the project. Here we have assumed that both resource type A and B each cost £1,000 per week. This is called the project budget or planned cost (Figure 9.6).

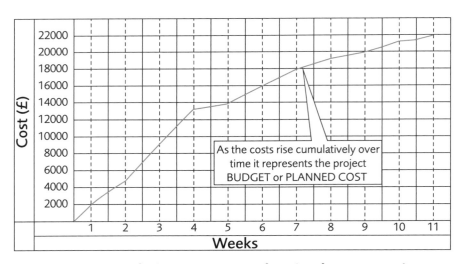

Figure 9.6 Cumulative cost curve showing how costs rise over time

These diagrams help to explain the overall process, but there is a lot more to it than meets the eye. In the next few sections we will look at the principles of how to produce a schedule and a fully costed budget.

The creation of a project schedule

We saw in earlier sections how the project work breakdown structure was created. The next diagram (Figure 9.7) demonstrates how a work breakdown structure is used to generate a precedence diagram. The method for doing this is called the precedence diagram method (PDM). Each of the lowest levels of work package is placed into a logical sequence working from left to right based upon task dependency. The lines between the nodes indicate a relationship and the typical relationship is that of finish to start as in Figure 9.8. This is the most common way of linking tasks and will usually be sufficient for simple plans, although there are more complex relationships available which are documented in Figure 9.9.

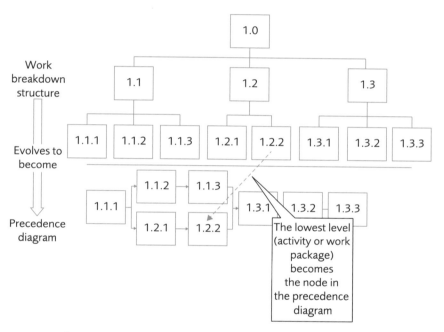

Figure 9.7 The creation of a precedence diagram from a WBS

Types of network node relationships

Figure 9.8 Finish to start relationship

This relationship simply means that 1.1.2 cannot start until 1.1.1 has finished. This is quite important as it means that, in theory, a gap in time can appear between the end of one task and the start of the next. This gap is referred to as 'float'. There are other types of relationships (other than finish to start), two of which are commonly used as shown in Figure 9.9:

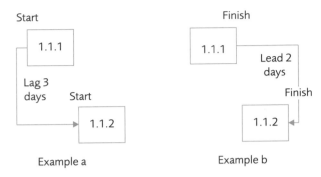

Figure 9.9 Start to start and finish to finish links

The examples of the use of these might be:

1. **Start to start** – (Example a) 1.1.2 can only start once 1.1.1 has started; so, for example, we can only start testing the software once the software has begun to be produced.

2. **Finish to finish** – (Example b) 1.1.2 can only finish, once 1.1.1 has finished; so, for example, the project management activities can only finish once the final acceptance has been achieved.

Once again it is important to note that the start(s) and finish(es) do not have to coincide in time, merely that they are dependent upon each other.

Any of these connections can have a modification with either a lag (delay) or a lead (concurrency) introduced.

In these two examples, the raw connectivity has been modified through the insertion of a Lag of 3 in a) and a Lead of 2 in b). The effect of this will be:

1. That in Example a, 1.1.2 can only start at least three days after 1.1.1 starts (Lag 3);

2. That in Example b, 1.1.1 can finish up to two days before 1.1.2 finishes (Lead 2).

Precedence diagramming or critical path analysis

So, utilising these various connections, we can start to connect all of the 'nodes' to provide a complete picture of the end to end logic of the project.

The 'nodes' in Figure 9.10 have now been expanded into a recognised format which is as follows:

Key:	
ES is the earliest that a task can start	EF is the earliest that a task can finish
LS is the latest that a task can start	LF is the latest that a task can finish
D is the duration	TF is the total float (discussed later)

If you apply the following process using these terms and complete a fully developed network, you can build up a working knowledge of the earliest the project can finish as well as a number of other key facts relating to the project such as total float, free float and the critical path through the network.

ES	D	EF
	Task ID	
LS	TF	LF

Figure 9.10 A template network node

Forward pass

We have taken the WBS from the earlier section (ignoring the level 4 work packages) and applied some fictitious durations to these work packages, and by using these durations we can produce an updated network as appears in Figure 9.11. We need to assume that the relationships between the nodes have been clarified and are correct.

In this example the duration box (middle top of each node) has been completed. The first thing when calculating the critical path through the network is to carry out a 'forward pass' through the network.

We do this by commencing far left and populating the early start, then we add the duration to calculate the early finish. In practical terms, think about a task that starts on Monday first thing, We know from our estimates that it should take 1 week, so the task should finish end of business on the Friday. In our network, we choose to start at week 0, add the 1 week of the task duration and arrive at week 1 for the earliest finish.

If we apply this principle to the network, we will end up with something like this (for the first node):

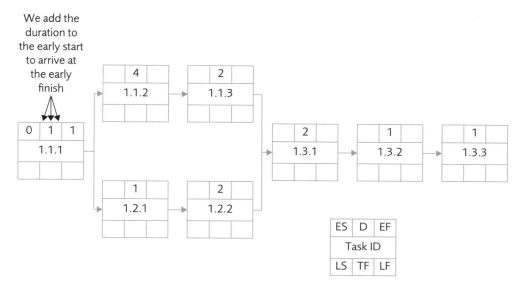

Figure 9.11 Network diagram showing early finish calculation

When we have done the first, we can continue with the forward pass and populate the top rows of all the nodes (see Figure 9.12). There are two key aspects:

MANAGEMENT

- The early finish from the predecessor node gets transposed into the early start in the subsequent node(s).

- In the forward pass, if you have a choice about which number to take from the early finish to the early start, you always choose the *higher* number (based on connected tasks only).

To move on, take a look at the shaded areas on the next diagram.

When you have finished adding all the way through, the last early finish box is the earliest date on which the project will finish. It is the sum of all the longer durations through the network.

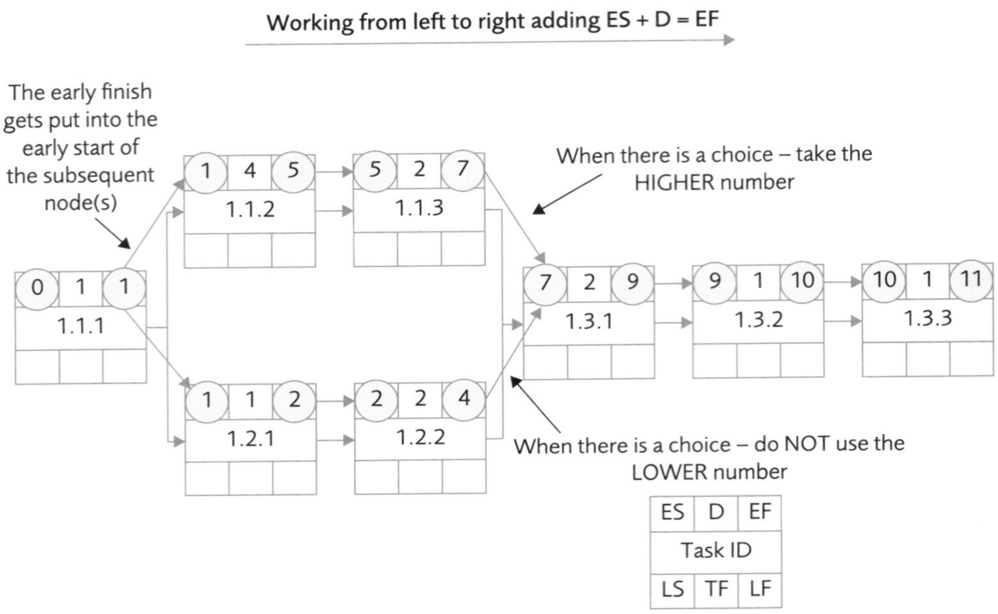

Figure 9.12 Network diagram showing early start and finish calculations

Backward pass

The next job is to carry out the backward pass (see Figure 9.13). Working from right to left this time, we subtract the duration from the latest finish to arrive at the latest start.

- The latest start from the successor node gets entered into the latest finish for the predecessor node.

- In the backward pass, if you have a choice about which number to take backwards from the latest start into the latest finish of the predecessor task, you always choose the lower number.

- In the cases for the exam and to make life a bit easier in these examples, the earliest finish from the last node in the network becomes the latest finish for that (last) node.

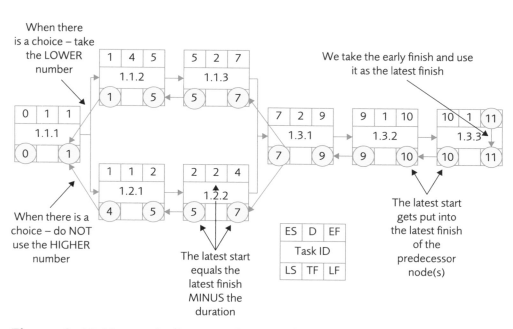

Figure 9.13 Network diagram showing latest start and finish calculations

Total float and critical path

What the diagrams have shown so far is that if we assume the latest finish is the same as the earliest finish and we work back from right to left we get back to a zero as the latest start in the first node. There is still a blank box in the middle on the bottom row of each of the nodes. This is reserved for the calculated total float. Total float is arrived at by subtracting the early finish of a given node from the latest finish of the same node. In the case of 1.1.3 above this equals 0, as it does for most of the other nodes, except 1.2.1 and 1.2.2, which both have 3 in the total float box.

The definition of the term total float is "*the amount of time by which a task (node) can be delayed before it affects the end date of the project*". In Figure 9.14, if 1.1.3 takes three weeks instead of two weeks the end date will be delayed. This is because it has 0 weeks total float, therefore no option to be lengthened or delayed.

Also in the diagram, if 1.2.2 is delayed by a week it will not affect the end date because it has three weeks total float.

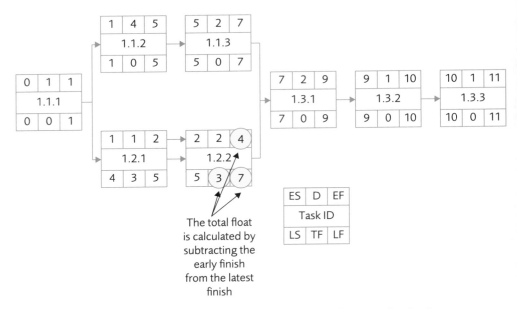

Figure 9.14 Network diagram showing total float calculations

The critical path

The critical path through the network is that path that demonstrates the LEAST TOTAL FLOAT. In the case of our example, it follows the path as defined in Figure 9.15. It is also the longest in terms of duration (it defines the end date).

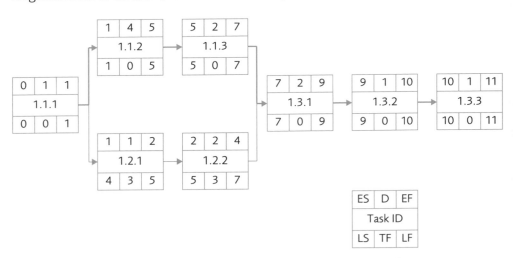

Figure 9.15 Network diagram showing the critical path

Free float

Free float is one more term mentioned in the syllabus for the APM Project Management Qualification. It is defined as being 'the amount of time by which the end of a task can be delayed before affecting any subsequent tasks'.

Free float is therefore concerned with the gap between the end of one task and the start of the next one(s), but here we are just concerned with affecting the next task and not the project end date as we were with total float considerations. If we want to gauge the gap between two tasks, we need to consider the gap between the earliest one task can finish and the earliest the next can start. So, for example in Figure 9.16, 1.2.2 can be delayed by three weeks before it 'bumps into' 1.3.1. Therefore, if we take the earliest finish of 1.2.2 away from the earliest start of the successor task (1.3.1) we arrive at 3 (weeks). This is said to be the free float of 1.2.2. If we carry out the same exercise with 1.2.1, however, and take the earliest finish of 1.2.1 from the earliest start of 1.2.2, we end up with 0 weeks free float – even though 1.2.1 has three weeks total float.

Determine free float

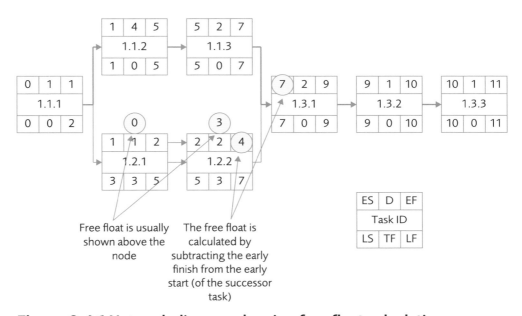

Figure 9.16 Network diagram showing free float calculations

The purpose of critical path

Critical path analysis (as described in Figures 9.10 to 9.16) is the accepted method for calculating the end date for a project. In doing so, it reveals the total float and free float values. These are important because:

1. Tasks with the lowest combined total float describe the critical path. If we understand which tasks are going to affect the end date we can pay a little more attention to them than some of the others. They are at the top of the project manager's list.

2. Tasks that affect another task need to be understood, as their delay will affect another task and as such may need managerial intervention. They won't affect the end date of the project though, and so are not as key as the ones with little or no total float. These are tasks with free float.

3. Tasks with total float and free float have a fair degree of flexibility in their timings and therefore do not need to be as closely scrutinised and managed as the others. They may also represent those tasks that can have resources reduced to redeploy elsewhere, as extending them may not have ramifications for the end date.

MANAGEMENT

4. By drawing the network we are actively engaged in thinking about the detail of the interdependencies, the estimates, the relationships between tasks, the implications of delays and so on. If the team are engaged in the process the quality of the planning will improve dramatically.

Once the networks have been produced, the next step is usually to convert it into a bar chart. The most common term used is that of the Gantt chart, as it is the one most widely reproduced in planning software. The principle is quite simple. A Gantt chart has the tasks down the left-hand axis and the timescale across the top and the tasks are represented by a bar or line going from left to right covering the start and end of that task. The migration of the network to a Gantt chart is described in Figure 9.17. They are really useful at:

- Providing a communication tool for portraying progress to others.

- Being able to relate the relative timings of the network diagram into absolute timings with reference to actual dates.

- Being able to be colour coded thus showing the relevant relationships and for example critical/non-critical activities.

- Showing milestones – key dates or deliverables – usually as a diamond (see Figure 9.17).

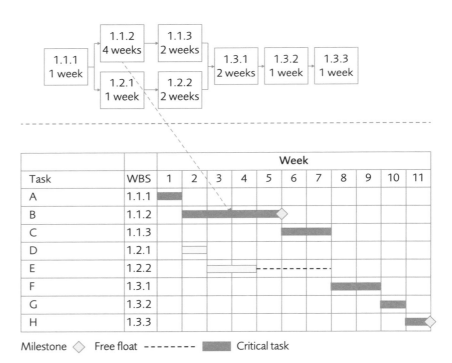

Figure 9.17 Showing the evolution of a network diagram into a Gantt chart

The use of software systems for planning

Over the past 30 years or so, the use of personal computers and the availability of corporate systems has increased dramatically. This ready availability of processing power has caused an explosion of software tools in many industries and project management is no exception.

The continual recalculation, storage of data and excellent rendering of the various charts and diagrams has led to a huge uptake of their use. There are a number of recognised advantages and disadvantages to their deployment.

Advantages

- Quick to use and relatively inexpensive. Most modern systems are intuitive and have a flexible user interface supported on most platforms and supported by widely available training.

- Able to support 'what if' modelling. It is possible to dynamically change the resource loadings, the dependencies and so on, to provide quick and easy manipulation of numerous potential scenarios.

- Able to continually recalculate as circumstances change. They can be used throughout the project to continually review and update the thinking without laborious changes and detailed recalculations by hand.

- Easily customised to conform to most standards. Most packages will integrate into corporate standards and will be flexible enough to be adapted to most needs.

- Can be used in multi-user mode to support large workgroups. Enterprise planning software can be hosted on a server and is a quick and relatively easy way of ensuring that corporate planning standards are followed.

- Excellent range of reports and displays are available. These help to make sure that the monthly and other regular reporting is relatively quick and painless.

- Corporate systems can usually be readily interfaced with financial and other systems. This means that financial and other data can flow up and down the managerial hierarchy of the organisation.

Disadvantages

- Can 'dumb down' the area of planning, leading to poor plans. This can lead to people just following the software blindly without really thinking through the implications of what they are doing.

- Can be seen as authoritative simply because of the use of a computer. Garbage in means garbage out.

- Can be overly systemised, requiring large amounts of data simply to operate them and sometimes the plan can become the project.

- Corporate systems can limit the flexibility of the project manager who has to conform to standards that do not add value to their role.

 Quick quiz (answers on page 283)

	Question	Options	Your answer
1	The top axis of a Gantt chart contains the . . .?	a) Tasks b) Time periods c) Resources d) Work packages	
2	Total float is the difference between latest finish and . . .?	a) Early start b) Latest start c) Early finish d) Free float	
3	Free float is the difference between the early start of the successor activity and the early finish of the activity in question.	True or false?	
4	A lag shows the time a task must be delayed after the preceding task.	True or false?	
5	A milestone has what amount of time associated with it?	a) One day b) One week c) Nothing d) Depends	
6	The critical path is the longest path through the network.	True or false?	
7	The early finish is the early start plus . . .?	a) Duration b) Latest start c) Latest finish d) Early finish	
8	Milestones can be used to trigger payments.	True or false?	
9	Work packages become nodes in the network.	True or false?	

	Question	Options	Your answer
10	The middle box on the bottom row of a network node contains . . .?	a) Total float b) Free float c) Early start d) Early finish	

Use this space to make some notes

....

....

....

....

....

....

....

....

....

....

....

....

MANAGEMENT

1 List and describe <u>five</u> ways in which a software tool can help in planning a project.

50 marks (10 marks each)

2 This question has <u>four</u> parts. Answer all parts.

Only the answer sheet will be marked, any workings on the question paper will be ignored.

Explain how total float is calculated.

10 marks

Explain why it is important to understand the projects' critical path and how this knowledge might be used when running a project.

10 marks

Explain the importance of understanding the free float associated with tasks and how this knowledge might be used when running a project.

10 marks

Analyse the following network and determine the following:

a) The earliest finish of the project
b) The total float for task D
c) The free float for task B
d) The critical path

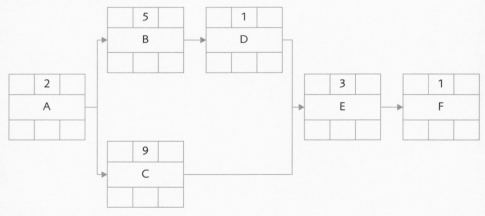

20 marks (5 marks each for a, b, c and d)

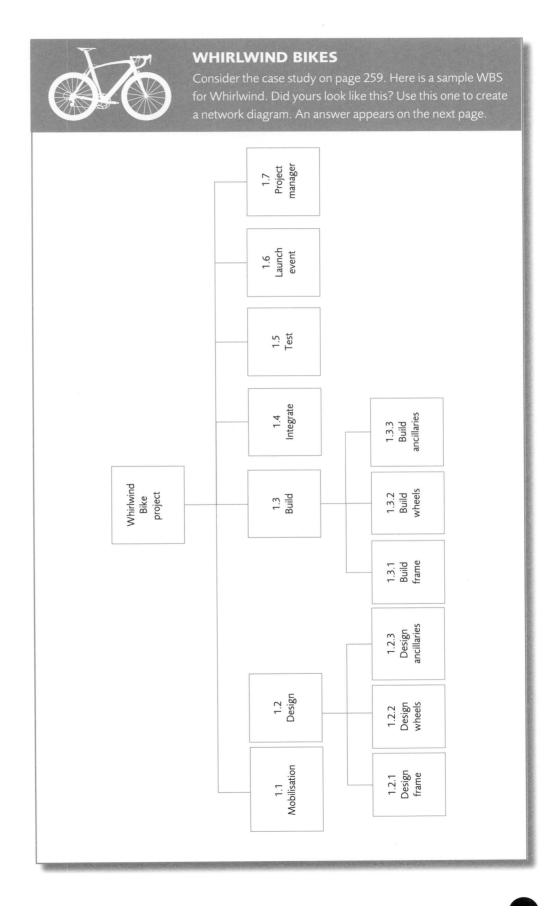

WHIRLWIND BIKES

Consider the case study on page 259. Here is a sample WBS for Whirlwind. Did yours look like this? Use this one to create a network diagram. An answer appears on the next page.

MANAGEMENT

WHIRLWIND BIKES

Consider the case study on page 259. Here is a network diagram from the data you have in the previous WBS. See if you can populate the boxes and work out a schedule. (we have made some assumptions about the frame design and build work packages).

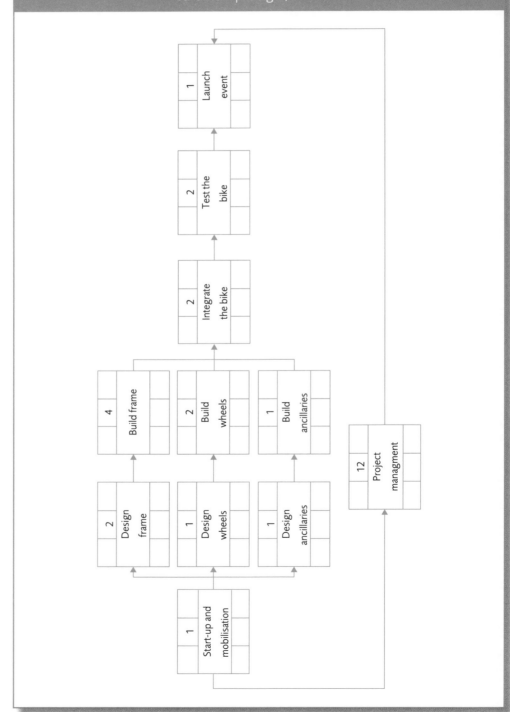

9.2 | Resource management

By completing this subsection you will be able to:

■ explain categories and types of resources (such as human resources, consumable and reusable equipment, materials, space);

■ describe how resources are allocated to a schedule;

■ differentiate between resource smoothing and resource levelling.

Again, these three assessment criteria have been amalgamated as they are all concerned with the management of resources and their use against a project schedule.

Resource management

Resource management is the term used to describe the proactive management of the various human and other project resources in an efficient manner. In doing so, the project manager will need to consider a large number of different things, including:

■ The availability of the resources in terms of timing and quantity. There might be a limit on how many people can contribute to the task in hand at any one time.

■ Awareness of any specific individual or scarce components that will be critical to the ability to deliver the project. For example, sometimes there is a certain piece of equipment of which there is only one in existence, such as a super-sized crane.

■ Limits and constraints that might impinge upon the totally flexible deployment (and redeployment) of resources. For example, there is no point in having three tunnel-boring machines if there are only two access points to the tunnel (each end).

■ The costs involved and creative ways of profiling the project budget to minimise any impacts from cash flow or the availability of funds.

There are a number of types of resource to consider. Each will be treated differently.

Consumable resources are those things that once used need to be replaced. Examples of these are fuel and money. The project manager must make appropriate arrangements for these to be replaced as they are used up. They do this by creating budgets and plans to ensure that all stakeholders are aware of the implications of their use and what the consequences are when they are used up.

Reusable resources can be redeployed when no longer needed, examples include people, accommodation, vehicles, etc. The project manager will need to make appropriate arrangements for the redeployment of resources, especially the human ones. Care should be taken of any material that can be redeployed to avoid scrappage costs and unnecessary expense.

Equipment used on the project needs to be planned for. If a tunnel is being dug then a boring machine may be required. This is not a direct cost to the customer but a machine will need to be ordered to fulfil the project activities.

Materials are used in the same way as equipment except they contribute directly towards the finished product. If we are building a new website, the artwork we purchase becomes a deliverable. These are direct costs associated with the creation of the website.

Space is often required to temporarily house the project teams, for an IT project office space will be required to accommodate the machines, people and support services.

Creating a resource histogram

The major mechanism for the project manager to understand the resources available and to proactively manage them is the resource histogram (Figure 9.18). The principle being that each resource can be charted showing the amount that each of them is planned to be used and viewed across the life of the project. The timescale is along the x axis and the number of resources used per time period is on the y axis.

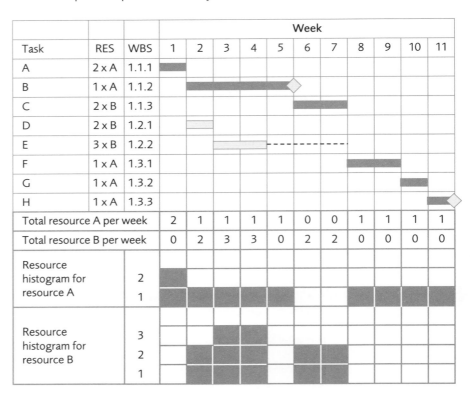

Figure 9.18 Example resource histogram

Figure 9.18 demonstrates the principles of the resource histogram. The Gantt chart appears at the top of this diagram only to help describe the bottom half, which is the resource histogram itself. The shaded areas in the bottom half are there to reflect the value of resources planned week by week. Varying amounts of resource type 'A' and 'B' have been allocated to each task and require two B's in week 2 and three in week 3 for example.

The purpose of this is to see at a glance where resources are planned to be used, such that action can be taken to make sure that they are available according to the plan and if this is impossible, to take steps to deal with it before it becomes a problem.

Resource smoothing

In some circumstances it may be possible to swap resources around and increase the number on one particular task at the expense of others. It may also be possible to simply allocate more people to the task, thus making it shorter.

For the purposes of explaining resource smoothing let's assume that there are only two resource type B's available (see Figure 9.18). There would therefore be an over-allocation of these resource types during weeks 3 and 4. On the face of it, the project plan is not viable simply because we cannot go into the project knowing that we cannot resource it. The project manager should therefore undertake a process of resource smoothing.

The purpose of smoothing is to seek to resolve any over allocation issues without affecting the end date. The presumption is that the end date is paramount and should not be compromised. However, if we assume that all of the network and task interdependencies are correct, and the estimates and allocation of resources is similarly accurate, then there is not much that can be done without modifying the schedule.

The potential solution to this dilemma is through the use of float. Total float is the amount of time by which a task may be delayed or extended before it affects the target finish date. The dotted line on the Gantt chart in Figure 9.18 demonstrates the float that is available for task E, which has three resources of type B used for two weeks. At the end of this task there is a gap before it starts to interfere with the task that follows it (task F). Task E is responsible for the limit of resources being breached, but because there is some float there are a couple of things that we could consider doing to solve the problem (assuming we definitely cannot get more resource B's).

The project manager investigates the nature of task E and after discussions with the team decides that instead of three resources for two weeks, an alternative might be to have two resources for three weeks. The resultant plan might look like that shown in Figure 9.19.

Notice how task E now takes three weeks, but the limit of two resource type B's has been adhered to. This now represents a viable project schedule. The end date has not been compromised and the project can proceed on this basis. The total float for E has been reduced by a week to accommodate the extended duration.

Splitting tasks

One other technique a project manager may be able to deploy when coming up with a viable schedule is that of splitting tasks. By doing this, a task is started, stopped and restarted, leaving a break in the middle, possibly to conform to any resource availability constraints. There are certain instances where in the real world splitting tasks is inevitable (during public holidays, factory shutdowns, etc.), but the project manager may choose to split a task at other times simply to conform to resource constraints.

Generally speaking though, splitting tasks is not to be recommended as it inevitably introduces a demobilisation and remobilisation overhead. Individuals will put one task down and then pick it up again sometime later. This usually introduces delay and risk. It is an option but not one that should be considered until all other smoothing options have been discounted.

MANAGEMENT

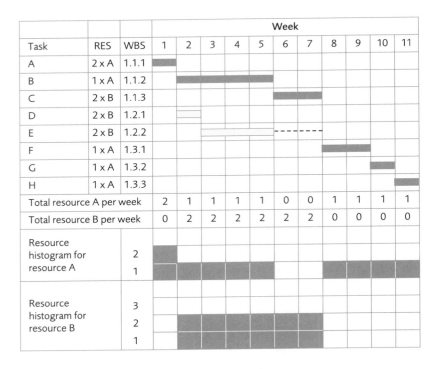

Task	RES	WBS	Week 1	2	3	4	5	6	7	8	9	10	11
A	2 x A	1.1.1	▮										
B	1 x A	1.1.2		▮	▮	▮	▮						
C	2 x B	1.1.3						▮	▮				
D	2 x B	1.2.1		▭									
E	2 x B	1.2.2			▭	▭	▭	- - -	- - -				
F	1 x A	1.3.1								▮			
G	1 x A	1.3.2										▮	
H	1 x A	1.3.3											▮
Total resource A per week			2	1	1	1	1	0	0	1	1	1	1
Total resource B per week			0	2	2	2	2	2	2	0	0	0	0
Resource histogram for resource A		2	▮										
		1	▮	▮	▮	▮	▮			▮	▮	▮	▮
Resource histogram for resource B		3											
		2		▮	▮	▮	▮	▮	▮				
		1		▮	▮	▮	▮	▮	▮				

Figure 9.19 Example of resource smoothing

Resource levelling

Consider Figure 9.18 again. Let us assume this time that there is only one of resource type A available. There is an over-allocation in week one as the plan is showing the need for two A's in that week. The project manager can do some investigation, but the problem with the over-allocation is that it is caused by task A, which is on the critical path. By definition, therefore, task A cannot be extended or delayed because it will cause a delay to the end date of the project. If task A can be extended and the resources reduced (in the same manner as we looked at for smoothing above), we will delay the project by a week, making it a 12-week project instead of an 11-week one.

Other considerations

If after levelling and smoothing have been done there is still a demand for resources that cannot be satisfied, the project manager may be faced with some tough choices. They would probably have to consult with all the stakeholders but they may be faced with having to:

■ Do less – descope the work to reduce the amount of effort required.

■ Seek efficiency – look for areas where resources can be optimised, they may choose to train staff better, look for ways of improving performance through good leadership perhaps.

■ Look for removing bottlenecks and delays, perhaps going to the suppliers and asking them to streamline deliveries.

■ Ask staff to work longer hours – overtime and weekends. Care will be needed as this will not be popular and the project manager will need to be on their guard so as not to overly stress the team.

WHIRLWIND BIKES

Consider the case study on page 259. Here is a complete network diagram. We have also added a Gantt chart as well on the next page. See if you can recognise how the Gantt has been produced.

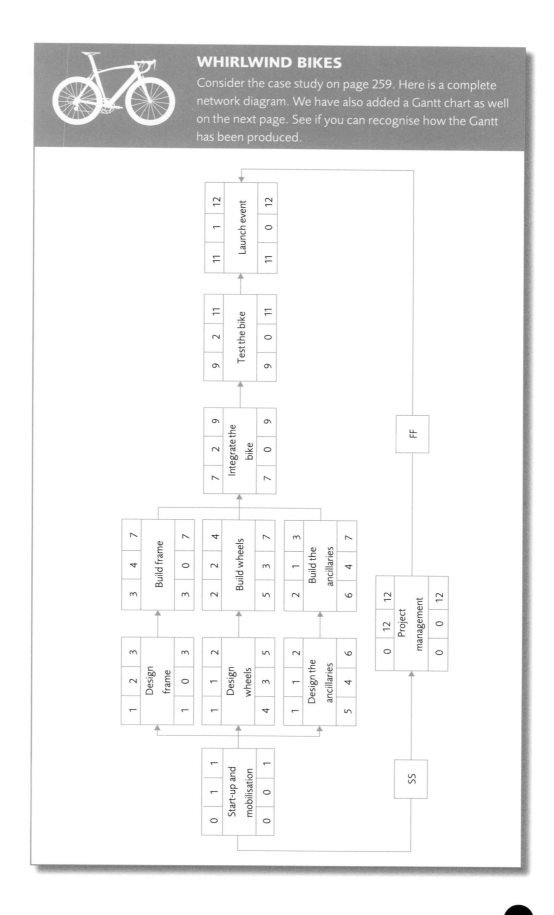

WHIRLWIND BIKES

Consider the case study on page 259. Here is the project Gantt chart. See if you can produce a resource histogram on the template on the next page.

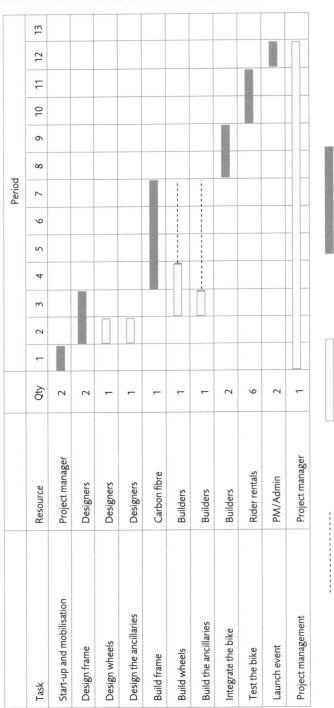

WHIRLWIND BIKES

Consider the case study on page 259. Here is a blank resource histogram template. Have a go at populating it from the data in the Gantt chart.

Resource histogram

Per period												
7												
6												
5												
4												
3												
2												
1												
Period	1	2	3	4	5	6	7	8	9	10	11	12

WHIRLWIND BIKES

Consider the case study on page 259. Here is a completed resource histogram. Did yours look like this?

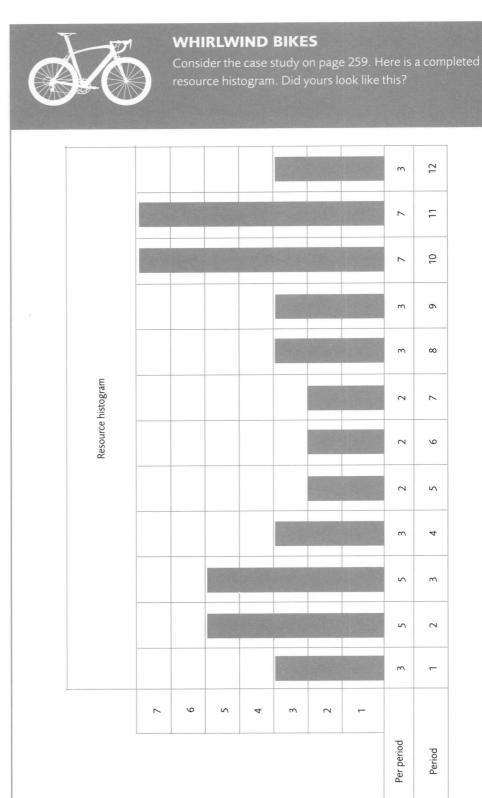

Per period	3	5	5	3	2	2	2	3	3	7	7	3
Period	1	2	3	4	5	6	7	8	9	10	11	12

Use this space to make some notes

Quick quiz (answers on page 284)

	Question	Options	Your answer
1	The two ways of dealing with resource over allocation are . . .?	a) Levelling and settling b) Lightening and strengthening c) Levelling and smoothing d) Building and moving	
2	Resource levelling has the potential to extend the project end date.	True or false?	
3	Resource smoothing has the potential to extend the end date.	True or false?	
4	Resource planning can be iterative.	True or false?	
5	Which technique provides the precursor to producing a resource histogram?	a) Precedence diagram b) WBS c) RAM chart d) Gantt chart	

MANAGEMENT

	Question	Options	Your answer
6	Which of these is a type of resource?	a) Fixed b) Cost-based c) Replenishable d) Unused	
7	Splitting a task will incur which kinds of overheads?	a) Mobilisation and demobilisation b) Total float c) Free float d) Lag	
8	Examples of replenishable resources are all of these except . . .?	a) Fuel b) Labour c) Money d) Time	
9	Which of these is NOT a consideration that the project manager would take into account when producing an initial resource histogram?	a) Costs b) Availability c) Constraints d) Skills	
10	A resource histogram can apply to all types of resources separately or collectively.	True or false?	

What kind of questions might there be in the exam?

1

This question has <u>two</u> parts. Answer both parts.

Only the answer sheet will be marked, any workings on the question paper will be ignored.

Explain what is meant by the term 'resource management'.

10 marks

From the Gantt chart provided below draw a resource histogram.

		Week										
Task	RES	1	2	3	4	5	6	7	8	9	10	11
A	2 x A	■										
B	1 x B		■	■								
C	2 x A		□									
D	2 x A				■	■	■					
E	2 x B			□	□							
F	1 x A							■	■			
G	2 x A									■	■	
H	2 x A											■

40 marks

2

This question has <u>two</u> parts. Answer both parts.

Explain the terms 'resource levelling' and 'resource smoothing'.

20 marks (10 marks each)

List and describe <u>three</u> implications of splitting tasks.

30 marks (10 marks each)

9.3 Budgeting and cost control

By completing this subsection you will be able to:

- explain what is meant by budgeting and cost control.

The project budget

The use of the resource histogram is to help identify and understand where the spending peaks and troughs are. An extension of this principle would be to consider the resources together and arrive at a total figure for time period and then combine them all to provide a cumulative figure for the life of the project. Consider Figure 9.20 (we have reverted to the pre-levelled schedule from earlier as in Figure 9.18).

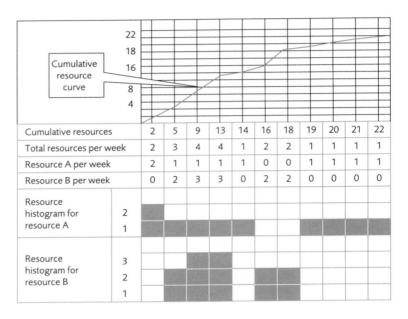

	2	5	9	13	14	16	18	19	20	21	22
Cumulative resources	2	5	9	13	14	16	18	19	20	21	22
Total resources per week	2	3	4	4	1	2	2	1	1	1	1
Resource A per week	2	1	1	1	1	0	0	1	1	1	1
Resource B per week	0	2	3	3	0	2	2	0	0	0	0

Figure 9.20 Cumulative resource curve

This shows how these two different resources have been added together to provide a single cumulative value, which is translated in the upper part of the diagram as a cumulative (or summation) curve.

As a principle this is going to be very useful during the project. An obvious extension to it, however, is to take the resources and apply the relative costs to each of them. Having done this, instead of merely having a number of days described by the curve, we can start to understand the costs or the budget and how it gets profiled over the life of the project.

Using our examples from earlier sections, if we assume that resource A costs £1,000 per week and resource B costs £500 per week, we can multiply out the figures as in Table 9.1.

The graphical representation of these figures has been produced in Figure 9.21.

This is the final step in the planning exercise. It provides the project manager with a definitive budget against which all expenditure can be compared and managed. When we introduce the concept of earned value later, this budget curve (also referred to as the planned cost) will be used to compare with the actual costs and earned value amounts to provide not only the performance against cost budgets, but also an index to describe progress against the time schedule as well.

As with all the plans, an initial estimate will have been described in the business case. As the project progresses, this is further iterated, refined and developed, so that a fully considered plan can be produced. These budgets will have had an input from the risk management process (Section 10).

Table 9.1 The example project budget

Week	Resource Type	Units	Rate (£) per week	Cost (£)	Total cost per week (£)	Cumulative cost (£)
1	A	2	1,000	2,000	2,000	2,000
2	A	1	1,000	1,000		
	B	2	500	1,000	2,000	4,000
3	A	1	1,000	1,000		
	B	3	500	1,500	2,500	6,500
4	A	1	1,000	1,000		
	B	3	500	1,500	2,500	9,000
5	A	1	1,000	1,000	1,000	10,000
6	B	2	500	1,000	1,000	11,000
7	B	2	500	1,000	1,000	12,000
8	A	1	1,000	1,000	1,000	13,000
9	A	1	1,000	1,000	1,000	14,000
10	A	1	1,000	1,000	1,000	15,000
11	A	1	1,000	1,000	1,000	16,000
				Total	**16,000**	

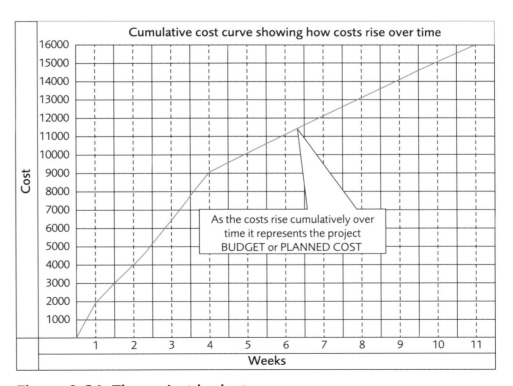

Figure 9.21 The project budget

Benefits of budgeting and cost management

By producing a budget the project manager will be better placed to:

- Record progress against a known baseline and spot early deviations and variances, thus being able to make alternative arrangements before things become too far from plan.

- Describe to others the need for project funding requirements, thus being able to justify the expenditure with clear analysis underpinning the business case.

- Introduce an effective change control procedure as there will be a definite baseline about which change can be controlled, so the changes can be clearly delineated from any variance.

- Closely link it with the cost breakdown structures and in this way the actual expenditures can be closely mapped to the estimates. This is an invaluable aspect in the ability to learn lessons for the future.

- Provide a key input into the project review cycles, making the analysis of variations possible again aiding corrective actions.

- Provide careful cost management, which is the key in the organisation understanding its own liabilities and provide information to help 'balance the books'.

Commitments

The budget is extremely useful in understanding the nature of the costs we anticipate. However, consider the following example:

We are running a project with £24,000 cost budget for accommodation. At the start of the project we commit to lease a building for a year. The costs are £2,000 per month. In month 0 we sign the lease and are contractually committed to this expenditure with no 'get out clause'. At this point in time our commitment is £24,000. Our project budget is reduced by £24,000 to £0. We have not spent anything. We are said to have a committed cost of £24,000.

At the start of month 1, for the 12 months of our project, the commitments look like Table 9.2 (not including any other considerations). As time goes by (assuming the incurred costs are paid), the legal commitment reduces.

Table 9.2 Commitments

Month	0	1	2	3	4	5	6	7	8	9	10	11	12
Uncommitted budget	24	0	0	0	0	0	0	0	0	0	0	0	0
Committed cost		24	22	20	18	16	14	12	10	8	6	4	2

The reasons we need to monitor committed costs are that:

- We need to be aware of our total liability so that we do not exceed our budget. These records are kept in the project accounts and will be able to be taken into account by the project manager when reviewing costs to date and future uses of the remainder.

- They give us the ability to understand the costs that we cannot avoid if at any point the project is halted. If you sign a mobile phone contract for 12 months, the provider will expect to receive payment for each of the 12 months even if you do not want the service. You are therefore committed to the expenditure (but only that amount you have not yet paid).

- They allow the organisation to properly prepare cash flow forecasts. If they know that something will need to be paid for at some point in the future then they can make sure the money will be available.

- The decisions to spend that money are no longer negotiable. Stakeholders need to be aware of this as the decision to commit the money will undoubtedly be significant in that once made is irrevocable.

Accruals

An accrual is an accounting entry that represents our best estimate of expenditure that has not been invoiced or paid in a given period. They allow expenditure to be properly estimated for that period. Without accruals, we would not get a true picture of the costs of a project at that time, because it would depend when other organisations sent us invoices and when they in turn get paid, which can be some time after the work has been completed. These accruals, when combined with the actual expenditure, give us the best estimate of our total actual costs to date.

If we consider the position of our project at the end of month 2, we will have recorded the actual expenditure from month 1 as a result of an invoice we have received and paid. The invoice for month 2 may not have been received yet so we make an accrual for this cost (Table 9.3).

Actual expenditure is the money that has already been paid, and the convention is to record that against the period to which the costs relate by removing the accrual and replacing it with an actual.

Table 9.3 Accruals

Month	0	1	2	3	4	5	6	7	8	9	10	11	12
Budget in month		2	2	2	2	2	2	2	2	2	2	2	2
Cumulative budget		2	4	6	8	10	12	14	16	18	20	22	24
Actual expenditure		2	0	0	0	0	0	0	0	0	0	0	0
Accrual		0	2	0	0	0	0	0	0	0	0	0	0
Cumulative actual and accrued costs		2	4										
Forecast cost in month				2	2	2	2	2	2	2	2	2	2
Forecast cumulative cost				6	8	10	12	14	16	18	20	22	24

The advantages of making accruals are that:

- The project manager can ensure that the costs expended are taken into account when reviewing the project accounts at the end of the month.

- The reporting process is improved because the organisation can be assured that the costs they are seeing are as true to the actual position as possible.

- Nothing gets forgotten, the project manager is close to the business of the project and they can recognise costs that have been incurred and document them in this formal way so there are no surprises later.

Forecasts

The budget and actual figures are very important from cash and cost management points of view. The other main area that project managers are frequently asked to report on is a forecast. The principle here is that it is inadequate to merely report on things that have happened in the past, and the real key to effective management is to, as far as is possible, plan for the future and then seek to follow the plan. You can only manage the things you haven't done yet.

The forecasting by a project manager is crucial to the sponsoring business, as it provides key financial information so that the organisation can properly manage its portfolio of projects and programmes and also its cash flow.

Let's say that on our project (from before) we are aware that because of certain factors the rent will rise on the building (perhaps energy prices have risen and the contract stipulates that we will pay such increases). Without action we will encounter a problem as we have no allowance for the increase in the budget. At the end of month 7 we are told that our rent will rise by £1,000 per month from month 8 onwards. We cannot change what has already gone before, but we can change our perspective of the future. Our new forecasts will change to a new forecast outturn of £29,000, compared to a budget (and original forecast outturn) of £24,000.

At the end of month 7:

Table 9.4 Forecasts

Month	0	1	2	3	4	5	6	7	8	9	10	11	12
Budget in month		2	2	2	2	2	2	2	2	2	2	2	2
Cumulative budget		2	4	6	8	10	12	14	16	18	20	22	24
Actual expenditure		2	2	2	2	2	2	0	0	0	0	0	0
Accrual		0	0	0	0	0	0	2	0	0	0	0	0
Actual and accrued costs in month		2	2	2	2	2	2	2	0	0	0	0	0
Cumulative actual and accrued costs	2	4	6	8	10	12	14						
Forecast cost in month									3	3	3	3	3
Forecast cumulative cost									17	20	23	26	29

In Table 9.4, the project manager and the sponsoring organisation have a choice as to whether they change the budget (perhaps call down some contingency) and effectively change the cost baseline to avoid showing any variances, or simply record it as a variance, which, if within tolerance, can be managed through existing management arrangements. They may of course have alternative courses of action, such as renegotiating leases, use less energy, etc.

Cash flows

Think about your bank account. It is preferable to be paid at the start of the month and pay all the bills and hopefully have a credit balance at the end rather than the opposite, i.e. when you pay all your bills during the month and get your salary at the end. The latter situation leads you to run up an overdraft which costs money in interest and penalties. Organisations are precisely the same. It is preferable to be paid before expenditure is incurred.

Consider the diagrams in Figures 9.22 and 9.23.

Of course not all projects are funded by genuine income (i.e. from a client), but nevertheless the money to cover the costs has to come from somewhere, and the sponsoring organisation will need to borrow from the bank if the cash is not immediately available. Either way, running a deficit will not go down well with your accounting colleagues if it can be avoided. Poor cash flow situations have been instrumental in the downfall of a number of organisations where it has never been managed and at a given point in time an organisation is not able to pay all of its bills on time.

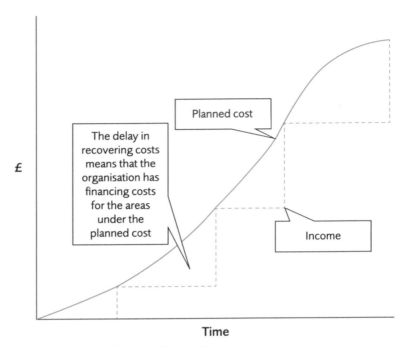

Figure 9.22 A type of cash flow situation

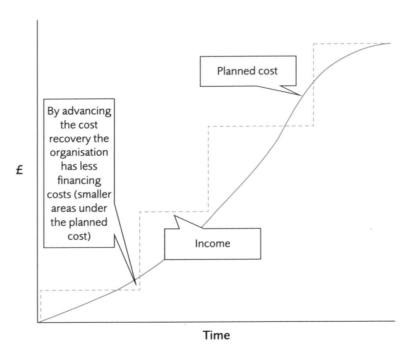

Figure 9.23 Another type of cash flow situation

WHIRLWIND BIKES

Consider the case study on page 259. Use this costed Gantt chart to produce a cumulative cost curve on the template provided on the next page.

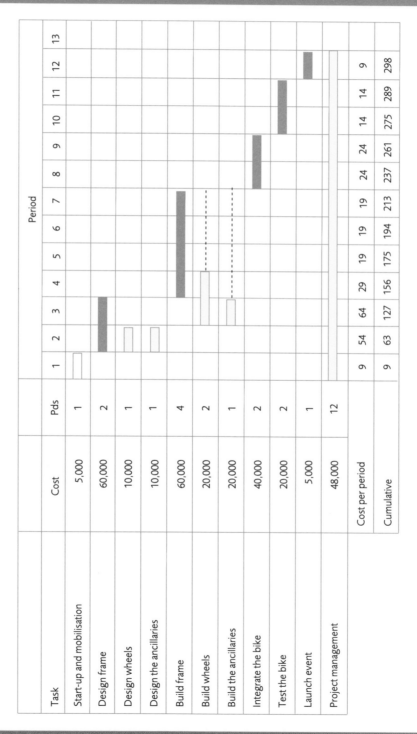

Task	Cost	Pds	P1	P2	P3	P4	P5	P6	P7	P8	P9	P10	P11	P12	P13
Start-up and mobilisation	5,000	1													
Design frame	60,000	2													
Design wheels	10,000	1													
Design the ancillaries	10,000	1													
Build frame	60,000	4													
Build wheels	20,000	2													
Build the ancillaries	20,000	1													
Integrate the bike	40,000	2													
Test the bike	20,000	2													
Launch event	5,000	1													
Project management	48,000	12													
Cost per period			9	54	64	29	19	19	19	24	24	14	14	9	
Cumulative			9	63	127	156	175	194	213	237	261	275	289	298	

Period

MANAGEMENT

WHIRLWIND BIKES

Consider the case study on page 259. Template for you to draw a cost curve on.

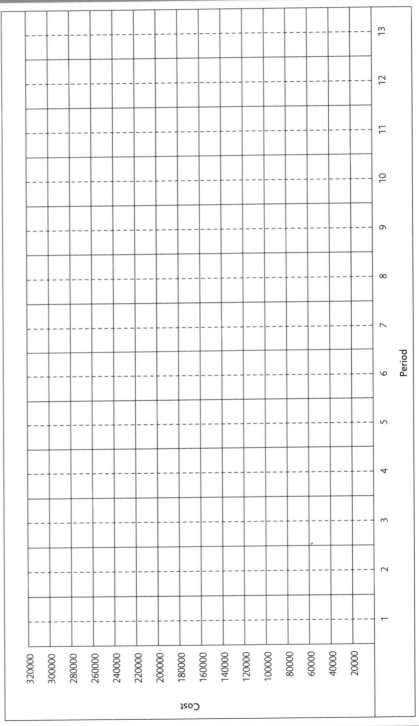

Use this space to make some notes

....

....

....

....

....

Quick quiz (answers on page 284)

	Question	Options	Your answer
1	A resource histogram shows the quantity of resources used over time as a horizontal bar.	True or false?	
2	The estimated cost to complete a project is reflected in all of these except——?	a) Budget b) Planned cost c) Actual cost d) Estimates	
3	The objective of cash flow management is to _____ the amount of time costs exceed income?	a) Reduce b) Increase c) Normalise d) Determine	
4	What term describes the technique for making sure that predicted costs are recorded in the project accounts in the appropriate time period?	a) Budget b) Forecast c) Accrual d) Actual	
5	The project manager is responsible for identifying the predicted out-turn (forecast) for the project.	True or false?	

	Question	Options	Your answer
6	The cumulative cost curve gets carried forward into the earned value calculations.	True or false?	
7	Which term describes monies legally due on a project?	a) Actual b) Forecast c) Commitments d) Negative	
8	Who is responsible for making sure that costs are properly managed on the project?	a) The sponsor b) The project manager c) The client d) The project manager and the sponsor	
9	Budgets are only a guide and do not really matter.	True or false?	
10	Cumulative resources rise over the time of the project.	True or false?	

What kind of questions might there be in the exam?

1 List and describe <u>five</u> things a project manager might do to manage costs.

50 marks (10 marks each)

9.4 Earned value

By completing this subsection you will be able to:

- describe advantages and disadvantages of earned value management;
- perform earned value calculations and interpret earned value data.

These two assessment criteria have been brought forward from earlier sections.

What is earned value?

Earned value is a term used to describe a value placed on the products that have been produced or belong to a project that cannot be taken away. It is a calculated figure derived by multiplying the budget allocated to produce the product and the percentage complete of that product.

Consider the diagram in Figure 9.24. In this scenario, the costs of the project were predicted at the outset to rise steadily up to the original budget at completion (BAC). Armed with this information, we can derive details about any difference between the money we had anticipated to spend (planned cost) and the money we have actually spent (actual cost), both recorded at the time now or actual time expended (ATE).

In isolation, you could draw the conclusion that the project is just fine as the actual cost is below where we thought we would be in terms of cost. On the face of it, very good news! However, if we have actually not produced anything, this graph is exceptionally bad news.

The concept of earned value can be used to help understand more about the true nature of the project performance and, if applied correctly, it can provide indicators as to a) what might be going wrong; and b) where the project might end up in terms of cost and time if it carries on as it is.

Earned value management is the proactive management of the project performance using earned value as a key input.

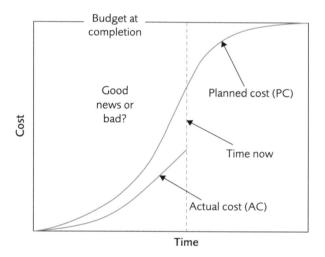

Figure 9.24 The need for earned value

Consider an example:

A builder is building a wall; it is three metres high, two metres long, is intended to take three weeks to build and we pay the builder £100 per week while he is working for us building it. We have to pay the builder even if he is off sick.

The budget at completion is £300; the planned completion is three weeks.

After two weeks, we measure the wall and find it is only one metre high (but two metres long) so we can clearly tell we are behind schedule. We have paid the builder £200 as he has been working for two weeks and we would expect it to be two metres high. In a simple case like this, a subjective analysis may be sufficient to spot the problem. Earned value gives us the tools to do more than that.

We can take an objective measure (using a tape measure) of the height of the wall (one metre). It is demonstrably one-third finished (33 per cent). On the basis that the wall cannot be taken from us and it belongs to us we can classify this as having earned value equalling 33 per cent × the budget at completion or 33 per cent × £300. **The earned value we have on our project is £100 even though we have spent two-thirds of the time scheduled and £200 getting it**.

Using this example therefore, we would appear to have a problem. We are now going to be late as the builder needs to build two metres of wall in one week, which probably won't happen if past experience is anything to go by, and this means we will probably go over budget. On the face of it, one metre in two weeks may well mean three metres in six weeks. If this turns out to be true, we will take twice as long and spend twice as much. This we can do in our head. On a large project, with many work packages, these relatively simple principles need earned value techniques to help us keep track.

Earned value terminology

The terms in Table 9.5 are derived from *Earned Value Management: APM Guidelines*, 2nd edition (APM, 2008, pp. 26–31) and will be used consistently from here on in this guide.

Table 9.5 Terms for calculating earned value

Acronym	Term	Definition
ATE	Actual time expended	The time now (at which the earned value calculations are done, including all the data up to that point).
EV	Earned value	The value of the useful work done at any given point in a project. The value of completed work expressed in terms of the budget assigned to that work. It is calculated by multiplying the original budget at completion for the given work package by the % complete (for that work package). **EV = BAC (for that work package) × % complete (of that work package)**
PC	Planned cost	This is the rate at which the project expects to spend its costs. It is effectively the cost we expected to incur at any point in time rising to the project BAC at the planned completion date.

Acronym	Term	Definition
AC	Actual cost	The costs incurred by the project up to the ATE in carrying out the planned activities.
		AC is derived as part of the normal project accounting procedures and is a record of cost incurred to date.
BAC	Budget at completion	Describes either the individual work package BAC or the sum of all of the individual work package budgets at completion.
EAC	Estimate at completion	The final estimated cost at completion (derived from the earned value calculations). $\textbf{EAC} = \textbf{BAC} / \textbf{CPI}$
	Planned completion	The date the project was originally planned to be finished.
	Actual completion	The date at which it is predicted, as a result of the earned value calculations, that the project will finish.
		Actual completion = planned completion / SPI
CV	Cost variance	The difference between the earned value of the products produced to date and the actual cost incurred in doing that work to date. $\textbf{CV} = \textbf{EV} - \textbf{AC}$
SV	Schedule variance	The difference between the earned value of the products produced to date and the planned cost of doing that work to date. $\textbf{SV} = \textbf{EV} - \textbf{PC}$
CPI	Cost performance Index	The ratio of the earned value and the actual cost (both as at the ATE) expressed as a decimal. $\textbf{CPI} = \textbf{EV} / \textbf{AC}$
SPI	Schedule performance index	The ratio of the earned value and the planned cost (both as at the ATE) expressed as a decimal. $\textbf{SPI} = \textbf{EV} / \textbf{PC}$

It is usual to demonstrate the earned value principles in a diagram such as in Figure 9.25.

A more complex example

We considered earlier the construction of a cumulative cost curve for a sample project and called it the planned cost or budget. As a reminder, Figure 9.21 is reproduced overleaf.

This is the basis for our earned value calculations. It is the planned cost curve. When we calculated it earlier we used the weekly figures to plot the curve. In Table 9.6 we

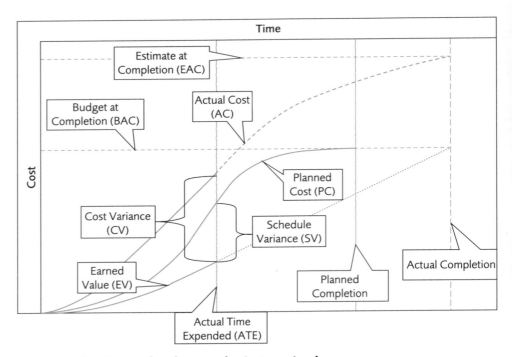

Figure 9.25 Earned value analysis terminology

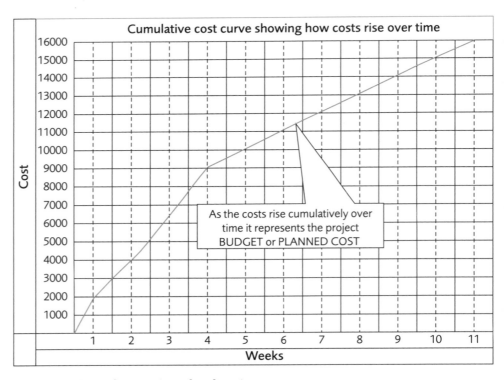

Figure 9.21 The project budget*

* As an example, Figure 9.21 is reproduced here to help with calculations in this section.

have re-analysed the data to give us a perspective based upon the work package details, rather than on a weekly basis. The curve will remain the same. By doing it now this way around, we are able to attribute progress figures to individual work packages (WP), so that a true picture of progress can be calculated. Please note we have fabricated all of these numbers to provide a viable example. The durations and BAC for the work packages are fictitious, but used to demonstrate the technique.

Table 9.6 Work packages and their BACs

Work Package	Duration	BAC
A	1	2,000
B	4	4,000
C	2	2,000
D	1	1,000
E	2	3,000
F	2	2,000
G	1	1,000
H	1	1,000
Total		**16,000**

Please remember that the budget at completion (BAC) for the project is the sum of all the period-based costs for all of the constituent work packages. A planned cost of £100 in week 1, £300 in week 2 and £200 in week 3 will mean a BAC for the project of £600.

So let's now move to the end of week 5, check the graph and you can see we should have spent (according to the planned cost curve) £10,000 (Figure 9.21). We are going to introduce some more figures so we can work through an earned value calculation for our project.

Let's say that we have gone through the project and, as part of our regular record keeping (undertaken by the project office perhaps), we have ascertained the progress and cost data (shown in Table 9.7) relating to the project at the end of week 5.

Don't forget that the earned value = BAC for the work package × % complete

We are only concerned with data up to week 5 we have assumed that work packages C, F, G and H are yet to start.

So, we now have the data we need to plot the remaining curves and try and understand where we are on the project. You will see on the diagram in Figure 9.26 that the planned cost curve is above both the earned value and the actual costs. The actual costs are above the earned value. This is not particularly good, in fact it is bad. We have overspent for the things we have produced and we have delivered those things more slowly than we should.

Table 9.7 Earned value data

Work Package	Duration	Planned Cost (£)	Earned Value % Complete	Earned Value (£)	Actual costs booked to WP (£)
A	1	2,000	100	2,000	2,100
B	4	4,000	25	1,000	1,800
D	1	1,000	80	800	1,600
E	2	3,000	70	2,100	2,000
Total		**10,000**		**5,900**	**7,500**

This latter fact is the bit that people sometimes have trouble grasping. That the earned value is below the planned cost means that (in this example) we should have produced £10,000 worth of products but we have only actually produced £5,900 worth of products in that time. So we need to catch up – another way of saying we are late.

Earned value displayed graphically for the example project

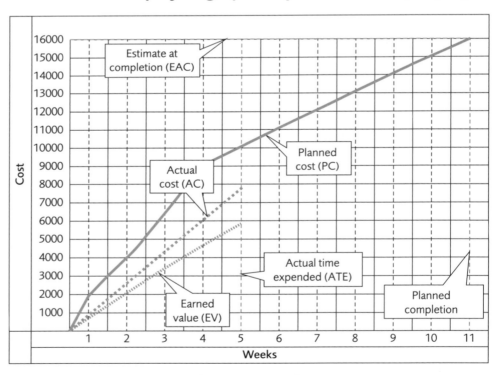

Figure 9.26 Earned value for the example project

We can now consider the formulae we need to know to be able to analyse this in more detail (Table 9.8).

Table 9.8 Earned value calculations

Formula	From the example	Value
CV = EV – AC	CV = 5,900 – 7,500	£–1,600
SV = EV – PC	SV = 5,900 – 10,000	£–4,100
CPI = EV/AC	CPI = 5,900/7,500	0.79 (or 79%)
SPI = EV/PC	SPI = 5,900/10,000	0.59 (or 59%)
EAC = BAC/CPI	EAC = 16,000/0.79	£20,200
Actual completion = planned completion/SPI	Actual completion = 11 (weeks)/0.59	18.6 (weeks)

Please note that a **negative cost variance (CV) or schedule variance (SV) is BAD. A schedule performance Index (SPI) or cost performance index (CPI) of less than 1 is also BAD.**

The CPI and SPI can sometimes be thought of as cost and schedule 'efficiencies'. If something is running at less than 100 per cent it might be considered to be inefficient.

We are going to need a bigger graph to demonstrate graphically what is going to happen with this project (see Figure 9.27).

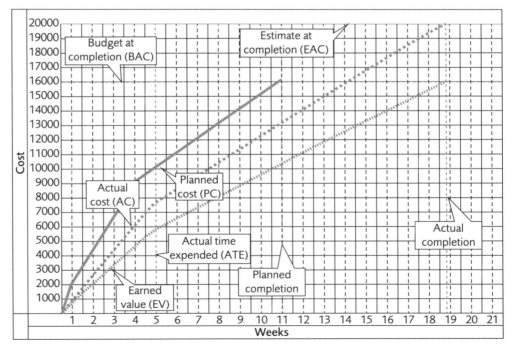

Figure 9.27 Earned value graph showing actual completion

MANAGEMENT

Note: the earned value NEVER exceeds the original budget at completion, but will be achieved at the new actual completion.

In essence, the example project is not doing very well at all. It is late (projected to finish in week 19 and not week 11 as planned) and will overspend (£20,200 instead of £16,000 as planned). The project team will have quite a bit of work to do to pull this back.

Interpreting earned value

In the example used above, the project appears to be in a fairly poor state. It will require significant activity and effort to pull back on track. This, of course, is not true of every project, indeed very often quite the opposite in fact. Earned value is a well-developed and objective mechanism for understanding what is going wrong (or right).

Consider the graphs in Figures 9.28 to 9.31. Can you work out whether the projects are in good (or bad) shape and what might be going wrong (or right)?

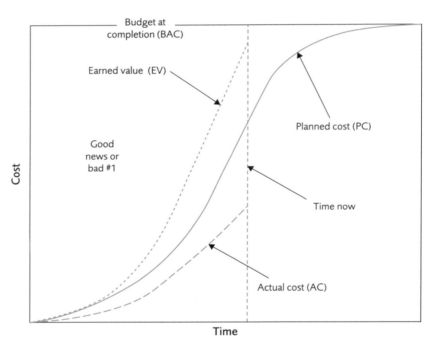

Figure 9.28 Good news or bad #1

The project is storming ahead, the earned value is relatively high and the actual costs relatively low (below the PC and EV). The project has nearly finished with dramatically lower costs than estimated. There can be downsides to this though, as dramatically poor estimating can cause organisations to take on less risk than they might otherwise do, thereby potentially missing out on opportunities. Alternatively, the team may just be very efficient, which should be applauded.

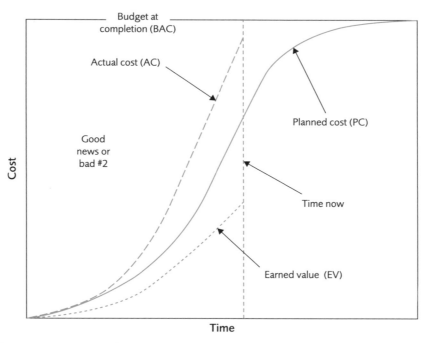

Figure 9.29 Good news or bad #2

Completely the opposite of example #1. The actual costs are way above budget and the delivery is very late. There are inefficiencies in here; the team are exerting a lot of effort but not getting very far. Again, perhaps the estimates were wrong, or perhaps we need some training or a good hard look at how to speed things up and save costs. This could also be an indicator of poor morale.

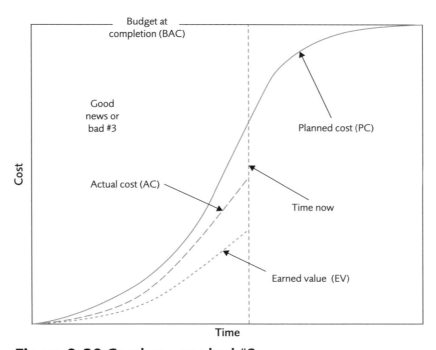

Figure 9.30 Good news or bad #3

The actual costs are below the planned costs but above the earned value. Here we are delivering slowly and spending more than we should for what we deliver. Once again, the team may be in need of motivation or possibly some reinforcement. Perhaps we have too many junior members of staff and could do with some more skilled people to recover the schedule and utilise the under spend. We might consider overtime working.

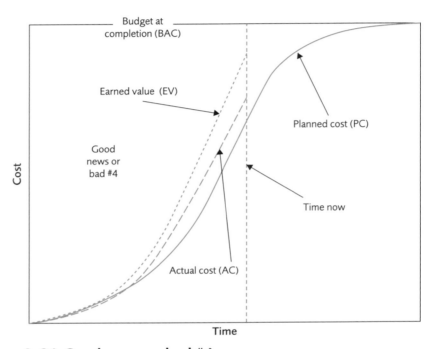

Figure 9.31 Good news or bad #4

The earned value is above the actual cost and way above the planned cost. This means once again that the project is roaring ahead. Perhaps it could slow down a little, maybe redeploy some of its staff to cut back on costs as it can afford to deliver a bit more slowly.

The advantages of using earned value

■ It provides an index that can be used to help understand whether the project is going to fulfil its success criteria and parameters.

■ It provides an insight into how the project has been performing to date and is able to be represented as a couple of key performance indicators of schedule performance index and cost performance index.

■ Helps provide clues as to what needs to be investigated in order that corrective action can be taken as the relative positions of the various curves on the graph provide an insight.

■ Helps communicate the situation through the use of graphs and diagrams in a consistent way to stakeholders.

The disadvantages of using earned value

■ Needs rigour and tight control of costs.

■ Requires a properly established baseline WBS so that costs can be tracked accurately.

■ Requires openness and honesty and not hiding things 'under the carpet'.

■ Has a huge reliance on the assessment of percent complete, which in physical products is relatively straightforward, but presents a huge challenge where the products are less well-defined (for example, software).

■ Limited understanding of EVM in project context, e.g. sponsors.

Use this space to make some notes

WHIRLWIND BIKES

Consider the case study on page 259. For Whirlwind, we have introduced some data and 'rolled the project forward' to period 6 at which the planned cost is £194,000 (derived from the earlier cost curve calculations). Calculate the earned value, the CPI, SPI and actual completion, and estimate at completion based on the data provided. Draw the other two curves (EV and AC) on the template provided.

Work package	Duration	Work package BAC	Earned value % complete	Earned value	Actual costs booked to WP
Start-up and mobilisation	1	5,000	100		5,000
Design frame	2	60,000	95		57,000
Design wheels	1	10,000	100		12,000
Design the ancillaries	1	10,000	100		15,000
Build the frame	4	60,000	0		
Build the wheels	2	20,000	70		14,000
Build the ancillaries	1	20,000	90		17,000
Integrate the bike	2	40,000	0		
Test the bike	2	20,000	0		
Launch the bike	1	5,000	0		
Project management	12	48,000	50		22,000
Total		298,000			142,000

CPI =

SPI =

SV=

CV=

Actual completion

Estimate at completion

WHIRLWIND BIKES

Consider the case study on page 259. Earned value graph template.

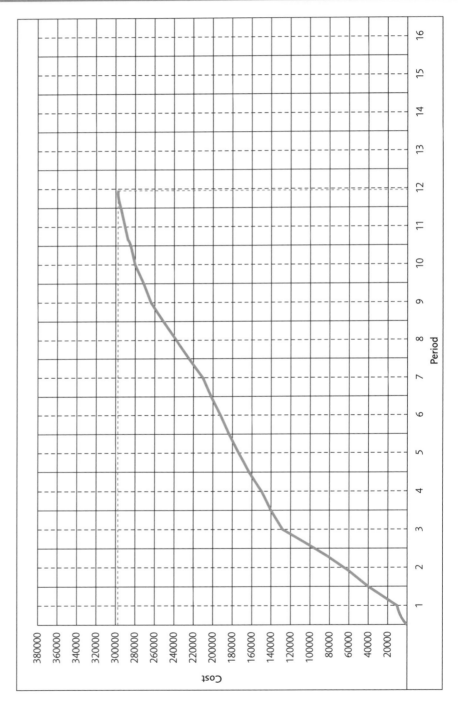

Use this space to make some notes

Quick quiz (answers on page 285)

	Question	Options	Your answer
1	An SPI more than 1 is bad.	True or false?	
2	A CPI less than 1 is good.	True or false?	
3	Earned value management cannot be used to tell whether we are . . .?	a) Ahead or behind of schedule b) Ahead or behind on cost c) Actual costs d) None of the above	
4	CV = EV – ?	a) SV b) CPI c) AC d) PC	
5	BAC stands for . . .?	a) Budget at cost b) Budget after completion c) Bonus at completion d) Budget at completion	

	Question	Options	Your answer
6	Earned value management needs a very well-considered WBS in order to be operated effectively.	True or false?	
7	Which of these is an advantage of earned value management?	a) It requires very detailed data b) It requires a robust system to administer it c) It provides a forecast out-turn for the project d) It requires skilled interpretation	
8	If the EV is above the AC, is this . . .?	a) Good b) Bad c) Awful d) Can't tell	
9	The actual costs are usually provided by the accounts department (or project accountants).	True or false?	
10	Changes to the budgets will affect EV calculation.	True or false?	

What kind of questions might there be in the exam?

1

This question has <u>four</u> parts. Answer all parts.

Only the answer sheet will be marked, any workings on the question paper will be ignored.

State a definition of the term 'earned value'.

5 marks

State a definition of the term 'budget at completion'.

5 marks

Consider the data provided below produced at week seven of a 12-week project, which has a budget at completion of £21,000. Determine the CPI, SPI, estimate at completion and planned completion for the project.

Work Package	Budget at completion (BAC)	% complete at week 7	Earned Value at week 7	Planned cost at week 7	Actual Costs at week 7
A	2,000	100	2,000	2,000	2,100
B	4,000	25	1,000	3,000	1,800
C	2,000	25	500	1,000	600
D	6,000	10	600	500	1,000
E	7,000	0	0	0	0
Total	21,000		4,100	6,500	5,500

20 marks (5 marks for each of SPI, CPI, estimate at completion and planned completion)

From the data in part (c) explain <u>two</u> reasons why the project may be exhibiting these figures.

20 marks (10 marks each)

2

This question has <u>three</u> parts. Answer all parts.

Explain the primary use of earned value.

10 marks

Explain <u>two</u> advantages of using earned value analysis technique.

20 marks

Explain <u>two</u> disadvantages of using earned value analysis technique.

20 marks (10 marks each)

10

Risk and issue management

Subjects covered in this section

10.1 Risk management

10.2 Issue management

10.1 ## Risk management

By completing this subsection you will be able to:

- explain each stage in a risk management process (such as initiate, identify, assess, plan and implement responses);

- compare the responses to risk in terms of risk as a threat or opportunity (such as avoid, reduce, transfer or accept and exploit, enhance, share or reject);

- explain the benefits of project risk management.

These assessment criteria have been amalgamated together as they refer primarily to risk, whereas the next subsection refers to issues.

What is a risk?

"A risk event is an uncertain event or set of circumstances that, should it occur will have an effect on the achievement of one or more of the project's objectives."

Project Risk Analysis and Management Guide
(APM, 2004, p. 17)

The APM *Body of Knowledge 6th edition* focuses attention on the overall impact of risk to the whole project outcome, including the benefits. This overall risk is made up of specific project risk events, such as 'possible failure of acceptance testing', which we would record on the risk register, AND other sources of uncertainty, such as estimating. These latter areas we suspect may be potential risks that may need more investigation but are not quantifiable at this stage.

It is important to differentiate between the causes of risks, the risk itself and the effect of a risk. Take a simple example. There is a risk that we may not have enough of a specific resource for a critical stage in the project, such as commissioning or going live with a system. The causes may be failure of the transport system due to extreme weather, inability to recruit sufficient people with the right skills or that there is a flu pandemic. Because of one or all of these causes, the risk transpires and the effects occur which might be that we are unable to deliver the critical stage product on time, we get sued by the client and we all lose our jobs.

We need to focus on the causes and the effects rather than the terminology of the risk itself. Causes may in themselves have other causes (extreme weather may or may not be caused by global warming). The causes also have a probability associated with them. If they are already happening then they are not a risk but an issue. Issues occur when work will exceed, or has exceeded, limits agreed on the plan. All risks have to have an element of uncertainty associated with them. We indicate this uncertainty using probability.

If the risk occurs there will be an impact, which we measure in terms of time, cost or failure to meet performance criteria.

There is a tendency to merely think of risks as threat-based (i.e. what might go wrong). You are also encouraged to consider the opposite (i.e. what might go better than right) and these are referred to as opportunities.

Why do we need a proactive risk management process?

A risk management process is intended to encourage the team to identify and pre-empt the things that might affect the project. Using a formal process allows thought and energy to be applied at the time when it has the most value – at the beginning. The benefits of adopting a proactive approach to risks would include the following:

■ It is the process which will define the way in which risks are dealt with, the objectives and the roles of the various stakeholders.

■ It is the mechanism to achieve continual improvement through a proper feedback loop throughout the process itself.

■ It will help make sure that a proper contingency is in place by calculating the relevant allowances against a quantified and fully considered risk profile.

■ It is a process that ensures everyone is doing the same things in the same way as it is documented in the PMP.

■ It provides a common reference point for any audit and assurance processes.

■ It will make sure that the sponsoring organisation enters into projects with a clear perspective of the risks, in the knowledge that all the avenues have been covered and due process has been followed, and the resultant data on which decisions are made is accurate.

The PRAM process

The *Project Risk Analysis and Management Guide* (APM, 2004, p. 19) advocates a generic risk management life cycle and it is reproduced (with annotations) in Figure 10.1. The arrows around the boxes are significant and imply that the steps are not isolated but are in fact iterative in a number of ways. Following the process blindly is not going to be sufficient to manage risks effectively on the project. It is merely a framework around which the project manager and teams will need to use their skill, knowledge and ingenuity on an ongoing basis to pre-empt the things that might interfere with the achievement of objectives.

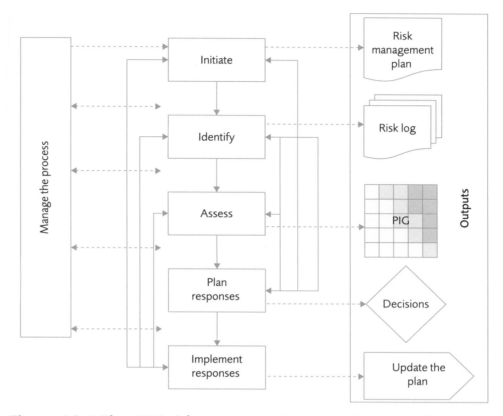

Figure 10.1 The APM risk management process (annotated)

These stages are discussed below:

Initiation

The main output from the initiation phase is the risk management plan. This document describes the following key elements of how risk management will be implemented on the project:

- Scope – of the risk management process, what are the objectives of having the process and which elements of the project are in (and which out of) scope of the process. For example, a risk study may focus on the risk to a particular milestone, such as a product launch, in isolation from the rest of the project.

- Objectives – what is the process trying to achieve, what level of risk reduction are we trying to achieve? What are the legislative or industry standards applicable to the industry in which we are operating?

- Roles – who has a role in the risk management process; who are our advisors? Is there a corporate component to be taken into account; is the project part of a programme or portfolio? If so, there are probably already roles in place.

MANAGEMENT

■ Process – what steps will we follow for the identification, assessment and management of the risks (i.e. what is the process and how can we demonstrate we are following it)?

■ Tools – what tools are available and what techniques are going to be supported in the process?

Identification

The next stage is to identify the risks (Figure 10.2).

Figure 10.2 Risk identification techniques

■ **Brainstorming** is the use of facilitated workshops to elicit 'blue sky' ideas from participants with a view to identifying risks that may be significant. Brainstorming gets a lot of good ideas out in the open quickly, but because of the number of people involved it can be expensive and requires careful management.

■ **Interviewing** is where specific subject experts in their respective fields are interviewed to help focus in on specific components or activities in the project. Experts will tend to use their own subjective perspective of what are risks and what are not. These views may differ from other 'experts'. They do yield a lot of detailed data and insights though and capitalise on experience.

■ **Delphi** This is a form of expert analysis where a number of identified 'experts' are consulted about a specific problem or set of circumstances and they then discuss and debate within groups or plenary what the nature of the resultant risks may be. This is easily done remotely using email or web-based technology and will provide a large amount of expert input but will doubtless cost quite a lot of money and will be tricky to co-ordinate.

- **Prompt lists** These are a form of checklist but more generic in nature and are used to help identify the nature of a risk rather than provide a pre-existing 'category' as such. They can include things like a categorisation (e.g. technical, commercial, etc). They do in some cases limit thought and creativity though as time can be consumed discussing the headings rather then the risks themselves.

- **Checklists** are widely used to help identify risks. They appear in all walks of life and are borne out of a systematic process done once to analyse potential areas of risk and deployed into repetitive situations to speed up the identification process. They are quick and relatively cheap, but sometimes it can be felt that doing the checklist is doing the risk management and significant risks are overlooked simply because they are not on the list.

- **Assumptions analysis** is a mechanism of going through previous lists of assumptions and breaking them down to understand which risks may be a consequence of them. This is relatively quick and easy, and draws on work that has gone before; there is a danger that assumptions are not managed otherwise.

As risks are identified they must be recorded on a risk log and be annotated with some basic information, such as:

- **Identification number** – usually sequential within a given project or programme.

- **Description** – a detailed description, which should include the cause and effect.

- **Category** – this aids communication and might include: strategic (risks that would interfere with the organisation's interests); project (those that might cause the project to fail); operational (risks that would interfere with the organisation's business); and technical (potential problems with the products and their manufacture).

- **Potential impact** on the project objectives pre-mitigation (only possible after the assessment step – see below).

- **Probability pre-mitigation** (only possible after the assessment step – see below).

- **Potential actions** to mitigate the risk (only possible after the plan response step – see below).

- **Assignment of an owner** – a risk owner is the person or individual who is perceived to be best placed to manage the risk.

Assessment

A common output from the risk assessment process is the probability and impact grid (PIG), an example of which appears in Figure 10.3. The use of this example is to show that a risk is evaluated on two axes; that of probability (how likely is it to happen) and that of impact (what will happen if it does).

MANAGEMENT

Each of the two axes has two forms of scale. The VHI, HI, MED, LO, VLO is an example of a **qualitative** scale. Whether a risk is a very low probability is a personal evaluation. One person's view of very low is different from another person's view. This is a perfectly viable scale though and should not be dismissed. It has the advantage of being accessible to lay people and encourages individuals to become engaged in the process, which can sometimes otherwise be seen as complicated and obscure.

The numbered scale on the other hand is an attempt to put a **quantitative** assessment on the risks and it encourages thinking about specific numbering, providing potential to input these numbers into some form of modelling and analysis tool.

It is normal to take the probability score and multiply it with the impact score to arrive at what is often termed the Severity. It is usual at this time to also record their ranking on the risk log, and in an automated system the most significant risks will 'bubble to the top'. So on the grid below, the following maths can be exercised:

Risk A = 0.5 × 0.1 = 0.05
Risk B = 0.9 × 0.8 = 0.72
Risk C = 0.1 × 0.8 = 0.08
Risk D = 0.9 × 0.05 = 0.045

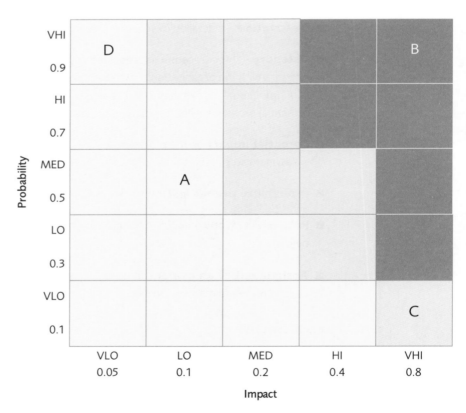

Figure 10.3 Probability impact grid

Note that the impact score is non-linear. This is because the impact of a risk is usually considered to be more significant than the probability. If a potential impact has a calamitous outcome (e.g. nuclear core meltdown) we want to see it much higher up the ranking (probably at the top) than it might otherwise do if the scores were simply linear (1–5 perhaps).

Plan response

Having prioritised the risk, it is now necessary to determine a potential response for the higher risk. There are two things to do here. One is to determine what can be done to reduce the probability of the risk occurring (thereby reducing its probability). The second is to determine a plan and set aside contingencies to deal with it if it does. Some examples appear in Table 10.1:

Table 10.1 Risk events and responses

Risk event	Consequence	Mitigation action to reduce probability	Contingency actions to deal with it if it still does occur
Bad weather happens on a key date	There may be delays in replacing the roof, thereby causing delays and potential overspend.	Do roofing work during the drier months.	Erect protective sheeting above roof while work takes place. Stop work and move workers inside during bad weather.
The new server does not arrive in time.	The software testing cannot take place.	Make sure it is purchased from a reputable supplier.	Provide a delay between planned delivery and testing starting. Purchase two, one as a spare.
The staff do not accept the new working practices.	Poor customer service and morale.	Make sure staff are communicated with early in the process.	Have a long transition phase. Hire temporary staff while changes and alterations are made.

Generally speaking there are a number of different words used to describe what can be done to improve risk. The following eight are options of ways to describe them (four for threats and four for opportunities). There are more (you may have come across Terminate, Treat,

Tolerate, Absorb, Pursue, for example which are also fine to use in the exam) but these are ones fully described for the purpose of providing you with at least a few valid ones for the exam.

Threats

■ Accept – Here we accept the risk and take no proactive action other than putting monitoring processes in place to make sure that the potential for damage does not change. Once risks are accepted it is generally necessary to provide for some form of contingency to provide funds or time to accommodate the risk should it happen (despite its lower probability/impact).

■ Avoid – The only real way to avoid a risk is to change the project scope or approach – what we do or the way we do it. Remove a particular chemical from the process, for example.

■ Transfer – We seek to move the risk from our risk log onto someone else's risk log. We seek to transfer the potential for harm to another, usually through an insurance policy or a contract.

■ Reduce – Either the probability or the impact (or both). For example, provide training to staff so they know how to operate a process (reduces probability) or perhaps test all output so that if a poor-quality product is produced, we do not deliver it to the client (reduces the impact of the risk).

Opportunities

■ Reject – Choose not to take advantage of the opportunity, possibly because it is worth too little or requires too much work to capitalise upon.

■ Enhance – Take proactive steps to try to enhance the probability of an opportunity being able to be exploited. If there is a chance of finishing the hotel refurbishment early through some proactive intervention, then we can seek to sell the rooms earlier.

■ Exploit – This involves changing the scope of the project to encompass some aspect, hitherto not considered, that will achieve some extra benefit for the stakeholders. Typically engagement with these types of opportunities is more prevalent during the concept phase.

■ Share – Seek partners with whom we can actively capitalise on the circumstances. Often a joint venture, perhaps where an opportunity exists for an extra retail outlet in the bus station, but as it is not core business, we may seek a partner to help capitalise on it.

Care is needed when arriving at any response to risk because whatever action we take has the potential to generate other risks. For example when changing the type of chemical used in a particular process with another to avoid risks of corrosion to the containers, we may introduce the secondary risk of that replacement chemical not being as efficient as the original, leading to a risk of a less than optimal result. This is an example of a secondary risk.

Implement responses

Once the specific responses have been decided upon they should be included within the project plan. A project does not have a risk plan and a separate project plan. It simply has a new version of the plan. Therefore, once the responses have been scoped and planned, they are included within the work breakdown structures, schedules, budgets, and so on.

You also need to establish a separate activity if there needs to be a contingency or fall back plan created to make sure that there is a proper course of action to be followed in the event of a risk materialising. This plan does have a separate budget formulated from the calculated contingencies for the project. If a risk occurs, then the contingency is disbursed by the sponsor when required. Contingency is only set aside to deal with the known and quantified effects of risk.

Make sure that the process is alive and continually reviewed. Risk reviews should take place at prescribed intervals, proper records kept, and escalation and advice sought where necessary. Make sure the team are engaged and that all available information is utilised where practical to improve the quality of the evaluations.

 Use this space to make some notes

....

....

....

....

....

Quick quiz (answers on 285)

	Question	Options	Your answer
1	The axes of a risk assessment grid are...?	a) Power and influence b) People and information c) Probability and influence d) Probability and impact	

	Question	Options	Your answer
2	Which of these is not a response to a threat-based risk?	a) Accept b) Avoid c) Share d) Reduce	
3	If a risk has a probability score of 0.4 and an impact score of 0.05, its risk score (severity) is. . .?	a) 0.01 b) 0.02 c) 0.04 d) 1.01	
4	Which of these is NOT a stage in the APM risk management process?	a) Initiate b) Plan response c) Quantitative d) Assess	
5	The risk management plan may be part of the overall project management plan.	True or false?	
6	Brainstorming is a way of identifying risks.	True or false?	
7	Expert judgement will never affect an individual's view of a risk probability.	True or false?	
8	Throughout the project, risk scores will never change.	True or false?	
9	Which of these is not a risk identification technique?	a) Brainstorming b) Expert judgement c) Assumptions analysis d) Guesswork	
10	A risk owner is the person who carries out the risk mitigation actions.	a) Yes b) No c) Manages them d) Avoids them	

What kind of questions might there be in the exam?

1

This question has <u>two</u> parts. Answer both parts.

Only the answer sheet will be marked, any workings on the question paper will be ignored.

Consider the diagram below and list the top five risks in order of severity.

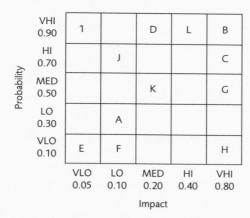

10 marks (2 marks for each in the correct order)

List and describe <u>four</u> responses to risks or opportunities.

40 marks (10 marks each)

2

List and describe <u>five</u> steps in a risk management process.

50 marks (10 marks each)

10.2 | # Issue management

By completing this subsection you will be able to:

- Distinguish between risks and issues
- Explain the benefits of the escalation process

These are the two assessment criteria associated with issues.

A definition of an issue

This is one of the key roles of a project manager – see definition below:

> *"A formal issue occurs when the tolerances of delegated work are predicted to be exceeded or have been exceeded. This triggers the escalation of the issue from one level of management to the next in order to seek a solution."*
>
> APM Body of Knowledge 6th edition (APM, 2012, p. 238)

A project manager would normally be allowed a tolerance to make decisions to keep the project going along. They are not required to resort to a sponsor decision as soon as something minor occurs. One of the key pieces of judgement a project manager will need to apply is that of when to seek assistance to sort out a problem and when to make that decision themselves. This has a lot to do with the relationship between the project manager and the sponsor but also needs to be recorded in a manner of a formal process. The issue management plan is one of those documents that finds its way into the PMP.

The issue log

Recognition of an issue should be swiftly followed by the recording of it on some form of template, maintained by the project manager (potentially supported by the project office). An example of such a template (the issue log) appears in Figure 10.4:

			Issue log					
				Impact				
ID	Description	Date	Time	Cost	Owner	Status	Agreed actions	

Figure 10.4 Issue log

The headings are very similar to those on a risk log and there are a lot of synergies. One significant source of issues is simply risks that have occurred. Issues can appear under other circumstances, but it can be argued that this is simply a failing on the part of the risk management process having not predicted them!

A couple of things to note on this sample issue log are:

- There is no probability column. An issue has a probability of 100 per cent (i.e. it has happened).

- The status would reflect whether it was perhaps Open or Resolved. These headings would be spelt out in the issue management plan.

However, given that they have occurred, they need to be managed in a systematic way. Key failings in this process are often:

- Not recognising an issue for what it is and not escalating it, believing it can be resolved by the project manager.

- Failing to track an issue once escalated to make sure it has or is in the process of being resolved.

- Losing track of 'ownership' resulting in the project manager ending up trying to fix everything.

As well as the project manager, the sponsor and steering group have a key role in dealing with issues as they will be the bodies to whom the issues are raised if necessary. Failure on the part of the steering group or sponsor to deal with the issue leaves very little other option. The project manager needs a good solid network of support from these two entities.

The benefits of issue management and escalation

- If left unattended, issues will slowly grow in number and build up to be a wave of difficulty that can submerge a project. Dealing with them as soon as they become apparent (or at least identify how they will be resolved) will help prevent failure of the project.

- Stakeholders will be properly informed, as issues can be shared among the individuals or groups that can best deal with them, possibly through the use of specialist support.

- Contingencies allocated in the risk management process need to be drawn down to deal with the issues as they present themselves.

- There is a clear hierarchy of responsibility required to be sure where ownership lies. Allocation of an owner is an important process in itself and it will ensure that a suitably capable person or group has been delegated to sort out the issue.

- Project process encourages open reporting, active resolution.

Use this space to make some notes

....

....

....

....

....

Quick quiz (answers on page 286)

	Question	Options	Your answer
1	An issue is a threat that the project manager cannot readily deal with and needs to be escalated for assistance.	True or false?	
2	To whom would a commercial issue normally be escalated?	a) Client b) Sponsor c) Steering group d) Team	
3	Which of these is NOT a heading on the issue log?	a) Date b) Number c) Owner d) Probability	
4	Not escalating an issue early enough is a common cause of projects running into difficulties.	True or false?	
5	The project manager may choose to write the issue management process in the PMP.	True or false?	

What kind of question might there be in the exam?

1	This question has <u>two</u> parts. Answer both parts.

Explain the purpose of managing issues on a project.

10 marks

List and describe <u>four</u> stages in an issue management process.

40 marks (10 marks each)

11

Quality

Subjects covered in this section

11.1 Quality planning, assurance and control

11.1 Quality planning, assurance and control

By completing this subsection you will be able to:

- define quality management;
- define quality planning, assurance, control and continual improvement;
- describe the benefits of the quality management process.

A definition of quality

Quality is an assessment of a product's fitness for purpose. While this definition appears to be limited to the products that the project will produce, importantly, quality applies not only to these products, but also to the processes and procedures deployed in managing the project itself. There is great deal of significance to the term quality and it is worth spending a little more time looking at it in more detail.

If I want to travel cheaply and easily by car, then a small hatchback may be just what is required. In this respect the car conforms to my requirements and specification and is therefore deemed to be a 'quality' product. If I wish to transport a family of six in comfort I may need some form of larger vehicle. This then would be a quality car and the hatchback would not be. Quality is a binary decision. The product either fulfils the specification, or it does not. Clearly this requires an irrefutable description of the product requirements to start with.

Often the term quality is applied to the assessment of a product without such a requisite specification. In these cases, the perspective will be totally subjective and open to interpretation. Inevitably, there are occasions when a subjective analysis carries a lot more weight than the purely objective analysis against a pre-agreed specification, such as a stay in a hotel, where the customer experience is more than just the size of the room.

The nature of the product is specified as part of the work package descriptions and will carry associated acceptance criteria. It is the achievement of these acceptance criteria that formally acknowledges that the requirements have been met.

Quality pervades everything we do and what we produce. It is an integral component of professional project management directed full square at producing the right product first time, every time.

MANAGEMENT

Quality management

The term quality management applies to four main components, each of which we consider later. However, it is worth considering the interaction of quality with other components of the syllabus. Consider Figure 11.1.

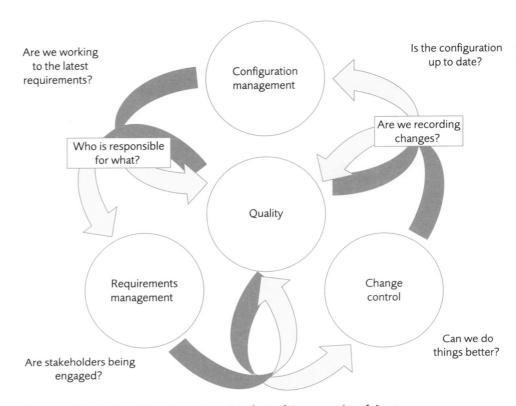

Figure 11.1 Quality is not an isolated 'cameo' subject

There is a value in managing quality proactively on a project. It can also be argued that quality is in fact free, in that it pays for itself; as the organisation becomes more mature, it makes less faulty goods that need to be replaced and repaired less often. As the prevention costs slowly rise, the failure and prevention costs fall dramatically. This phenomena was described as 'The Cost of Quality' (Crosby, 1979).

There are four stages in quality management:

Quality planning

The project manager must produce a quality plan (part of the PMP) and in it describe how the project will produce quality products and how it will manage itself. It will describe all of the following:

■ The roles and responsibilities concerned with quality – these might include quality assurance, testing, supervision and management roles.

- The processes that will be followed – these will be documented in a systematic way and will govern the mechanisms for the production of the product specifications and testing procedures, for example.

- How continual improvement will be carried out – this will include making adjustments to processes where they are proven to be unsatisfactory.

- What project assurance techniques will be deployed, such as audit, supplier vetting, specification writing, etc.

- What quality control techniques will be used, such as Pareto analysis, control charts, inspection test and measurement, etc.

- Interactions with other processes (e.g. configuration management) and how these links will be established and managed and in a suitable manner.

The project manager owns the PMP and therefore owns the subsidiary plans of which the quality plan is one. In drawing it up, the project manager needs to draw on the organisation's existing processes, tools and techniques. External influences will need to be taken into account that impact on the nature of the quality environment.

- ISO 9000 – is the company an ISO 9000 accredited organisation?

- TQM – is there adherence to a total quality management system?

- Are Investors in People accreditation principles in place?

- Are any quality maturity models being actively managed, such as the European Foundation Quality Model?

- Are there external industry standards that need to be adhered to?

- Is Six Sigma used as a quality control technique?

The project is not operating in a vacuum and, as such, all or any of the above may have a direct bearing on the way in which the project is commissioned and run.

Quality assurance

Quality assurance is the process associated with demonstrating and providing confidence to all stakeholders that the quality requirements will be achieved. Quality assurance will provide satisfaction that the plans are being followed and in the absence of any external distractions a quality product will be produced.

Assurance usually incorporates components of:

- **Training** – are the team properly trained? Are training records in place? Are there clear job requirements and are we able to vouch for the fact that the post holder is competent?

- **Audit** – can be used to make sure in a formal and external way whether or not the processes and principles of the PMP are being followed. Commissioned by sponsors, steering groups and others they will provide evidence of the fact that things are being executed in the way intended.

■ **Lessons learned** – the assurance processes make sure that the lessons learned during the project are properly communicated and that a properly formulated feedback loop is in place, making sure that mistakes and poor quality are removed at the root of the problem; the illnesses cured not the symptoms.

■ **Supplier accreditation** – the supplier base may need to demonstrate their quality credentials. Where goods and materials are shipped in for incorporation into the project's products (steel in a building perhaps) it may be necessary to ensure that those materials are of a suitable quality and will not cause a failure of testing further down the line.

Quality control

Quality control techniques are many and varied and are generally influenced to a very large degree by the nature of the project. For example, you would not rely on a visual inspection of safety-critical software code, whereas for a small brick wall it may well be appropriate.

There are a number of these techniques, some of which are discussed below. In all cases, quality control must be undertaken using an objective mechanism comparing the finished product against a specification to confirm acceptability. Work packages will all have associated acceptance criteria relating to the products.

Inspection and measurement – as discussed above, very often a simple sight check will be sufficient, looking through a document before it is sent out or looking at the way a playing surface has been laid may be all that is required, perhaps measuring the height of the goal posts using some form of gauge or a tape to make sure the white lines are the right distance apart. In software, the use of various levels of specification can provide the means to develop ever more precise tests to turn what might be fairly subjective requirements into testable products and systems.

Walk-throughs – are a little more in-depth and these will usually involve a group of people stepping through the lines of code in a software program, literally perhaps walking through a finished arrivals hall to make sure the signs are in place as an example.

Pareto analysis – involves understanding the nature of the observable faults and understanding the nature of the root cause of those problems. Once these are understood, it will be beneficial to solve the causes that result in the most number of faults. There is little point in fixing the problems that never result in an observable fault. This is sometimes called the 80:20 rule; 80 per cent of the observable faults are caused by 20 per cent of the root causes. Focus attention on those and a big impact will be achieved. Once those are fixed the next 20 per cent (of a smaller sample) can be tackled and so on.

Process control charts – a process control chart plots the measurements of how the readings taken of a sample of product vary over time. With time on the x axis and the range of witnessed measurements on the y axis, a plot can be taken that describes how the readings fluctuate. There may be upper and lower control limits which are based on the specification requirements. The intention is to recognise that a problem is about to occur and various algorithms can be deployed to determine whether there is a significant problem or not.

Continuous (continual) improvement

This is a fundamental principle of quality. This requires the correct use of feedback and using the lessons of the past to drive the actions of the future. Projects can evolve their processes to tune and develop their approach, improving accuracy and conformance to requirements.

Continual improvement will require the collection of data, using some of the techniques above, such as Pareto analysis for example. Let's take an example of a project to build a bridge. The welds between the individual beams of the bridge are inspected and a lot of them are demonstrating faults during the x-ray analysis of those welds. Work is undertaken to examine why the faults are occurring and it is determined that the welder needs better training, but also that the welding equipment has not been serviced and is performing below its expected capability. If the welder is sent on a refresher training course and the equipment serviced then the number of faults will reduce. There may still be faults but they will be for other reasons perhaps. This is continual improvement. It will inform quality planning before and during the project but it refines the plan rather than replaces it. It is an ongoing process.

The benefits of a quality management process

The benefits of the quality management processes are that:

- Eventually, if followed to their ultimate conclusion, it will eradicate all problems and a perfect product will be produced. This will probably never happen in reality, but as we progress towards it, faults will occur less often.

- It engenders confidence on the part of the stakeholders that they will receive what they asked for because requirements are visibly and systematically recorded and processed. Stakeholders can therefore be more comfortable that their needs will be addressed.

- It reduces rework, thus ultimately reducing costs. This is because there will be clear specifications and direction to the effort with clear statements of anticipated results that can be assured and checked.

- In safety-critical systems, it provides confidence that those processes will not introduce risk through faulty deliverables. Testing will be thorough and rigorous and any deviations from the specification will be spotted and dealt with at an early stage and completely.

- With a strong ethos of continual improvement, quality will improve efficiency and effectiveness over time as lessons will be learnt and used to provide diagnostic information and guidance for the establishment of better processes going forward.

MANAGEMENT

Use this space to make some notes

....

....

....

....

....

....

WHIRLWIND BIKES

Consider the case study on page 259. See if you can spot some fundamental requirements in the case study and try and identify a mechanism for testing to see if they have been achieved.

Quick quiz (answers on page 286)

	Question	Options	Your answer
1	Quality is best described as what?	a) The best we can do b) Gold plated c) Posh d) Fitness for purpose	
2	Acceptance criteria are associated with work package deliverables.	True or false?	
3	Which of these is not a component of a quality management process?	a) Continual improvement b) Planning c) Control d) Finishing	
4	An 80:20 diagram is a demonstration of the what?	a) Perverse method b) Machiavelli method c) Pareto method d) Italian method	
5	A process control chart records samples against upper and lower control limits.	True or false?	
6	Pareto analysis is a quality control technique.	True or false?	
7	Changes to specifications need to be controlled by which other process?	a) Requirements management b) Configuration management c) Change control d) Project management plan	

	Question	Options	Your answer
8	Which of these is not a quality assurance component?	a) Training b) Lessons learned c) Audit d) Resource management	
9	As the cost of prevention rises slowly, the cost of failure and prevention drop dramatically.	True or false?	
10	Who is responsible for quality on a project?	a) The project manager b) The project sponsor c) The project team d) Everyone	

? What kind of questions might there be in the exam?

1	List and describe <u>five</u> reasons why it is important to manage quality on a project. 50 marks (10 marks each)
2	This question has <u>two</u> parts. Answer both parts. Explain the term quality management. 10 marks Explain the following aspects of quality management: quality planning, quality assurance, quality control and continual improvement. 40 marks

Procurement

12

☑ **Subjects covered in this part**

12.1 Planning and managing procurement

12.1 Planning and managing procurement

By completing this subsection you will be able to:

- explain the purpose, typical content and importance of a procurement strategy;

- distinguish between different methods of supplier reimbursement (including fixed price, cost plus fee, per unit quantity, target cost);

- distinguish between different contractual relationships;

- explain a supplier selection process.

Procurement strategy

Procurement is the process by which an organisation acquires goods and services. It includes the development of a procurement strategy, preparation of contracts, selection and acquisition of suppliers and management of the contract.

Procurement is a process that is followed and most organisations will already have a significant amount of material and systems associated with it. The project will need to make sure that it has a clear interaction with the business components and this needs to be properly documented in a procurement strategy.

The procurement strategy is a project document that describes the mechanics of how the project will go about procuring and subsequently managing services and goods. The procurement strategy defines how the project procurement will take place and as such needs to be considered when the project is being formulated alongside the business case. There will be numerous procurement implications for the project manager throughout the life of the project, so the procurement strategy may also be a component of the PMP. There are a number of key sections that it should contain:

Make or buy decision – should the goods be made in-house or could we procure them elsewhere at a lower cost or better quality? To do this, we will need a well-developed understanding of the specification, because in order to derive a solid price, we will need to be specific about what it is we want.

Contractual relationship – should we buy from one supplier or many? There are many types of different contractual arrangements that we can end up with and some are mentioned here. Please note that a contract type is different from a payment term (see reimbursement methods later). The types of contractual arrangement shown in Figure 12.1 might be considered when drafting the procurement strategy:

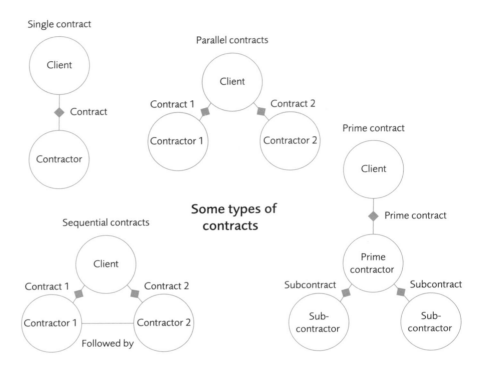

Figure 12.1 Types of contractual relationships

- Single contracts are where a single client purchases from a single supplier with a single contract between them. This is the simplest form of arrangement.

- Parallel contracts are an arrangement where there are a number of single contracts with a number of suppliers all doing the same work. We may have a number of house builders all building houses on the same site to the same design for example.

- Sequential contracts are where we have one supplier doing one element of the work (e.g. design) and another doing the next (e.g. build).

- Prime and subcontracts are where we allocate one single contract to a main supplier who then 'subcontracts' that work to others.

- Turnkey contracts (no diagram) are where a single supplier undertakes to provide everything needed to meet the requirements. It is called turnkey because the principle is that the client merely turns the key and it works.

- Partnering (no diagram) is where two or more organisations agree to work together to achieve the project. They both have separate skills and areas of expertise; in isolation they are unable to deliver the finished product, but collectively they can.

■ It should not be forgotten that there may be a raft of internal suppliers with whom the project manager will need to negotiate goods and services (for example the IT department supplying PCs to the project team). These arrangements are no more or less contracts but there will be no legal paperwork, replaced instead usually by service level agreements (SLAs).

Reimbursement methods – the project and the sponsoring organisation will need to decide on the mechanism it would prefer to use to pay for the goods procured under the contract. These are referred to as payment terms and are different from the contract type.

There are a number of factors to be taken into account when deciding which type to use. Often the decision is based on risk (Figure 12.2). If the client is unsure about exactly what is to be purchased, they would probably not be in a position to demand a fixed price from the supplier. If there are new innovative techniques involved, the client may not wish to have a fixed price and may pay the supplier to innovate, which may need a more flexible payment regime.

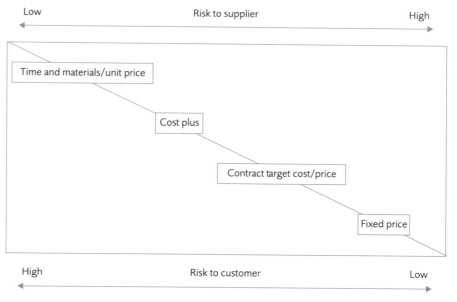

Figure 12.2 Types of supplier reimbursement terms

■ Time and materials payment or unit price is where a price is agreed for a unit of cost (e.g. an individual work day, a ton of concrete) and the client pays per unit. The problem with this approach, of course, is that if the job is estimated to take 20 days and takes 30, the client will pay for 30. Thus the risk of overrun lies with the client. These can be useful, however, when the client genuinely does not have a fixed view about the costs and the specification is vague. The project management here would often have to be a shared responsibility or rest with the client.

■ Fixed price payment is where a fixed price is agreed for a fixed scope of work to be carried out by the supplier. If the job is contracted at 20 days and it actually takes 30, the client still only pays for 20. Fixed price may be appropriate if you know exactly what is required and there is a precise requirement. Fixed price contracts tend to cost more as the supplier will normally look for some form of reimbursement for carrying the risk of overrun.

■ Cost plus payment is where the supplier gets reimbursed their cost (not price) and the client agrees to pay a certain amount over the costs to cover the supplier's profit. These arrangements can include cost plus fixed fee or cost plus percentage. Both of these will have a slightly different impact on the way the supplier is motivated because cost plus fixed fee will only allow the same fixed fee regardless of actual cost, whereas the percentage fee rises at the same percentage with the cost, thus protecting the contractor's margin.

■ Target cost/price payment is where a target price (or cost) is agreed up front and the supplier and client agree to work to try and achieve it. It has a big impact on the way the contract is managed as usually any over or under performance is shared between the parties and they agree to share it at an agreed rate. There is potentially therefore the opportunity to provide motivation on both parties to work corroboratively to maximise under spend and minimise overspend.

Supplier selection – a key consideration for the procurement strategy is how to go about engaging the right supplier. There are usually a number of steps to go through and most organisations will already have some rules and guidelines to help the project on its way. Very often these processes are used to manage a competitive tender process where a number of suppliers are asked to submit prices for a specified piece of work in a commercially competitive manner with the objective of achieving best value for the price charged. These procedures will almost certainly involve most of the following key stages:

■ Research the market, define the requirement and make sure that there is a suitable level of definition for the scope of work. Document it as part of the project documentation and record it in appropriate systems for later reference.

■ Pre-qualify suppliers and reduce the list of potential suppliers to a manageable number, check their capability, financial stability and references.

■ Issue an invitation to tender (ITT) which may follow an advertising process to determine who the likely suppliers might be. The ITT usually has a response period and should include enough information for the potential bidders to respond. It should also include the criteria on which the responses will be judged, perhaps some form of compliance matrix. ITTs are sometimes referred to as invitation to bid or request for tender.

■ Answer the queries the bidder has raised. It is normal to make sure that if one bidder asks a question then all the bidders see the answer. Sometimes a bidders' conference can be held where there is an interactive opportunity to ask questions and seek clarification.

■ Receive and evaluate bids and review against the selection criteria. The bidders may well provide a lot of 'extras' over and above the specification and these can be considered, but straightforward compliance to the ITT is the minimum.

■ Award a contract to the successful bidder(s), making sure that the scope is as per the tender, binding documents are relevant and all parties understand the nature of the arrangement and their respective liabilities. There are a number of key components of a contract depending on the nature of the industry and the demands of the work:

Offer, the client offers to buy; **Acceptance**, the supplier agrees to sell; **Consideration**, money or some other form of value changes hands; **Form**, generally contracts do not need to be in writing, but best practice dictates that they are in case they need to be referenced; **Intent**, both parties need to be intent on being bound; **Legal entity**, both parties need to be able to undertake a contract; **Capacity**, both parties must be in a position to fulfil the bargain. **Authority**, each party must be entitled to sign/commit.

■ Other areas that need to be considered are duration, termination, intellectual property rights, warranties, indemnities and guarantees. The advice generally is to seek advice from a qualified person before entering into any legally binding arrangements. Warranties need to be considered as do the terms of penalty if either side break their part of the bargain and breach the contract.

Contract administration should be carried out often throughout the contract award to make sure that both parties are conforming and discharging their duties accordingly. Any recourse to enforcement of the contract will need to be supported by evidence that both parties were engaged and trying to make the agreement work as planned.

Feedback and review, a key ingredient for any strategy, is a lessons learned and feedback process to understand what has gone well and what has not gone so well. Procurement departments are usually happy to become engaged in feedback so that processes can be improved for next time.

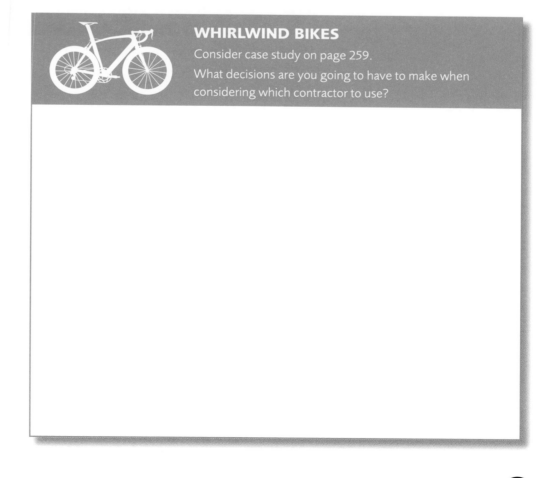

WHIRLWIND BIKES

Consider case study on page 259.

What decisions are you going to have to make when considering which contractor to use?

MANAGEMENT

Use this space to make some notes

Quick quiz (answers on page 287)

	Question	Options	Your answer
1	With fixed price payment terms, the supplier holds the risk of overrun.	True or false?	
2	Which of these is not a payment term?	a) Fixed price b) Target cost c) Unit price d) Parallel	
3	In a sequential contract, two different suppliers can each provide their own component of the project simultaneously.	True or false?	
4	Which of these is not a component reimbursement method?	a) Time and materials b) Fixed price c) Negotiated d) Cost plus	

	Question	Options	Your answer
5	A procurement strategy forms part of which document?	a) Neither b) PMP c) Business case d) Needs to be considered for both	
6	In a unit price contract, who pays for the extra work if the actual effort goes up?	a) The client b) The supplier c) Both d) Neither	
7	In writing the procurement strategy, which of these components is most important?	a) Selection of supplier b) Payment terms c) Contract type d) All of them	
8	If a contract is not performed it is called a breach.	True or false?	
9	How many parties can there be to a contract?	a) One b) Two c) Any number d) Four	
10	Who writes the project procurement strategy?	a) The project manager b) The sponsor c) The users d) The project manager in consultation with the procurement department	

MANAGEMENT

What kind of questions might there be in the exam?

1

Explain <u>five</u> components of a procurement strategy.

50 marks (10 marks each)

2

This question has <u>three</u> parts. Answer all parts.

Explain what is meant by the term 'procurement'.

10 marks

List and describe <u>two</u> contractual relationships.

20 marks (10 marks each)

List and describe <u>two</u> project reimbursement (payment) methods.

20 marks (10 marks each)

Case study

WHIRLWIND BIKES

You work for Whirlwind Bikes, a bicycle manufacturer in the north-east of England who has just been awarded a grant of €300,000 from the European Union's 'Cycling for Health Agency' (EUCHA) and who wants you to come up with a radical new design for a pedal bike.

EUCHA believe many people are put off cycling because the current designs are the same, and cycling is perceived as old-fashioned and not 'cool'. They hope to get half a million people into cycling with this new design as the focal point for a huge publicity campaign. The award was the result of Whirlwind's successful bid to the EU where they managed to convince them that Whirlwind's status as one of the leading specialist bike designers in the country meant they were ideally placed to carry out this work. Whirlwind won the business in the face of exceptionally strong competition from other EU bike manufacturers including a number of household names.

These competitors are unsurprisingly not best pleased (in fact very annoyed) about Whirlwind's appointment and are actively lobbying the EU to have the agreement cancelled. They see you as inexpert in such a high-profile politically charged activity. Also, provided the bike is a success, you will of course license the design and as such enjoy significant revenues in the future, which they would like to get.

Whirlwind is jointly owned by the original founder (James McKee), who is a real traditionalist and is firmly against new technologies, and a venture capitalist (Zak Shallow), who managed to buy into the business a few years ago when times were hard. It is Zak who is driving this piece of work.

Whirlwind is now required to come up with a radical new design for this pedal cycle, one that is light, cheap, with low rolling resistance, extremely adjustable and safe. Whirlwind identified in its submission that a carbon fibre composite would be a good option for the frame, as once in full-scale production it will be less expensive for similar specification than aluminium. They have identified a specialist contractor (Carbon Fibre Products) in America who is experienced in the field, but last time they used them they delivered poor-quality products. Alternatively, there is a specialist carbon fibre manufacturer just down the road (Carbon Concepts), but they seem expensive.

To satisfy the stringent EU bike safety tests, Whirlwind will have to demonstrate that the new design (once built) has been thoroughly tested on the roads all over Europe in varying conditions. Whirlwind have used the local bike club, The Chain Gang, before (James McKee is chairman of the club) and they are keen to get involved in the road trials. There is also another firm called Rider Rentals, who have submitted a bid to do the work using inexperienced people from mainland Europe. Both will be required to file reports on their experiences and any issues arising. Whirlwind have not worked with either of them before.

Other information

- Twenty prototypes are to be built based on a design once finished and agreed by EUCHA.

- Every individual who takes up regular cycling has been shown to save the economy €800 per annum in health costs savings, increased productivity and lower carbon emissions.

- Whirlwind normally keep their product introduction cycle to three main work streams: design, build and integrate and test.

- The main components of the bike are frame, wheels and ancillaries (such as pedals, seat, etc.).

- The bike must be usable by people between 1.4 metres and 2.10 metres in height and up to 160kg in weight.

- The bike must cover over 20,000km of road tests in varying weather and terrain conditions, without any major mechanical failures or any failure-related accidents. Once demonstrated and audited, the design will be awarded type approval for the EU and may be sold for profit in industrial quantities. The test reports will be a vital component in achieving this accreditation.

- Whirlwind have not decided yet whether to build the frame in-house or to get the US contractor to do it. If it is done in the US, the payment will be made in US dollars.

- The decision about whether to use The Chain Gang bike club or Rider Rentals for the testing has not been made. If the European organisation is used, the payment will be made in Euros.

- Exchange rates (both with the US and Europe) are subject to fluctuations.

- While Whirlwind have grant funding to cover the work, all of their design efforts will be consumed on this one job possibly at the expense of other customers (including the British Olympic Cycling Team).

- Health and Safety and insurance arrangements are a major factor in this type of contract.

- The launch of the campaign when the bike is required is now 12 periods away.

- A successful bike design will earn Whirlwind £200,000 in profits per annum if market volumes are achieved.

- You are the appointed project manager.

Whirlwind have received indicative pricing and estimates of durations from the various internal and external suppliers as follows:

Case study

WBS Number	Work Package	Time (periods)	Cost	Predecessor	Resource
1.1	Start-up and mobilisation	1	£5,000		PM
1.2.1	Design the frame	2	£60,000	1.1	Designer
1.2.2	Design the wheels	1	£10,000	1.1	Designer
1.2.3	Design the ancillaries	1	£10,000	1.1	Designer
1.3.1 (*)	Build the frame	4	£60,000	1.2.1	Carbon Fibre Products
1.3.1 (*)	Build the frame	3	£80,000	1.2.1	Carbon Concepts
1.3.2	Build the wheels	2	£20,000	1.2.2	Builder
1.3.3	Build the ancillaries	1	£20,000	1.2.3	Builder
1.4	Integrate the bike	2	£40,000	1.3.1, 1.3.2, 1.3.3	Builder
1.5 (*)	Testing	2	£20,000	1.4	Rider Rentals
1.5 (*)	Testing	1	£40,000	1.4	The Chain Gang
1.6	Launch event	1	£5,000	1.5	PM
1.7	Project management and administration	The length of the project	£48,000	1.1 (SS), 1.6 (FF)	PM
	Exchange rate info when budgeting: €1 = £1; $1 = £0.67				
	(*) Tasks are alternatives				

Exam questions

Answering questions – general approach

There are sample questions on the APM website and these are used in this exam section of the guide. You will also find questions in this guide that have been prepared to mimic the style of the 'official ones', to give you more practice before facing the real ones. Beware of learning so-called 'model answers' as these can easily constrain you and seem to drive you down a certain route. There are no model answers as such and the closest is the examiners' marking guidelines. These are not shared outside the markers' community though so you should aim for a well-rounded in-depth understanding of the majority of the subjects in this guide, rather than rote learning of standard answers to hypothetical questions.

Questions should be answered in full, in a legible form (decisions regarding legibility will be made by APM and will be final). You should start each answer on a new sheet of paper and each sheet should be clearly marked at the top with your candidate number, the number of the question you are covering and the number of the sheet. Questions that require calculations (Determine – see later) should include each formula used and show workings as well as the final answer. Please note that in all cases:

■ The candidate may answer from the perspective of the purchaser (i.e. you are the client employing a supplier), the supplier (i.e. you are working for a client), a project manager (for either the client or the supplier or as a third party acting for the client managing the supplier on their behalf), or any other legitimate stakeholder.

■ The most important point about any exam is fairly obvious – make sure you read the question and answer it. If it is asking for benefits of something, give benefits; if the question asks you to describe a process then describe it. A lot of failures seem to stem from a poor relationship between the answer and the question as asked.

■ Diagrams are typically not required (unless specified) and therefore do not attract extra marks. There may be information contained in them that may attract marks if it incidentally relates to a part of the question. Some people use a diagram to trigger recall and drawing them will not detract from your marks, just be aware that it may not add to your score either.

■ Where a number of items such as steps in a process are sought these can appear in any order.

■ If a specific number of points are requested then any further points will be ignored even if they are correct and earlier ones that have been marked are incorrect.

■ Anything you write on the question paper will not be marked.

■ Although examples are not explicitly requested in the question, they are accepted as relevant means of demonstrating understanding of the answer. You can use examples from public, professional or media so long as they help substantiate the answer.

■ Start each question (or part) on a new page. You will feel like you are wasting paper with only a couple of sentences at the top of some of the pages, but it means you can go back and change things without making your paper look a mess.

- The easier it is to mark, the better. You do not get more marks for neat handwriting, but if the marker cannot read it at all they are going to have difficulty marking it.

- If you are answering any 'Determine' question, make sure you show your workings, there may be marks awarded if the end result is wrong, but some of the logic and rationale made sense. It may not turn a fail into a pass, but all the marks go into the total.

- Leave a big gap between bullet points so you can annotate and add things as you go. You can go back (remember to try and keep 15 minutes at the end to review what you have written). This way your answer is not all crammed into a limited space and you will have no trouble adding anything else or making it clearer later.

- Ensure any graphs and diagrams are clear, with a title and scales clearly identified and explained. Again, please note that while delegates are free to write as they wish on the examination question sheet only the answer sheets will be marked.

- If you do use acronyms, write what they stand for out in full at first use, so that the meaning is clear to the examiner.

- Answers can be written in longhand but it is not essential to do this and each of the constituent sentences can in themselves be a bullet point. Bullet points are perfectly acceptable, but care is needed to ensure that the examiner is clear which question (or part) is being answered and the answer does not become too brief. Bullet point answers still need to satisfy the criteria set out below. You will NOT score 10 marks for just a few written words.

- If you have not sat a three-hour paper recently, one of your major issues is going to be simply writing for that period of time. The only answer, regrettably, is practice. When you have a go at the sample questions in this guide, do not simply skip through, thinking to yourself what you might write. Get organised, sit down in private and actually answer the question by writing a longhand answer.

Marking schemes and pass marks

There will be no marking schemes identified to you on the question papers in the exam, but the apportionment of marks between sections will be provided along with some other guidance. Please see the sample paper at the back of this guide. The total marks in the exam are 500 (10 questions worth 50 marks per question). The pass mark for the exam is 55 per cent. You will need therefore to obtain 275 marks overall. It is worth remembering that even if you only score a few marks on an individual question it will still go into the total pot of marks awarded and contribute to you passing.

Time management

Given the need to answer 10 questions in 180 minutes (three hours), you will need a strategy. Try this:

- When told to do so, open the paper and skip through all of the questions, ticking (on the question paper) those you think you can do.

- For those ticked, you may want to put a scale against each to indicate how comfortable you are with your ability to answer the question ('A' might mean you know the subject inside out while 'C' might mean you should pick another). Category 'B's' are those that you are less confident with. They are the ones where you can pick up those marks that will transform your script from a fail to a pass. You should aim for at least five category 'A's' from all the 12 learning outcomes. You will not really get away with having more than three or four 'C's' especially from the larger assessment criteria sections.

■ Once you have all the questions prioritised in this way, take a piece of the exam script paper and write down the questions you want to answer in order. Leave at least five lines between each. You will now have a list of questions in order. Alternatively use the exam question paper itself.

■ For each question, read the wording carefully and write down the key distinct points that you think will fully answer the question as asked; if you are unable to, it means you may not be as good at that topic as you thought.

■ Build confidence by tackling your 'A's' first.

These steps may well take you 15 minutes of your 180. Don't panic! You do not want to get halfway through a question only to find your points are merging together, you don't really know any features/benefits/advantages of the topic in question, or you have simply dried up.

Planning is crucial to success. You will be left with about 15 minutes to answer each question.

It's not possible to suggest how many pages you should write for each question, as it depends on many variable factors, and in any event the examiners are more interested in the quality of what you write and its accuracy in answering the question. Ultimately it's not about how much you write, but how well you answered the question posed.

Some questions will have split marks (e.g. 20 marks for part (a) and 30 for part (b)). These work the same as above with marks apportioned as necessary. It is not a numbers game but you will need to have a plan to answer the questions fully and within the time you have.

Make sure you are properly prepared

In the run up to the exam, you might be nervous and stressed; it is easy to say but try not to let this get in the way:

■ Avoid alcohol.

■ Get a good night's sleep.

■ Arrive early, select a decent seat near the window, out of the sun and not right under the air conditioning unit (noisy and cold).

■ Read the exam guidance from APM and make sure you have everything you need (coloured pens, writing pens, ruler, calculator and photo ID).

■ Avoid last-minute panic by arriving in plenty of time.

■ There are concessions for previously advised medical conditions – check the latest guidance notes.

MANAGEMENT

Revision tips

■ Make sure you have read the quick quizzes at the end of each section in this guide to be sure you know the basics (e.g. the difference between success criteria, critical success factors and key performance indicators).

■ If you are not very good at remembering equations, try writing them on an index card, turning it over and writing them again. Check if you got them right. Keep doing this and hopefully, eventually it will stick. Just before the exam do it a few times, and when you get into the exam, before writing any plans or answers, write them again on a blank sheet of script paper. You have practised and your memory will be fresh. Remember – you cannot take any study guide materials into the exam room.

■ Try and set yourself a reasonable revision plan – little and often, set a time frame for revising and stick to it.

■ Try not to just keep revising the things you already know, try learning the things you don't know. Avoid the comfort of familiar territory. Push yourself to explore new areas that you may have considered too obscure or difficult. Some of the less popular subject areas can in fact be relatively straightforward with the right approach.

■ If one assessment criteria is completely inaccessible to you, at a pinch you could leave it out of your revision schedule. Avoid leaving too many out though, there are 73 assessment criteria and you answer 10 from 16 questions. You might end up with a paper full of questions you have consigned to the 'too hard box' and spend three hours twiddling your thumbs.

■ Go onto the web and look up a phrase or a topic, or look at the *APM Body of Knowledge 6th edition* and recommended texts. They may give you an alternative view of something that helps you describe it a bit better. Make sure you use reputable sites.

Sample questions

Question 1

Learning outcomes	Understand project life cycles
Warning	This question has <u>two</u> parts. Answer both parts.
Question part (a)	Explain the importance of project reviews.
	10 marks
Question part (b)	List and describe <u>four</u> different types of review that may be carried out during a project, and their main purposes.
	40 marks (10 marks each)

Question 2

Learning outcomes	Understand project scope management
Question	List and describe <u>five</u> key activities typically performed as part of an effective configuration management process.
	50 marks (10 marks each)

Question 3

Learning outcomes	Understand planning for success
Warning	This question has <u>two</u> parts. Answer both parts.
Question part (a)	Within the context of earned value management (EVM), explain the term earned value (EV).
	10 marks
Question part (b)	Explain <u>four</u> benefits of using earned value management.
	40 marks (10 marks each)

Question 4

Learning outcomes	Understand project procurement
Question	List and describe <u>five</u> typical stages in the process for selection of a supplier via competitive tender.
	50 marks (10 marks each)

Question 5

Learning outcomes	Understand schedule and resource management
Warning	This question has <u>two</u> parts. Answer both parts.
Question part (a)	Explain the following approaches to resource scheduling:
	• Resource smoothing
	• Resource levelling
	Ensure that your answer distinguishes between the two approaches.
	20 marks (10 marks each)
Warning	Do not repeat resource smoothing and resource levelling cited in part (a)
Question part (b)	Explain <u>three</u> approaches/responses which a project manager might consider when optimising the resource allocation for a project. Identify in your answer any assumptions and implications made.
	30 marks (10 marks each)

Question 6

Learning outcomes	Understand how organisations and projects are structured
Warning	This question has <u>two</u> parts. Answer both parts.
Question part (a)	List and describe <u>three</u> advantages of a matrix organisation structure when used in a project environment.
	30 marks (10 marks each)

Question part (b)	List and describe <u>two</u> disadvantages of a matrix organisation structure when used in a project environment.
	20 marks (10 marks each)

Question 7

Learning outcomes	Understand the principles of leadership and teamwork
Warning	This question has <u>two</u> parts. Answer both parts.
Question part (a)	Explain what is meant by situational leadership in a project environment.
	10 marks
Question part (b)	List and describe <u>four</u> benefits of adapting leadership styles during a project.
	Ensure you include at least <u>one</u> beneficiary in each description.
	40 marks (10 marks each)

Question 8

Learning outcomes	Understand contexts and environments in which projects can be delivered
Question	List and describe <u>five</u> important environmental legislative requirements which the project manager must take into account when planning a project.
	50 marks (10 marks each)

Question 9

Learning outcomes	Understand planning for success
Warning	This question is in <u>two</u> parts. Answer both parts.
Question part (a)	Explain the prerequisites required for each of the following <u>three</u> estimating methods:
	• Comparative
	• Bottom-up/analytical
	• Parametric
	30 marks (10 marks each)
Question part (b)	State <u>four</u> practical problems of initial estimates for a project with a long timescale.
	20 marks (5 marks each)

Question 10

Learning outcomes	Understand governance of project management and the use of structured methodologies
Question	List and describe <u>five</u> typical contents (e.g. processes, components, techniques) of a structured project management method.
	50 marks (10 marks each)

Question 11

Learning outcomes	Understand how organisations and projects are structured
Question	List and describe <u>five</u> activities which the project sponsor performs during the project life cycle.
	50 marks (10 marks each)

Question 12

Learning outcomes	Understand communication within project management
Question	List and describe a source of conflict arising within each of the following parts of the extended project life cycle:

- Concept
- Definition
- Development
- Handover and closure
- Benefits realisation

50 marks (10 marks each)

Question 13

Learning outcomes	Understand project quality management
Warning	This question has <u>two</u> parts. Answer both parts.
Question part (a)	Explain the difference between continual improvement and project quality planning.
	10 marks
Question part (b)	List and describe <u>four</u> aspects of project quality assurance.
	40 marks (10 marks each)

Question 14

Learning outcomes	Understand project scope management
Warning	This question is in <u>two</u> parts. Answer both parts.

MANAGEMENT

Question part (a)	Explain <u>two</u> reasons why the scope of a project may need to be changed.
	20 marks (10 marks each)
Question part (b)	Explain <u>three</u> ways that change control can reduce and manage scope creep on a project.
	30 marks (10 marks each)

Question 15

Learning outcomes	Understand risk management and issue management
Question	List and describe <u>five</u> benefits to an organisation of adopting a formal risk management process.
	50 marks (10 marks each)

Question 16

Learning outcomes	Understand the principles of leadership and teamwork
Warning	This question has <u>two</u> parts. Answer both parts.
Question part (a)	Explain the concept of teamwork.
	10 marks
	This question requires <u>four</u> explanations.
Question part (b)	From the following team or social roles listed, explain <u>four</u> of these, including how they contribute to an effective team.

- Opponent/Challenger/Antagonist
- Creator/Innovator/Plant
- Team Builder/Worker
- Completer/Finisher
- Collaborator
- Controller/Inspector/Implementer

40 marks (10 marks each)

Multiple choice answers

| 1.1 | Projects and business-as-usual | page 4 |

Question	Answer and rationale
1	c) Essential, if the relationship between the two is not taken into account then the business may not be properly prepared for the implementation of the products.
2	True, all projects require a business case.
3	False, projects are unique, there may be similarities with other projects but they will never be the same.
4	True, projects have a distinct time frame.
5	False, projects are there to make a difference.
6	True, business operations are generally repetitive and continuous. A project is unique and limited to a fixed timescale.
7	a) The time it takes, success criteria are those things that are being sought and will be those things that the final result will be measured against.
8	b) The others are example of operations (or business-as-usual).
9	True, risk management is arguably at the root of all project management practices.
10	True, the business case justifies the spending on a project.

| 1.2 | Projects, programmes and portfolios | page 14 |

Question	Answer and rationale
1	False, programme managers have a much bigger role than that, they need to be strategic in their approach and heavily focused on the business and the delivery of benefits.
2	False, programmes extend beyond the bounds of single projects, they may have multiple projects across a broad range of disciplines with multiple customers.

MANAGEMENT

Question	Answer and rationale
3	b) Crucial to the effectiveness of the delivered product.
4	False, most programmes are multi-year and will have altering customers, stakeholders, focus and scope. The last projects in a programme may not be well understood at the start.
5	True, portfolio management is very often linked with the implementation of the corporate governance principles.
6	True, these are all very relevant to programmes.
7	False, they are continual and will extend throughout the life of the need for them within the organisation.
8	False, portfolio management is to do with choosing the appropriate mix of projects and programmes, programmes are vehicles to deliver benefit through multiple projects.
9	True, these are all within the remit of the portfolio manager.
10	a) The other two are limited in scope and not strategic.

1.3 The project environment page 20

Question	Answer and rationale
1	False, the context considers both internal and external factors.
2	True
3	True, but not to be confused with the environmental aspects of projects (recycling, energy use, etc.).
4	b) Sociological, the human factor.
5	True, only by exploring the wider aspects of the project can the project team be fully appraised of the potential risks.

1.4 | The legislative aspects of project management | page 27

Question	Answer and rationale
1	True, the employer as part of their 'duty of care' is required to make sure that all personal protective equipment is suitable and available.
2	True, the Health and Safety Executive set policy.
3	d) All of these can cause stress
4	c) Near misses
5	a) ISO 14001
6	a) Intellectual property rights
7	True
8	c) Whistle-blowing
9	True, not just construction, all projects are governed by the acts.
10	True, they cannot just be imposed.

2.1 | Organisation structures | page 34

Question	Answer and rationale
1	True, it has that characteristic as staff are employed within a given area or department and that will be their professional development home.
2	True, while a matrix organisation does retain skills a purely functional organisation has the most focus on vertical (silo) management structures.
3	False, a project organisation will form, utilise skills from outside and generally disband losing the skills and knowledge built up.
4	a) Staff will tend to follow the direction of their line manager.
5	d) Excessive paperwork does not have a home anywhere.
6	a) The functional heads as they are the only ones with a remit across the business.
7	False, as more projects are contemplated and run the functional head's role diminishes in authority over the project activities.

MANAGEMENT

Question	Answer and rationale
8	True, all resources across the business are visible and potentially able to be deployed across the projects thus avoiding under-utilisation.
9	True, the teams are focused on the delivery of the project.
10	True, they work across multiple lines of business.

2.2   Organisational roles   page 41

Question	Answer and rationale
1	Maybe, there is no particular rule either way.
2	b) Contract, the project manager would normally be able to steer and guide the suppliers in this way.
3	b) The sponsor owns the business case but it will be approved by the project board/steering group.
4	a) The project manager owns the PMP but the sponsor will generally approve it.
5	d) The users generally do not deliver the work itself as they are in effect the customers.
6	a) Yes and the steering group will support them in the execution of their duties.
7	a) One
8	b) The governance framework for the organisation would normally indicate how sponsors are appointed, although in practice they may well be nominated from within a steering group and this decision ratified by the organisation.
9	a) The sponsor, they approve the business case and must therefore approve changes that may affect it.
10	True

2.3	Project office	page 46

Question	Answer and rationale
1	False, it can be a 'virtual' function spread across different departments in a business.
2	False, a project office manager may have many projects to look after and may not therefore report directly to multiple project managers.
3	b) The project office is an administrative function not directly involved in the activities of the teams in their delivery activities.
4	a) If the project office team report to the sponsor or the steering group they will not be able to deputise for the project manager as this will bring them into an area of conflicting interests.
5	b) Enterprise project management office
6	True
7	False, they take direction from the project manager.
8	True
9	True, they are a cost that needs to be accommodated within the estimates for the project.
10	b) Any number.

3.1	Project life cycles	page 57

Question	Answer and rationale
1	False, each industry, discipline or company may have a range of life cycles appropriate for the job in hand.
2	True, the inclusion of operations and termination allow these considerations.
3	True, there is not a 'one size fits all' mentality. Building software would be very different in nature to building a power station.
4	a) During operations the beneficial aspects of the products will become known.
5	False, they are external to the project.

Question	Answer and rationale
6	a) The operations phase.
7	True, it is too late to wait until the end to record and communicate lessons learned.
8	False, it is usually for the organisation to avoid bad news being covered up.
9	True
10	False, this is a conceptual model and can be adapted to suit local needs.

4.2 Methods and procedures   page 69

Question	Answer and rationale
1	c) Methods can only ever help to guarantee success.
2	False, a method may contain a life cycle.
3	True, an organisation will usually describe a method to be used by its projects.
4	d) Methods should not be seen as simply more paperwork.
5	False, the method really needs to be consistent across the piece. If a number of methods need to be merged to form a hybrid method that everyone then follows this will be fine.

5.1 The communication plan   page 75

Question	Answer and rationale
1	b) The project manager owns the communications plan as it is a component of the project management plan.
2	True, the communications plan contains the things that the project manager must do to ensure communications are properly managed.
3	False, the project manager should try and become part of the project's informal networks.
4	a) The communications plan will be developed from the very start of the project and will evolve to final sign-off within the PMP.

Question	Answer and rationale
5	b) There has to be a feedback mechanism to ensure that communications have been effective.
6	d) Risk management is not usually considered a barrier to communications.
7	a) Hand gestures are a type of body language.
8	c) Information management overlaps with communications management.
9	True
10	True

5.2 Conflict and negotiation — page 82

Question	Answer and rationale
1	c) Bargaining is not considered to be part of a negotiation process, however, it may be something done within the steps of a process.
2	True, this is a common step when negotiating. You can seek approval from someone who has not been part of the negotiation thus maintaining a good working relationship.
3	True, a project manager negotiates all the time, it is not limited to formal meetings and quite often involves one-to-one discussion.
4	True
5	c) Accommodating

6.1 Leadership — page 91

Question	Answer and rationale
1	b) Advancement, this is the only true 'motivator' according to Maslow.
2	False, these are the steps in Situational Leadership from Hersey and Blanchard.
3	c) Salary is not (according to Maslow) a motivator but a hygiene factor.
4	False, clearly the project manager must play a huge part in motivating their team.

MANAGEMENT

Question	Answer and rationale
5	d) Sickness, poor quality of work and absenteeism are all potential problems if motivation is not dealt with properly.

6.2	Teams and teamwork	page 97

Question	Answer and rationale
1	True, the others are Storming, Norming, Performing.
2	d) Operator
3	True, changes or too much negative conflict can cause a team to regress backwards around the Tuckman model.
4	d) Norming
5	c) Hopefulness, the others are potential problems while the team is storming.
6	d) 9–Plant, Completer Finisher, Shaper, Teamworker, Implementer, Resource Investigator, Co-ordinator, Monitor Evaluator, Specialist.
7	b) Completer finisher
8	True
9	False, this would be a performing team in the Tuckman model.
10	True.

7.1	Defining and managing project scope	page 107

Question	Answer and rationale
1	a) Organisational breakdown structure.
2	d) Work breakdown structure.
3	True, normally the naming convention will use a numbering structure to achieve this.
4	a) Which sites are included. This would steer the work involved whereas the other options are to do with who, when, etc.
5	True, they may not undertake the detailed work but they will certainly need to make sure the activity is completed.

Question	Answer and rationale
6	b) The task and the person involved in it.
7	True, although it may also appear in the business case.
8	True
9	a) Work package
10	True

7.2 Requirements and configuration management   page 116

Question	Answer and rationale
1	False, requirements are the things to be achieved, benefits are the value placed on those outcomes.
2	True, it is a subsidiary plan in the PMP.
3	b) The governance framework would normally have guidance to accommodate the collection of requirements.
4	c) Products will be checked as to their suitability throughout the project.
5	a) Work breakdown structures, the others are part of the PICSA components of configuration management.
6	d) The users specify the requirements of the products in the first place so they will therefore need to specify any changes to them.
7	d) Procurement specialists
8	c) Reiterate
9	True
10	a) WBS number, it may include the PBS number as it is concerned with products rather than work.

| 7.3 | **Change control** | **page 125** |

Question	Answer and rationale
1	c) Initial investigation and update plans.
2	True, they may be requested by the users but it is the sponsor who will determine whether they should be implemented or not.
3	False, although in most cases they may have tolerance within which to work and act on behalf of the sponsor.
4	a) Morale, all the others are components that need to be considered.
5	d) Although there will come a point where it becomes unacceptable.
6	c) Absorption
7	d) Generally the WBS number is not appropriate as these relate to the work packages rather than changes.
8	d) The probability would normally be something to do with risk management.
9	True
10	True, they would be able to contribute invaluable information about other products that might be affected or what steps the process requires to be followed.

| 8.1 | **Business case** | **page 132** |

Question	Answer and rationale
1	d) The project sponsor
2	True, the basic reason for doing a project is that you get more back than it costs.
3	True
4	a) The benefits are realised during the operations phase.
5	True, they may add significant new ideas and proposals.

| 8.2 | Benefits management | page 137 |

Question	Answer and rationale
1	a) Identify and agree
2	True, only in this way can the value of them be recognised in relation to the costs.
3	True
4	True
5	False, it rarely is one monolithic document. It usually consists of a number of supporting and associated materials.

| 8.3 | Investment appraisal | page 142 |

Question	Answer and rationale
1	d) It is usually based on current figures without adjusting for how the value of money might vary moving forward.
2	True, it can be a bit daunting to understand.
3	True, it is easy to understand.
4	d) The accountants are much better able to help in this area.
5	False, the organisation must consider the risk of a project and not just the return.

| 8.4 | Information management | page 149 |

Question	Answer and rationale
1	d) Change control
2	False, there are requirements to make sure that personal information is not kept unless essential.
3	False, some small projects get by with paper-based systems although their ability to transfer data will be limited.

Question	Answer and rationale
4	a) The project manager writes all the subsidiary plans.
5	False, even the smallest projects need to consider it especially if they are dealing with public money or personal data.

8.5 Project management plan — page 156

Question	Answer and rationale
1	b) The project manager
2	a) The business case is usually considered to be a separate document with a different purpose to the PMP. The business case describes the 'WHY'.
3	a) The project sponsor as it is they who sign it off in the first place.
4	True, although you would have to check to make sure it is still appropriate.
5	c) Just about anyone ought to have sight of the plan if they are involved in the project.

8.6 Estimating — page 162

Question	Answer and rationale
1	True
2	b) At the beginning when high-level estimates are most useful.
3	c) WBS, each of the work packages is added up to derive the overall estimate.
4	d) As many views as possible are helpful to get as accurate a picture as possible.
5	a) The business case holds the initial figures and estimates.
6	d) PERT is an analysis of three estimates.
7	True $(1 \times O) + (4 \times M) + (1 \times P)$ all divided by 6.
8	True, as more information is known so this becomes easier.

8.7 | Stakeholder management | page 167

Question	Answer and rationale
1	a) Power and influence
2	d) Negotiate
3	d) Everyone with an interest in the project is a stakeholder.
4	True, everyone will assess things in their own way.
5	c) It will certainly help, as being able to relate to and manage the stakeholder community is vital to project success.

9.1 | Scheduling | page 182

Question	Answer and rationale
1	b) Time periods
2	c) Early finish
3	True
4	True
5	c) Nothing
6	True
7	a) Duration
8	True (either to you from the client or by you to contractors).
9	True
10	a) Total float

9.2	Resource management	page 195

Question	Answer and rationale
1	c) Resource levelling which may extend the end date and resource smoothing (which will not).
2	True
3	False
4	True, it inevitably will take a number of iterations and the plan must be reviewed all the time to accommodate changing circumstances.
5	d) Gantt chart
6	c) Replenishable
7	a) Mobilisation and demobilisation
8	d) Time can never be recovered
9	b) Availability, the first pass of a resourcing model will assume unlimited resources.
10	True

9.3	Budgeting and cost control	page 207

Question	Answer and rationale
1	True
2	c) Actual costs, these are only known when the work has been done.
3	a) Reduce the time that we are in a deficit situation.
4	c) An accrual is intended to reflect the actual point at which the costs were attributable.
5	True
6	True, it becomes the PC curve on the graph.
7	c) Commitments, the things that have been ordered and cannot be avoided.
8	b) The project manager

Question	Answer and rationale
9	False, they are the backbone baseline for the project and must be calculated with care.
10	True

9.4 | Earned value | page 223

Question	Answer and rationale
1	False
2	False
3	c) It provides a forecast of out-turn, it contributes to cost control but it does not in itself help us to control historical costs.
4	c) AC – actual costs
5	d) Budget at completion
6	True
7	c) Earned value allows the calculation of a forecast based on the current situation.
8	a) Good, we are producing products and spending less doing it than we expected.
9	True
10	True

10.1 | Risk management | page 235

Question	Answer and rationale
1	d) Probability and impact
2	c) Share is a response to an opportunity.
3	b) 0.02 – you multiply them together.
4	c) Quantitative, risk assessment is either this or qualitative.

Question	Answer and rationale
5	True, it is a subsidiary plan in the PMP.
6	True
7	False, most people are influenced by their own expertise on a particular subject.
8	False, they need to be continually monitored.
9	d) Guesswork
10	c) They manage them and are responsible for them being carried out.

10.2 Issue management   page 240

Question	Answer and rationale
1	True
2	b) The sponsor
3	d) Probability – this is more to do with risk management.
4	True
5	True, this is a subsidiary plan in the PMP.

11.1 Quality planning, assurance and control   page 249

Question	Answer and rationale
1	d) Fitness for purpose – does it conform to the specification?
2	True, they define the acceptability standards for the products produced.
3	d) Finishing
4	c) A pareto diagram – 80 per cent of the faults are caused by 20 per cent of the errors.
5	True
6	True
7	b) Configuration management
8	d) Resource management

Question	Answer and rationale
9	True, this is referred to as 'the cost of quality'.
10	d) Everyone, although the project manager will have overall accountability for quality.

12.1	Planning and managing procurement	Page 256

Question	Answer and rationale
1	True
2	d) Parallel – it is a contract type.
3	False – they follow each other's delivery.
4	c) The project management plan is not a part of the contract although it may be required to be produced under the terms of the contract.
5	d) Both
6	a) The client bears the risk and pays more if the effort goes up.
7	d) All of them are important to pin down.
8	True
9	c) Technically there is no limit to the number of parties in a contract.
10	c) Negotiated

References

Association for Project Management, 2012, *APM Body of Knowledge 6th edition*. Princes Risborough: Association for Project Management.

Association for Project Management, 2004, *Project Risk Analysis and Management (PRAM) Guide*, 2nd edition. Princes Risborough: Association for Project Management.

APM Earned Value Specific Interest Group, 2008, *Earned Value Management: APM Guidelines*, 2nd edition. Princes Risborough: Association for Project Management.

APM Governance of Project Management Specific Interest Group, 2011, *Directing Change: A guide to governance of project management*, 2nd edition. Princes Risborough: Association for Project Management.

Belbin, R.M., 2010, *Team Roles at Work*, 2nd edition. London: Butterworth Heinemann.

Crosby, P.B., 1979, *Quality is Free*. New York: McGraw-Hill.

Fazar, W., 1959, *Program Evaluation and Review Technique*. The American Statistician, 13(2).

Hersey, P.H. and Blanchard, K.H., 1977, *Management of Organizational Behavior: Utilizing human resources*, 3rd edition. New Jersey: Prentice Hall.

Herzberg, F., Mausner, B. and Snyderman B.B., 1959, *The Motivation to Work*, 2nd edition. New York: John Wiley.

International Institute of Business Analysis, 2009, *A Guide to the Business Analysis Body of Knowledge*. Toronto: International Institute of Business Analysis.

Kilmann R.H. and Thomas, K.W., 1977, *Developing a Forced-Choice Measure of Conflict-Handling Behavior: The 'MODE' Instrument*. Educational and Psychological Measurement, 37: 309–25.

Maslow, A.H., 1943, *A Theory of Human Motivation*. Psychological Review, 50(4): 370–96.

Maslow, A.H., 1987, *Motivation and Personality*, 3rd edition. Upper Saddle River, New Jersey: Pearson Education, Inc.

Thomas, K.W., 1992, "Conflict and Negotiation Processes in Organizations", in M.D. Dunnette and L.M. Hough (eds), *Handbook of Industrial and Organizational Psychology*, 2nd edition, Vol 3 (pp. 652–717). Palo Alto, California: Consulting Psychologists Press.

Tuckman, B., 1965, *Developmental Sequence in Small Groups*. Psychological Bulletin, 63(6): 384–99.

Further reading

British Standards Institution, 2010, *BS 6079-1: 2010 A Guide to Project Management*. London: BSI [online] Available at apm.org.uk/BoK6FurtherReading.

Office of Government Commerce, 2009, *Directing Successful Projects with PRINCE2®, 2009*. London: The Stationery Office.

Glossary

Accept
A response to a threat where no course of action is taken.

Acceptance criteria
The requirements and essential conditions that have to be achieved before a deliverable is accepted.

Accounting
The process of collecting and communicating financial information to meet legal requirements, business management requirements, plus internal and external stakeholders' needs.

Activity
1. A task, job, operation or process consuming time and possibly other resources.

2. The smallest self-contained unit of work in a project.

Activity duration
The length of time that it takes to complete an activity.

Activity-on-node network
A network diagram where the activities are represented by the nodes.

Actual expenditure
The costs that have been charged to the budget and for which payment has been made, or accrued.

Actual progress
A measure of the work that has been completed for comparison with the baseline.

Agile
A family of development methodologies where requirements and solutions are developed iteratively and incrementally throughout the life cycle.

Analogous estimating
See comparative estimating.

Analytical estimating
See bottom-up estimating.

Avoid
A response to a threat that eliminates its probability or impact on the project.

Balance
A phase in the portfolio life cycle where the component projects and programmes are balanced in terms of risk, resource usage, cash flow and impact across the business.

Baseline
The reference levels against which a project, programme or portfolio is monitored and controlled.

MANAGEMENT

Benefit
The quantifiable and measurable improvement resulting from completion of deliverables that is perceived as positive by a stakeholder. It will normally have a tangible value, expressed in monetary terms that will justify the investment.

Benefits management
The identification, definition, planning, tracking and realisation of business benefits.

Benefits realisation
The practice of ensuring that benefits are derived from outputs and outcomes.

Blueprint
A document defining and describing what a programme is designed to achieve in terms of the business and operational vision.

Board
A body that provides sponsorship to a project, programme or portfolio. The board will represent financial, provider and user interests.

Bottom-up estimating
An estimating technique that uses detailed specifications to estimate time and cost for each product or activity.

Breakdown structure
A hierarchical structure by which project elements are broken down, or decomposed. Examples include: cost breakdown structure (CBS), organisational breakdown structure (OBS), product breakdown structure (PBS), and work breakdown structure (WBS).

Brief
The output of the concept phase of a project or programme.

Budgeting and cost control
The estimation of costs, the setting of an agreed budget, and management of actual and forecast costs against that budget.

Buffer
A term used in a critical chain for the centralised management of contingencies.

Business case
Provides justification for undertaking a project or programme. It evaluates the benefit, cost and risk of alternative options and provides a rationale for the preferred solution.

Business change manager
The role responsible for benefits management from identification through to realisation.

Business risk assessment
The assessment of risk to business objectives rather than risk to achieving project, programme or portfolio objectives.

Business-as-usual
An organisation's normal day-to-day operations.

Categorise

A phase in the portfolio life cycle where the component projects and programmes may be grouped according to shared characteristics.

Change control

The process through which all requests to change the baseline scope of a project, programme or portfolio are captured, evaluated and then approved, rejected or deferred.

Change freeze

A point after which no further changes to scope will be considered.

Change management

Change management is a structured approach to moving an organisation from the current state to the desired future state.

Change register

A record of all proposed changes to scope.

Change request

A request to obtain formal approval for changes to the scope of work.

Closure

The formal end point of a project or programme, either because it has been completed or because it has been terminated early.

Collaborative negotiation

Negotiation that seeks to create a 'win–win' scenario where all parties involved get part or all of what they were looking for from the negotiation.

Committed expenditure

Costs that have not yet been paid but cannot be cancelled.

Communication

The means by which information or instructions are exchanged. Successful communication occurs when the received meaning is the same as the transmitted meaning.

Communities of practice

Groups of people who share a concern or passion for an aspect of P3 management and develop expertise through regular interaction.

Comparative estimating

An estimating technique based on the comparison with, and factoring from, the cost of similar, previous work.

Competence

The combined knowledge, skill and behaviour that a person needs to perform properly in a job or work role.

Competence framework

A set of competences and competencies that may be used to define a role.

MANAGEMENT

Competency

A personal attribute of an individual.

Complexity

Complexity relates to the degree of interaction of all the elements that comprise P3 management and is dependent on such factors as the level of risk, range of stakeholders and degree of innovation.

Concept

Concept is the first phase in the project or programme life cycle. During this phase the need, opportunity or problem is confirmed, the overall feasibility of the work is considered and a preferred solution identified.

Configuration

Functional and physical characteristics of a product as defined in its specification.

Configuration management

Configuration management encompasses the administrative activities concerned with the creation, maintenance, controlled change and quality control of the scope of work.

Conflict management

The process of identifying and addressing differences that, if left unresolved, could affect objectives.

Consumable resource

A type or resource that only remains available until consumed (for example a material).

Context

A collective term for the governance and setting of a project, programme or portfolio.

Contingency

Resources set aside for responding to identified risks.

Contract

An agreement made between two or more parties that creates legally binding obligations between them. The contract sets out those obligations and the actions that can be taken if they are not met.

Control

Tracking performance against agreed plans and taking the corrective action required to meet defined objectives.

Critical chain

A networking technique that identifies paths through a project based on resource dependencies, as well as technical dependencies.

Critical path analysis

The procedure for calculating the critical path and floats in a network diagram.

Critical path

A sequence of activities through a network diagram from start to finish, the sum of whose durations determines the overall duration. There may be more than one such path.

Criticality

Used in Monte Carlo analysis, the criticality index represents the percentage of calculations that resulted in the activity being placed on the critical path.

Cybernetic control

The form of control that deals with routine progress tracking and corrective action using a feedback loop.

Define

The phase of a portfolio life cycle where the projects, programmes and change to business-as-usual required to meet strategic objectives are identified and evaluated.

Defined

The third level of a typical maturity model where processes are documented and standardised.

Definition

The second phase of a project or programme life cycle where requirements are refined, the preferred solution is identified and ways of achieving it are identified.

Delegation

The practice of giving a person or group the authority to perform the responsibilities of, or act on behalf of, another.

Deliverable

A product, set of products or package of work that will be delivered to, and formally accepted by, a stakeholder.

Demobilisation

The controlled dispersal of personnel and disposal of assets when they are no longer needed on a project, programme or portfolio.

Dependency

A relationship between activities in a network diagram.

Disbenefit

A consequence of change perceived as negative by one or more stakeholders.

Do nothing option

The result or consequence of not proceeding with the project or programme. Usually explained in the business case.

Drawdown

The removal of funds from an agreed source resulting in a reduction of available funds.

Earned value

The value of completed work expressed in terms of the budget assigned to that work. A measure of progress which may be expressed in cost or labour hours.

Earned value management

A project control process, based on a structured approach to planning, cost collection and performance measurement. It facilitates the integration of project scope, time and cost objectives and the establishment of a baseline plan of performance measurement.

Enhance

A response to an opportunity that increases its probability, impact or both.

Enterprise project management office

An organisation that is responsible for the governance infrastructure of P3 management.

Environment

The circumstances and conditions within which the project, programme or portfolio must operate.

Escalation

The process by which issues are drawn to the attention of a higher level of management.

Estimate

An approximation of time and cost targets, refined throughout the life cycle.

Estimating

The use of a range of tools and techniques to produce estimates.

Estimating funnel

A representation of the increasing levels of estimating accuracy that can be achieved through the phases of the life cycle.

Ethics frameworks

Sets recognised standards of conduct and behaviour within the P3 profession.

Event-driven

Control actions or reports that are triggered by a specific event are referred to as 'event-driven'.

Exploit

A response to an opportunity that maximises both its probability and impact.

Extended life cycle

A life cycle model that includes the operation of outputs and realisation of benefits.

Financial management

The process of estimating and justifying costs in order to secure funds, controlling expenditure and evaluating the outcomes.

Finish-to-finish

A dependency in an activity-on-node network. It indicates that one activity cannot finish until another activity has finished.

Finish-to-start

A dependency in an activity-on-node network. It indicates that one activity cannot start until another activity has finished.

Float

A term used to describe the flexibility with which an activity may be rescheduled. There are various types of float, such as total float and free float.

Forecast expenditure
The estimated and predicted use of money.

Funding
The means by which the capital required to undertake a project, programme or portfolio is secured and then made available as required.

Gantt chart
A graphical representation of activity against time. Variations may include information such as 'actual vs. planned', resource usage and dependencies.

Gate
The point between phases, gates and/or tranches where a go/no-go decision can be made about the remainder of the work.

Go/No-go
A form of control where a decision is made whether or not to continue with the work.

Governance
The set of policies, regulations, functions, processes, procedures and responsibilities that define the establishment, management and control of projects, programmes or portfolios.

Handover
The point in the life cycle where deliverables are handed over to the sponsor and users.

Health and safety management
The process of identifying and minimising threats to workers and those affected by the work throughout the project, programme or portfolio life cycle.

Host organisation
The organisation that provides the strategic direction of the project, programme or portfolio and will be the primary recipient of the benefits.

Human resource management (HRM)
Managing people-related activities within an organisation to meet its strategic goals.

Influencing
The act of affecting the behaviours and actions of others.

Information management
The collection, storage, dissemination, archiving and destruction of information. It enables teams and stakeholders to use their time, resource and expertise effectively to make decisions and to fulfil their roles.

Infrastructure
Provides support for projects, programmes and portfolios, and is the focal point for the development and maintenance of P3 management within an organisation.

Initial
The first level of a typical maturity model where processes are typically ad hoc and occasionally chaotic.

MANAGEMENT

Integrated assurance
The co-ordination of assurance activities where there are a number of assurance providers.

Integrative management
The application of management processes that integrate some or all fundamental components of scope, schedule, cost, risk, quality and resources.

Interpersonal skills
The means by which people relate to, and interact with, other people.

Investment appraisal
A collection of techniques used to identify the attractiveness of an investment.

Issue
A formal issue occurs when the tolerances of delegated work are predicted to be exceeded or have been exceeded. This triggers the escalation of the issue from one level of management to the next in order to seek a solution.

Knowledge management
The systematic management of information and learning. It turns personal information and experience into collective knowledge that can be widely shared throughout an organisation and a profession.

Law
The relevant legal duties, rights and processes that should be applied to projects, programmes and portfolios.

Leadership
The ability to establish vision and direction, to influence and align others towards a common purpose, and to empower and inspire people to achieve success.

Learning and development
The continual improvement of competence at all levels of an organisation.

Lessons learned
Documented experiences that can be used to improve the future management of projects, programmes and portfolios.

Life cycle
The interrelated phases of a project, programme or portfolio and provides a structure for governing the progression of work.

Linear sequential model
See waterfall method.

Line-of-balance
A scheduling technique for delivery of repetitive products that shows how resource teams move from product to product rather than the detail of individual activities.

Managed
The fourth level of a typical capability maturity model where metrics are gathered on process performance and used to control future performance.

Management plan
A plan that sets out the policies and principles that will be applied to the management of some aspects of a project, programme or portfolio. Examples include a Risk Management Plan, a Communication Management Plan and a Quality Management Plan.

Management reserve
A sum of money held as an overall contingency to cover the cost impact of some unexpected event.

Maturity model
An organisational model that describes a number of evolutionary stages through which an organisation improves its management processes.

Milestone
A key event selected for its importance in the schedule.

Mobilisation
Ensures that the project, programme or portfolio has appropriate organisational and technical infrastructures and mechanisms for putting resources in place.

Monte Carlo analysis
A technique used to estimate the likely range of outcomes from a complex process by simulating the process under randomly selected conditions a large number of times.

Negotiation
A discussion between two or more parties aimed at reaching agreement.

Network analysis
A collective term for the different ways in which a network diagram may be analysed, including, for example, critical path analysis, program evaluation and review technique and critical chain.

Network diagram
A model of activities and their dependencies comprising nodes and links.

Objectives
Predetermined results towards which effort is directed. Objectives may be defined in terms of outputs, outcomes and/or benefits.

Operations management
The management of those activities that create the core services or products provided by an organisation.

Opportunity
A positive risk event that, if it occurs, will have a beneficial effect on achievement of objectives.

MANAGEMENT

Optimising

The fifth and last level of a typical maturity model where continual process improvement is enabled by quantitative feedback from the process and from piloting innovative ideas and technologies.

Organisation

The management structure applicable to the project, programme or portfolio and the organisational environment in which it operates.

Outcome

The changed circumstances or behaviour that results from the use of an output.

Output

The tangible or intangible product typically delivered by a project.

P3 assurance

The process of providing confidence to stakeholders that projects, programmes and portfolios will achieve their scope, time, cost and quality objectives, and realise their benefits.

P3 management

The collective term for project, programme and portfolio management.

P3 management team

A collective term for those involved in the sponsorship and day-to-day management of a project, programme or portfolio.

Parallel life cycle

A life cycle where phases are conducted in parallel.

Parametric estimating

An estimating technique that uses a statistical relationship between historic data and other variables to calculate an estimate.

Phase

The major subdivision of a life cycle.

Planning

Determines what is to be delivered, how much it will cost, when it will be delivered, how it will be delivered and who will carry it out.

Portfolio

A grouping of an organisation's projects, programmes. Portfolios can be managed at an organisational or functional level.

Portfolio management

The selection, prioritisation and control of an organisation's projects and programmes in line with its strategic objectives and capacity to deliver.

Precedence network

A network diagram in which activities are represented by rectangles (nodes) and their dependencies are represented by arrows.

PRINCE2®
A project management methodology. It is an acronym standing for Projects IN Controlled Environments.

Prioritise
The phase of a portfolio life cycle where priorities are set by strategic objective, return on investment or any other chosen metric.

Procurement
Procurement is the process by which products and services are acquired from an external provider for incorporation into the project, programme or portfolio.

Product
A tangible or intangible component of a project's output. Synonymous with deliverable.

Professionalism
The application of expert and specialised knowledge within a specific field and the acceptance of standards relating to that profession.

Programme evaluation and review technique
A network analysis technique that calculates standard deviations for the schedule based on three-point estimates of activity durations.

Programme
A group of related projects and change management activities that together achieve beneficial change for an organisation.

Programme management
The co-ordinated management of projects and change management activities to achieve beneficial change.

Project
A unique, transient endeavour undertaken to achieve planned objectives.

Project management
The application of processes, methods, knowledge, skills and experience to achieve the project objectives.

Project management plan (PMP)
The output of the definition phase of a project or programme.

Provider
A person or company that provides goods or services.

Provider selection and management
The processes of identifying and selecting management providers through the P3 life cycle.

Quality
The fitness for purpose or the degree of conformance of the outputs of a process or the process itself.

Quality management

A discipline for ensuring the outputs, benefits and the processes by which they are delivered, meet stakeholder requirements and are fit for purpose.

Reduce

A response to a threat that reduces its probability, impact or both.

Reject

A response to an opportunity where no action is taken.

Repeatable

The second level of a typical maturity model where basic processes are established and the necessary discipline is in place to repeat earlier successes.

Reports

1. The presentation of information in an appropriate format (e.g. management report).

2. A written record or summary, a detailed account or statement, or a verbal account.

Requirements management

The process of capturing, assessing and justifying stakeholders' wants and needs.

Resource allocation

The process by which resources are attributed to activities.

Resource availability

The level of availability of a resource, which may vary over time.

Resource levelling

A scheduling calculation that delays activities such that resource usage is kept below specified limits. It is also known as resource-limited scheduling.

Resource management

The acquisition and deployment of the internal and external resources required to deliver the project, programme or portfolio.

Resource scheduling

A collection of techniques used to calculate the resources required to deliver the work and when they will be required.

Resource smoothing

A scheduling calculation that involves utilising float or increasing or decreasing the resources required for specific activities, such that any peaks and troughs of resource usage are smoothed out. This does not affect the overall duration. It is also known as time-limited resource scheduling.

Resources

All those items required to undertake work including people, finance and materials.

Responsibility assignment matrix

A diagram or chart showing assigned responsibilities for elements of work. It is created by combining the work breakdown structure with the organisational breakdown structure.

Re-usable resource

A resource that when no longer needed becomes available for other uses. Accommodation, machines, test equipment and people are re-usable.

Reviews

A review is a critical evaluation of a deliverable, business case or P3 management process.

Risk

The potential of an action or event to impact on the achievement of objectives.

Risk analysis

An assessment and synthesis of risk events to gain an understanding of their individual significance and their combined impact on objectives.

Risk appetite

The tendency of an individual or group to take risk in a given situation.

Risk attitude

The response of an individual or group to a given uncertain situation.

Risk context

Describes the institutional and individual environment, attitudes and behaviours that affect the way risk arises and the way it should be managed.

Risk efficiency

The principle of risk-taking to achieve the minimum level of exposure to risk for a given level of expected return.

Risk event

An uncertain event or set of circumstances that would, if it occurred, have an effect on the achievement of one or more objectives.

Risk management

A process that allows individual risk events and overall risk to be understood and managed proactively, optimising success by minimising threats and maximising opportunities.

Risk register

A document listing identified risk events and their corresponding planned responses.

Risk response

An action or set of actions to reduce the probability or impact of a threat, or to increase the probability or impact of an opportunity.

Risk techniques

Used to identify, assess and plan responses to individual risks and overall risk.

Rolling wave planning

The process whereby short-term work is planned in detail and longer-term work is planned in outline only.

Schedule

A timetable showing the forecast start and finish dates for activities or events within a project, programme or portfolio.

Schedule management
The process of developing, maintaining and communicating schedules for time and resources.

Scope
The totality of the outputs, outcomes and benefits and the work required to produce them.

Scope management
The process whereby outputs, outcomes and benefits are identified, defined and controlled.

S-curve
A graphic display of cumulative costs, labour hours or other quantities, plotted against time.

Security
The identification, assessment and mitigation of the risks posed to information, assets and people.

Setting
The relationship of the project, programme or portfolio with its host organisation.

Share
A response to an opportunity that increases its probability, impact or both by sharing the risk with a third party.

Slip chart
A pictorial representation of the predicted completion dates of milestones or activities compared to their planned completion dates.

Solutions development
The process of determining the best way of satisfying requirements.

Spiral life cycle
A life cycle model that combines features of both iterative development and the waterfall method.

Sponsorship
An important senior management role. The sponsor is accountable for ensuring that the work is governed effectively and delivers the objectives that meet identified needs.

Sprint
A regular repeatable work cycle in agile development. Also known as an 'iteration'.

Stage
A subdivision of the development phase of a project created to facilitate approval gates at suitable points in the life cycle.

Stakeholder
The organisations or people who have an interest or role in the project, programme or portfolio, or are impacted by it.

Stakeholder management
The systematic identification, analysis, planning and implementation of actions designed to engage with stakeholders.

Start-to-finish

A dependency in an activity-on-node network. It indicates that one activity cannot finish until another activity has started.

Start-to-start

A dependency in an activity-on-node network. It indicates that one activity cannot start until another activity has started.

Statement of work

An annex to the main body of a contract that defines the detail of deliverables, timescales and management procedures.

Strategic management

The identification, selection and implementation of an organisation's long-term goals and objectives.

Sub-project

A group of activities represented as a single activity in a higher level of the same project.

Success criteria

The measures by which the success of a project is judged.

Success factors and maturity

Management practices that, when implemented, will increase the likelihood of success of a project, programme or portfolio. The degree to which these practices are established and embedded within an organisation indicates its level of maturity.

Sunk costs

Costs that are unavoidable, even if the remaining work is terminated.

Sustainability

An environmental, social and economically integrated approach to development that meets present needs without compromising the environment for future generations.

Teamwork

A group of people working in collaboration or by co-operation towards a common goal.

Termination

The decommissioning and disposal of a deliverable at the end of its useful life.

Threat

A negative risk event; a risk event that if it occurs will have a detrimental effect on the objectives.

Three-point estimate

An estimate in which optimistic, most likely and pessimistic values are given.

Time chainage

A form of graphical schedule that shows activity in relation to physical location as well as time.

MANAGEMENT

Time-driven

Control actions or reports that are triggered by the passage of a defined interval (e.g. monthly) are referred to as 'time-driven'.

Time scheduling

A collection of techniques used to develop and present schedules that show when work will be performed.

Timebox

The production of project deliverables in circumstances where time and resources, including funding, are fixed and the requirements are prioritised and vary depending on what can be achieved within the timebox.

Tolerance

A permissible variation in performance parameters.

Total float

Time by which an activity may be delayed or extended without affecting the overall duration or violating a target finish date.

Tranche

A subdivision of the delivery phase of a programme created to facilitate approval gates at suitable points in the life cycle.

Transfer

A response to a threat that reduces its probability, impact or both by transferring the risk to a third party.

Users

The group of people who are intended to receive benefits or operate outputs.

V life cycle

A graphical representation of a life cycle where horizontal lines connect related front- and back-end phases.

Value

A standard, principle or quality considered worthwhile or desirable. In value management terms value is defined as the ratio of 'satisfaction of requirements' over 'use of resources'.

Value engineering

Concerned with optimising the conceptual, technical and operational aspects of deliverables.

Value for money ratio

The ratio of monetary and non-monetary benefits to the investment made of resources committed.

Value management

A structured approach to defining what value means to the organisation. It is a framework that allows needs, problems or opportunities to be defined and then enables review of whether these can be improved to determine the optimal approach and solution.

Value tree

A graphical representation of the relationship between different factors that drive value.

Waterfall method

A type of life cycle where phases are sequential.

Work package

A group of related activities that are defined at the same level within a work breakdown structure.

Index

MANAGEMENT

MANAGEMENT